Department for Constitutional Affairs

Mental Capacity Act 2005

Code of Practice

Issued by the Lord Chancellor on 23 April 2007 in accordance with sections 42 and 43 of the Act

London: TSO

Published by TSO (The
Stationery Office) and available from:

Online
www.tsoshop.co.uk

Mail, Telephone, Fax & E-mail
TSO
PO Box 29, Norwich NR3 1GN
Telephone orders/General enquiries: 0870 6005522
Fax orders: 0870 600 5533
E-mail: customer.services@tso.co.uk
Textphone: 0870 240 3701

TSO Shops
123 Kingsway, London WC2B 6PQ
020 7242 6393 Fax 020 7242 6394
16 Arthur Street, Belfast BT1 4GD
028 9023 8451 Fax 028 9023 5401
71 Lothian Road, Edinburgh EH3 9AZ
0870 606 5566 Fax 0870 606 5588

TSO@Blackwell and other Accredited Agents

Foreword by Lord Falconer

Foreword by Lord Falconer, Secretary of State for Constitutional Affairs and Lord Chancellor

The Mental Capacity Act 2005 is a vitally important piece of legislation, and one that will make a real difference to the lives of people who may lack mental capacity. It will empower people to make decisions for themselves wherever possible, and protect people who lack capacity by providing a flexible framework that places individuals at the very heart of the decision-making process. It will ensure that they participate as much as possible in any decisions made on their behalf, and that these are made in their best interests. It also allows people to plan ahead for a time in the future when they might lack the capacity, for any number of reasons, to make decisions for themselves.

The Act covers a wide range of decisions and circumstances, but legislation alone is not the whole story. We have always recognised that the Act needs to be supported by practical guidance, and the Code of Practice is a key part of this. It explains how the Act will operate on a day-to-day basis and offers examples of best practice to carers and practitioners.

Many individuals and organisations have read and commented upon earlier drafts of the Code of Practice and I am very grateful to all those who contributed to this process. This Code of Practice is a better document as a result of this input.

A number of people will be under a formal duty to have regard to the Code: professionals and paid carers for example, or people acting as attorneys or as deputies appointed by the Court of Protection. But for many people, the most important relationships will be with the wide range of less formal carers, the close family and friends who know the person best, some of whom will have been caring for them for many years. The Code is also here to provide help and guidance for them. It will be crucial to the Code's success that all those relying upon it have a document that is clear and that they can understand. I have been particularly keen that we do all we can to achieve this.

The Code of Practice will be important in shaping the way the Mental Capacity Act 2005 is put into practice and I strongly encourage you to take the time to read and digest it.

Charlie

Falconer

Lord Falconer of Thoroton

Introduction

The Mental Capacity Act 2005, covering England and Wales, provides a statutory framework for people who lack capacity to make decisions for themselves, or who have capacity and want to make preparations for a time when they may lack capacity in the future. It sets out who can take decisions, in which situations, and how they should go about this. The Act received Royal Assent on 7 April 2005 and will come into force during 2007.

The legal framework provided by the Mental Capacity Act 2005 is supported by this Code of Practice (the Code), which provides guidance and information about how the Act works in practice. Section 42 of the Act requires the Lord Chancellor to produce a Code of Practice for the guidance of a range of people with different duties and functions under the Act. Before the Code is prepared, section 43 requires that the Lord Chancellor must have consulted the National Assembly for Wales and such other persons as he considers appropriate. The Code is also subject to the approval of Parliament and must have been placed before both Houses of Parliament for a 40-day period without either House voting against it. This Code of Practice has been produced in accordance with these requirements.

The Code has statutory force, which means that certain categories of people have a legal duty to have regard to it when working with or caring for adults who may lack capacity to make decisions for themselves. These categories of people are listed below.

How should the Code of Practice be used?

The Code of Practice provides guidance to anyone who is working with and/or caring for adults who may lack capacity to make particular decisions. It describes their responsibilities when acting or making decisions on behalf of individuals who lack the capacity to act or make these decisions for themselves. In particular, the Code of Practice focuses on those who have a duty of care to someone who lacks the capacity to agree to the care that is being provided.

Who is the Code of Practice for?

The Act does not impose a legal duty on anyone to 'comply' with the Code – it should be viewed as guidance rather than instruction. But if they have not followed relevant guidance contained in the Code then they will be expected to give good reasons why they have departed from it.

Certain categories of people are legally required to 'have regard to' relevant guidance in the Code of Practice. That means they must be aware of the Code of Practice when acting or making decisions on behalf of someone who lacks capacity to make a decision for themselves, and they should be able to explain how they have had regard to the Code when acting or making decisions.

The categories of people that are required to have regard to the Code of Practice include anyone who is:

- an attorney under a Lasting Power of Attorney (LPA) (see chapter 7)
- a deputy appointed by the new Court of Protection (see chapter 8)
- acting as an Independent Mental Capacity Advocate (see chapter 10)
- carrying out research approved in accordance with the Act (see chapter 11)
- acting in a professional capacity for, or in relation to, a person who lacks capacity working
- being paid for acts for or in relation to a person who lacks capacity.

The last two categories cover a wide range of people. People acting in a professional capacity may include:

- a variety of healthcare staff (doctors, dentists, nurses, therapists, radiologists, paramedics etc)
- social care staff (social workers, care managers, etc)
- others who may occasionally be involved in the care of people who lack capacity to make the decision in question, such as ambulance crew, housing workers, or police officers.

People who are being paid for acts for or in relation to a person who lacks capacity may include:

- care assistants in a care home
- care workers providing domiciliary care services, and
- others who have been contracted to provide a service to people who lack capacity to consent to that service.

However, the Act applies more generally to *everyone* who looks after, or cares for, someone who lacks capacity to make particular decisions for themselves. This includes family carers or other carers. Although these carers are not legally required to have regard to the Code of Practice, the guidance given in the Code will help them to understand the Act and apply it. They should follow the guidance in the Code as far as they are aware of it.

What does 'lacks capacity' mean?

One of the most important terms in the Code is 'a person who lacks capacity'.

Whenever the term 'a person who lacks capacity' is used, it **means a person who lacks capacity to make a particular decision or take a particular action for themselves at the time the decision or action needs to be taken.**

This reflects the fact that people may lack capacity to make some decisions for themselves, but will have capacity to make other decisions. For example, they may have capacity to make small decisions about everyday issues such as what to wear or what to eat, but lack capacity to make more complex decisions about financial matters.

It also reflects the fact that a person who lacks capacity to make a decision for themselves at a certain time may be able to make that decision at a later date. This may be because they have an illness or condition that means their capacity changes. Alternatively, it may be because at the time the decision needs to be made, they are unconscious or barely conscious whether due to an accident or being under anaesthetic or their ability to make a decision may be affected by the influence of alcohol or drugs.

Finally, it reflects the fact that while some people may always lack capacity to make some types of decisions – for example, due to a condition or severe learning disability that has affected them from birth – others may learn new skills that enable them to gain capacity and make decisions for themselves.

Chapter 4 provides a full definition of what is meant by 'lacks capacity'.

What does the Code of Practice actually cover?

The Code explains the Act and its key provisions.

- **Chapter 1** introduces the Mental Capacity Act 2005.
- **Chapter 2** sets out the five statutory principles behind the Act and the way they affect how it is put in practice.
- **Chapter 3** explains how the Act makes sure that people are given the right help and support to make their own decisions.
- **Chapter 4** explains how the Act defines 'a person who lacks capacity to make a decision' and sets out a single clear test for assessing whether a person lacks capacity to make a particular decision at a particular time.
- **Chapter 5** explains what the Act means by acting in the best interests of someone lacking capacity to make a decision for themselves, and describes the checklist set out in the Act for working out what is in someone's best interests.

- **Chapter 6** explains how the Act protects people providing care or treatment for someone who lacks the capacity to consent to the action being taken.

- **Chapter 7** shows how people who wish to plan ahead for the possibility that they might lack the capacity to make particular decisions for themselves in the future are able to grant Lasting Powers of Attorney (LPAs) to named individuals to make certain decisions on their behalf, and how attorneys appointed under an LPA should act.

- **Chapter 8** describes the role of the new Court of Protection, established under the Act, to make a decision or to appoint a decision-maker on someone's behalf in cases where there is no other way of resolving a matter affecting a person who lacks capacity to make the decision in question.

- **Chapter 9** explains the procedures that must be followed if someone wishes to make an advance decision to refuse medical treatment to come into effect when they lack capacity to refuse the specified treatment.

- **Chapter 10** describes the role of Independent Mental Capacity Advocates appointed under the Act to help and represent particularly vulnerable people who lack capacity to make certain significant decisions. It also sets out when they should be instructed.

- **Chapter 11** provides guidance on how the Act sets out specific safeguards and controls for research involving, or in relation to, people lacking capacity to consent to their participation.

- **Chapter 12** explains those parts of the Act which can apply to children and young people and how these relate to other laws affecting them.

- **Chapter 13** explains how the Act relates to the Mental Health Act 1983.

- **Chapter 14** sets out the role of the Public Guardian, a new public office established by the Act to oversee attorneys and deputies and to act as a single point of contact for referring allegations of abuse in relation to attorneys and deputies to other relevant agencies.

- **Chapter 15** examines the various ways that disputes over decisions made under the Act or otherwise affecting people lacking capacity to make relevant decisions can be resolved.

- **Chapter 16** summarises how the laws about data protection and freedom of information relate to the provisions of the Act.

What is the legal status of the Code?

Where does it apply?

The Act and therefore this Code applies to everyone it concerns who is habitually resident or present in England and Wales. However, it will also be possible for the Court of Protection to consider cases which involve persons who have assets or property outside this jurisdiction, or who live abroad but have assets or property in England or Wales.

What happens if people don't comply with it?

There are no specific sanctions for failure to comply with the Code. But a failure to comply with the Code can be used in evidence before a court or tribunal in any civil or criminal proceedings, if the court or tribunal considers it to be relevant to those proceedings. For example, if a court or tribunal believes that anyone making decisions for someone who lacks capacity has not acted in the best interests of the person they care for, the court can use the person's failure to comply with the Code as evidence. That's why it's important that anyone working with or caring for a person who lacks capacity to make specific decisions should become familiar with the Code.

Where can I find out more?

The Code of Practice is not an exhaustive guide or complete statement of the law. Other materials have been produced by the Department for Constitutional Affairs, the Department of Health and the Office of the Public Guardian to help explain aspects of the Act from different perspectives and for people in different situations. These include guides for family carers and other carers and basic information of interest to the general public. Professional organisations may also produce specialist information and guidance for their members.

The Code also provides information on where to get more detailed guidance from other sources. A list of contact details is provided in Annex A and further information appears in the footnotes to each chapter. References made and any links provided to material or organisations do not form part of the Code and do not attract the same legal status. Signposts to further information are provided for assistance only and references made should not suggest that the Department for Constitutional Affairs endorses such material.

Using the code

References in the Code of Practice

Throughout the Code of Practice, the Mental Capacity Act 2005 is referred to as 'the Act' and any sections quoted refer to this Act unless otherwise stated. References are shown as follows: section 4(1). This refers to the section of the Act. The subsection number is in brackets.

Where reference is made to provisions from other legislation, the full title of the relevant Act will be set out, for example 'the Mental Health Act 1983', unless otherwise stated. (For example, in chapter 13, the Mental Health Act 1983 is referred to as MHA and the Mental Capacity Act as MCA.) The Code of Practice is sometimes referred to as the Code.

Scenarios used in the Code of Practice

The Code includes many boxes within the text in which there are scenarios, using imaginary characters and situations. These are intended to help illustrate what is meant in the main text. The scenarios should not in any way be taken as templates for decisions that need to be made in similar situations.

Alternative formats and further information

The Code is also available in Welsh and can be made available in other formats on request.

Contents

1.   What is the Mental Capacity Act 2005?   **15**

What decisions are covered by the Act, and what decisions
are excluded?   16

How does the Act relate to other legislation?   18

What does the Act say about the Code of Practice?   18

2   What are the statutory principles and how should they be applied? 19

Quick summary   20

What is the role of the statutory principles?   20

How should the statutory principles be applied?   20

Principle 1: *'A person must be assumed to have capacity unless
it is established that he lacks capacity.' (section1(2))*   20

Principle 2: *'A person is not to be treated as unable to make a
decision unless all practicable steps to help him to do so have
been taken without success.' (section1(3))*   22

Principle 3: *'A person is not to be treated as unable to make a
decision merely because he makes an unwise decision.' (section 1(4))*   24

Principle 4: *'An act done, or decision made, under this Act for or
on behalf of a person who lacks capacity must be done, or made,
in his best interests.' (section 1(5))*   26

Principle 5: *'Before the act is done, or the decision is made,
regard must be had to whether the purpose for which it is
needed can be as effectively achieved in a way that is less
restrictive of the person's rights and freedom of action.' (section 1(6))*   27

3   How should people be helped to make their own decisions?   **29**

Quick summary   29

How can someone be helped to make a decision?   30

What happens in emergency situations?   31

What information should be provided to people and how should
it be provided?   31

What steps should be taken to put a person at ease?   35

What other ways are there to enable decision-making?   38

4   How does the Act define a person's capacity to make a decision and how should capacity be assessed?   **40**

Quick summary   40

What is mental capacity?   41

What does the Act mean by 'lack of capacity'?   42

What safeguards does the Act provide around assessing someone's capacity?   43

What proof of lack of capacity does the Act require?   44

What is the test of capacity?   44

What does the Act mean by 'inability to make a decision'?   45

What other issues might affect capacity?   49

When should capacity be assessed?   52

Who should assess capacity?   53

What is 'reasonable belief' of lack of capacity?   55

What other factors might affect an assessment of capacity?   56

What practical steps should be taken when assessing capacity?   58

When should professionals be involved?   59

Are assessment processes confidential?   61

What if someone refuses to be assessed?   62

Who should keep a record of assessments?   62

How can someone challenge a finding of lack of capacity?   63

5   What does the Act mean when it talks about 'best interests'?   **64**

Quick summary   65

What is the best interests principle and who does it apply to?   66

What does the Act mean by best interests?   68

Who can be a decision-maker?   69

What must be taken into account when trying to work out someone's best interests?   71

What safeguards does the Act provide around working out someone's best interests?   73

How does a decision-maker work out what 'all relevant circumstances' are?   74

How should the person who lacks capacity be involved in working out their best interests?   75

How do the chances of someone regaining and developing capacity affect working out what is in their best interests?   77

How should someone's best interests be worked out when making decisions about life-sustaining treatment? 79

How do a person's wishes and feelings, beliefs and values affect working out what is in their best interests? 80

Who should be consulted when working out someone's best interests? 84

How can decision-makers respect confidentiality? 86

When does the best interests principle apply? 86

What problems could arise when working out someone's best interests? 88

6 What protection does the Act offer for people providing care or treatment? 92

Quick summary 92

What protection do people have when caring for those who lack capacity to consent? 93

What type of actions might have protection from liability? 94

Who is protected from liability by section 5? 100

What steps should people take to be protected from liability? 102

What happens in emergency situations? 104

What happens in cases of negligence? 105

What is the effect of an advance decision to refuse treatment? 105

What limits are there on protection from liability? 105

How does section 5 apply to attorneys and deputies? 110

Who can pay for goods or services? 111

7 What does the Act say about Lasting Powers of Attorney? 114

Quick summary 114

What is a Lasting Power of Attorney (LPA)? 115

How does a donor create an LPA? 117

Who can be an attorney? 117

How should somebody register and use an LPA? 119

What guidance should an attorney follow? 119

What decisions can an LPA attorney make? 120

Are there any other restrictions on attorneys' powers? 127

What powers does the Court of Protection have over LPAs? 127

What responsibilities do attorneys have? 128

What duties does the Act impose? 129

What are an attorney's other duties? 131

How does the Act protect donors from abuse? 134

What happens to existing EPAs once the Act comes into force? 135

8 What is the role of the Court of Protection and court-appointed deputies? 137

Quick summary 137

What is the Court of Protection? 138

How can somebody make an application to the Court of Protection? 139

What powers does the Court of Protection have? 141

What decisions can the court make? 145

What are the rules for appointing deputies? 146

When might a deputy need to be appointed? 147

Who can be a deputy? 149

Can the court protect people lacking capacity from financial loss? 151

Are there any restrictions on a deputy's powers? 151

What responsibilities do deputies have? 151

What duties does the Act impose? 152

What are a deputy's other duties? 153

Who is responsible for supervising deputies? 156

9 What does the Act say about advance decisions to refuse treatment? 158

Quick summary 158

How can someone make an advance decision to refuse treatment? 159

Who can make an advance decision to refuse treatment? 160

What should people include in an advance decision? 163

What rules apply to advance decisions to refuse life-sustaining treatment? 166

When should someone review or update an advance decision? 167

How can someone withdraw an advance decision? 167

How can someone make changes to an advance decision? 168

How do advance decisions relate to other rules about decision-making? 168

How can somebody decide on the existence, validity and applicability of advance decisions? 169

What should healthcare professionals do if an advance decision is not valid or applicable? 172

Contents

What happens to decisions made before the Act comes into force? 172

What implications do advance decisions have for healthcare professionals? 173

When can healthcare professionals be found liable? 174

What if a healthcare professional has a conscientious objection to stopping or providing life-sustaining treatment? 175

What happens if there is a disagreement about an advance decision? 176

10 What is the new Independent Mental Capacity Advocate service and how does it work? 178

Quick summary 178

What is the IMCA service? 179

Who is responsible for delivering the service? 181

Who can be an IMCA? 184

What is an IMCA's role? 185

What happens if the IMCA disagrees with the decision-maker? 189

What decisions require an IMCA? 191

When can a local authority or NHS body decide to instruct an IMCA? 196

Who qualifies for an IMCA? 198

11 How does the Act affect research projects involving a person who lacks capacity? 202

Quick summary 202

Why does the Act cover research? 203

What is 'research'? 203

What assumptions can a researcher make about capacity? 204

What research does the Act cover? 204

How can research get approval? 206

What responsibilities do researchers have? 210

What happens if urgent decisions are required during the research project? 212

What happens for research involving human tissue? 213

What should happen to research that started before the Act came into force? 214

12 How does the Act apply to children and young people? 216

Quick summary 216

Does the Act apply to children? 217

Does the Act apply to young people aged 16–17? 219

Do any parts of the Act not apply to young people aged 16 or 17? 219

What does the Act say about care or treatment of young people aged 16 or 17? 220

What powers do the courts have in cases involving young people? 223

13 What is the relationship between the Mental Capacity Act and the Mental Health Act 1983? 225

Quick summary 225

Who does the MHA apply to? 226

What are the MCA's limits? 227

When can a person be detained under the MHA? 228

How does the MCA apply to a patient subject to guardianship under the MHA? 231

How does the MCA apply to a patient subject to after-care under supervision under the MHA? 233

How does the Mental Capacity Act affect people covered by the Mental Health Act? 234

What are the implications for people who need treatment for a mental disorder? 235

How does the Mental Health Act affect advance decisions to refuse treatment? 237

Does the MHA affect the duties of attorneys and deputies? 238

Does the MHA affect when Independent Mental Capacity Advocates must be instructed? 240

What is the effect of section 57 of the Mental Health Act on the MCA? 241

What changes does the Government plan to make to the MHA and the MCA? 241

14 What means of protection exist for people who lack capacity to make decisions for themselves? 243

Quick summary 243

What is abuse? 244

How does the Act protect people from abuse? 247

How does the Public Guardian oversee LPAs? 249

How does the Public Guardian supervise deputies? 249

What happens if someone says they are worried about an attorney or deputy? 250

How does the Act deal with ill treatment and wilful neglect? 251

What other measures protect people from abuse? 253

Who should check that staff are safe to work with vulnerable adults? 253

Who is responsible for monitoring the standard of care providers? 254

What is an appointee, and who monitors them? 255

Are there any other means of protection that people should be aware of? 255

15 What are the best ways to settle disagreements and disputes about issues covered in the Act? 257

Quick summary 257

What options are there for settling disagreements? 258

When is an advocate useful? 259

When is mediation useful? 260

How can someone complain about healthcare? 261

How can somebody complain about social care? 264

What if a complaint covers healthcare and social care? 265

Who can handle complaints about other welfare issues? 265

What is the best way to handle disagreement about a person's finances? 266

How can the Court of Protection help? 266

Will public legal funding be available? 267

16 What rules govern access to information about a person who lacks capacity? 270

Quick summary 270

What laws and regulations affect access to information? 272

What information do people generally have a right to see? 273

When can attorneys and deputies ask to see personal information? 274

When can someone see information about healthcare or social care? 276

What financial information can carers ask to see? 278

Is information still confidential after someone shares it? 278

What is the best way to settle a disagreement about personal information? 278

Key words and phrases used in the Code 280

Annex A 292

Contents

1 What is the Mental Capacity Act 2005?

1.1 The Mental Capacity Act 2005 (the Act) provides the legal framework for acting and making decisions on behalf of individuals who lack the mental capacity to make particular decisions for themselves. Everyone working with and/or caring for an adult who may lack capacity to make specific decisions must comply with this Act when making decisions or acting for that person, when the person lacks the capacity to make a particular decision for themselves. The same rules apply whether the decisions are life-changing events or everyday matters.

1.2 The Act's starting point is to confirm in legislation that it should be assumed that an adult (aged 16 or over) has full legal capacity to make decisions for themselves (the right to autonomy) unless it can be shown that they lack capacity to make a decision for themselves at the time the decision needs to be made. This is known as the presumption of capacity. The Act also states that people must be given all appropriate help and support to enable them to make their own decisions or to maximise their participation in any decision-making process.

1.3 The underlying philosophy of the Act is to ensure that any decision made, or action taken, on behalf of someone who lacks the capacity to make the decision or act for themselves is made in their best interests.

1.4 The Act is intended to assist and support people who may lack capacity and to discourage anyone who is involved in caring for someone who lacks capacity from being overly restrictive or controlling. But the Act also aims to balance an individual's right to make decisions for themselves with their right to be protected from harm if they lack capacity to make decisions to protect themselves.

1.5 The Act sets out a legal framework of how to act and make decisions on behalf of people who lack capacity to make specific decisions for themselves. It sets out some core principles and methods for making decisions and carrying out actions in relation to personal welfare, healthcare and financial matters affecting people who may lack capacity to make specific decisions about these issues for themselves.

1.6   Many of the provisions in the Act are based upon existing common law principles (i.e. principles that have been established through decisions made by courts in individual cases). The Act clarifies and improves upon these principles and builds on current good practice which is based on the principles.

1.7   The Act introduces several new roles, bodies and powers, all of which will support the Act's provisions. These include:

- Attorneys appointed under Lasting Powers of Attorney (see chapter 7)

- The new Court of Protection, and court-appointed deputies (see chapter 8)

- Independent Mental Capacity Advocates (see chapter 10).

The roles, bodies and powers are all explained in more depth in the specific chapters of the Code highlighted above.

What decisions are covered by the Act, and what decisions are excluded?

1.8   The Act covers a wide range of decisions made, or actions taken, on behalf of people who may lack capacity to make specific decisions for themselves. These can be decisions about day-to-day matters – like what to wear, or what to buy when doing the weekly shopping – or decisions about major life-changing events, such as whether the person should move into a care home or undergo a major surgical operation.

1.9   There are certain decisions which can never be made on behalf of a person who lacks capacity to make those specific decisions. This is because they are either so personal to the individual concerned, or governed by other legislation.

1.10   Sections 27–29 and 62 of the Act set out the specific decisions which can never be made or actions which can never be carried out under the Act, whether by family members, carers, professionals, attorneys or the Court of Protection. These are summarised below.

Decisions concerning family relationships (section 27)

Nothing in the Act permits a decision to be made on someone else's behalf on any of the following matters:

- consenting to marriage or a civil partnership

- consenting to have sexual relations

- consenting to a decree of divorce on the basis of two years' separation

- consenting to the dissolution of a civil partnership

- consenting to a child being placed for adoption or the making of an adoption order

- discharging parental responsibility for a child in matters not relating to the child's property, or

- giving consent under the Human Fertilisation and Embryology Act 1990.

Mental Health Act matters (section 28)

Where a person who lacks capacity to consent is currently detained and being treated under Part 4 of the Mental Health Act 1983, nothing in the Act authorises anyone to:

- give the person treatment for mental disorder, or

- consent to the person being given treatment for mental disorder.

Further guidance is given in chapter 13 of the Code.

Voting rights (section 29)

Nothing in the Act permits a decision on voting, at an election for any public office or at a referendum, to be made on behalf of a person who lacks capacity to vote.

Unlawful killing or assisting suicide (section 62)

For the avoidance of doubt, nothing in the Act is to be taken to affect the law relating to murder, manslaughter or assisting suicide.

1.11 Although the Act does not allow anyone to make a decision about these matters on behalf of someone who lacks capacity to make such a decision for themselves (for example, consenting to have sexual relations), this does not prevent action being taken to protect a vulnerable person from abuse or exploitation.

How does the Act relate to other legislation?

1.12   The Mental Capacity Act 2005 will apply in conjunction with other legislation affecting people who may lack capacity in relation to specific matters. This means that healthcare and social care staff acting under the Act should also be aware of their obligations under other legislation, including (but not limited to) the:

- Care Standards Act 2000
- Data Protection Act 1998
- Disability Discrimination Act 1995
- Human Rights Act 1998
- Mental Health Act 1983
- National Health Service and Community Care Act 1990
- Human Tissue Act 2004.

What does the Act say about the Code of Practice?

1.13   Section 42 of the Act sets out the purpose of the Code of Practice, which is to provide guidance for specific people in specific circumstances. Section 43 explains the procedures that had to be followed in preparing the Code and consulting on its contents, and for its consideration by Parliament.

Section 42, subsections (4) and (5), set out the categories of people who are placed under a legal duty to 'have regard to' the Code and gives further information about the status of the Code. More details can be found in the Introduction, which explains the legal status of the Code.

What are the statutory principles and how should they be applied?

Section 1 of the Act sets out the five 'statutory principles' – the values that underpin the legal requirements in the Act. The Act is intended to be enabling and supportive of people who lack capacity, not restricting or controlling of their lives. It aims to protect people who lack capacity to make particular decisions, but also to maximise their ability to make decisions, or to participate in decision-making, as far as they are able to do so.

The five statutory principles are:

1. A person must be assumed to have capacity unless it is established that they lack capacity.

2. A person is not to be treated as unable to make a decision unless all practicable steps to help him to do so have been taken without success.

3. A person is not to be treated as unable to make a decision merely because he makes an unwise decision.

4. An act done, or decision made, under this Act for or on behalf of a person who lacks capacity must be done, or made, in his best interests.

5. Before the act is done, or the decision is made, regard must be had to whether the purpose for which it is needed can be as effectively achieved in a way that is less restrictive of the person's rights and freedom of action.

This chapter provides guidance on how people should interpret and apply the statutory principles when using the Act. Following the principles and applying them to the Act's framework for decision-making will help to ensure not only that appropriate action is taken in individual cases, but also to point the way to solutions in difficult or uncertain situations.

> In this chapter, as throughout the Code, a person's capacity (or lack of capacity) refers specifically to their capacity to make a particular decision at the time it needs to be made.

Quick summary

- Every adult has the right to make their own decisions if they have the capacity to do so. Family carers and healthcare or social care staff must assume that a person has the capacity to make decisions, unless it can be established that the person does not have capacity.

- People should receive support to help them make their own decisions. Before concluding that individuals lack capacity to make a particular decision, it is important to take all possible steps to try to help them reach a decision themselves.

- People have the right to make decisions that others might think are unwise. A person who makes a decision that others think is unwise should not automatically be labelled as lacking the capacity to make a decision.

- Any act done for, or any decision made on behalf of, someone who lacks capacity must be in their best interests.

- Any act done for, or any decision made on behalf of, someone who lacks capacity should be an option that is less restrictive of their basic rights and freedoms – as long as it is still in their best interests.

What is the role of the statutory principles?

2.1   The statutory principles aim to:

- protect people who lack capacity and

- help them take part, as much as possible, in decisions that affect them.

They aim to assist and support people who may lack capacity to make particular decisions, not to restrict or control their lives.

2.2   The statutory principles apply to any act done or decision made under the Act. When followed and applied to the Act's decision-making framework, they will help people take appropriate action in individual cases. They will also help people find solutions in difficult or uncertain situations.

How should the statutory principles be applied?

Principle 1: *'A person must be assumed to have capacity unless it is established that he lacks capacity.' (section1(2))*

2.3   This principle states that every adult has the right to make their own decisions – unless there is proof that they lack the capacity to make a particular decision when it needs to be made. This has been a fundamental principle of the common law for many years and it is now set out in the Act.

Chapter 2

What are the statutory principles and how should they be applied?

2.4   It is important to balance people's right to make a decision with their right to safety and protection when they can't make decisions to protect themselves. But the starting assumption must always be that an individual has the capacity, until there is proof that they do not. Chapter 4 explains the Act's definition of 'lack of capacity' and the processes involved in assessing capacity.

Scenario: Assessing a person's capacity to make decisions

When planning for her retirement, Mrs Arnold made and registered a Lasting Power of Attorney (LPA) – a legal process that would allow her son to manage her property and financial affairs if she ever lacked capacity to manage them herself. She has now been diagnosed with dementia, and her son is worried that she is becoming confused about money.

Her son must assume that his mother has capacity to manage her affairs. Then he must consider each of Mrs Arnold's financial decisions as she makes them, giving her any help and support she needs to make these decisions herself.

Mrs Arnold's son goes shopping with her, and he sees she is quite capable of finding goods and making sure she gets the correct change. But when she needs to make decisions about her investments, Mrs Arnold gets confused – even though she has made such decisions in the past. She still doesn't understand after her son explains the different options.

Her son concludes that she has capacity to deal with everyday financial matters but not more difficult affairs at this time. Therefore, he is able to use the LPA for the difficult financial decisions his mother can't make. But Mrs Arnold can continue to deal with her other affairs for as long as she has capacity to do so.

2.5   Some people may need help to be able to make a decision or to communicate their decision. However, this does not necessarily mean that they cannot make that decision – unless there is proof that they do lack capacity to do so. Anyone who believes that a person lacks capacity should be able to prove their case. Chapter 4 explains the standard of proof required.

Principle 2: *'A person is not to be treated as unable to make a decision unless all practicable steps to help him to do so have been taken without success.' (section1(3))*

2.6   It is important to do everything practical (the Act uses the term 'practicable') to help a person make a decision for themselves before concluding that they lack capacity to do so. People with an illness or disability affecting their ability to make a decision should receive support to help them make as many decisions as they can. This principle aims to stop people being automatically labelled as lacking capacity to make particular decisions. Because it encourages individuals to play as big a role as possible in decision-making, it also helps prevent unnecessary interventions in their lives.

2.7   The kind of support people might need to help them make a decision varies. It depends on personal circumstances, the kind of decision that has to be made and the time available to make the decision. It might include:

- using a different form of communication (for example, non-verbal communication)

- providing information in a more accessible form (for example, photographs, drawings, or tapes)

- treating a medical condition which may be affecting the person's capacity or

- having a structured programme to improve a person's capacity to make particular decisions (for example, helping a person with learning disabilities to learn new skills).

Chapter 3 gives more information on ways to help people make decisions for themselves.

Scenario: Taking steps to help people make decisions for themselves

Mr Jackson is brought into hospital following a traffic accident. He is conscious but in shock. He cannot speak and is clearly in distress, making noises and gestures.

From his behaviour, hospital staff conclude that Mr Jackson currently lacks the capacity to make decisions about treatment for his injuries, and they give him urgent treatment. They hope that after he has recovered from the shock they can use an advocate to help explain things to him.

However, one of the nurses thinks she recognises some of his gestures as sign language, and tries signing to him. Mr Jackson immediately becomes calmer, and the doctors realise that he can communicate in sign language. He can also answer some written questions about his injuries.

The hospital brings in a qualified sign-language interpreter and concludes that Mr Jackson has the capacity to make decisions about any further treatment.

Chapter 2

What are the statutory principles and how should they be applied?

2.8   Anyone supporting a person who may lack capacity should not use excessive persuasion or 'undue pressure'.[1] This might include behaving in a manner which is overbearing or dominating, or seeking to influence the person's decision, and could push a person into making a decision they might not otherwise have made. However, it is important to provide appropriate advice and information.

---

[1]   Undue influence in relation to consent to medical treatment was considered in *Re T (Adult: Refusal of Treatment)* [1992] 4 All E R 649, 662 and in financial matters in *Royal Bank of Scotland v Etridge* [2001] UKHL 44.

Scenario: Giving appropriate advice and support

Sara, a young woman with severe depression, is getting treatment from mental health services. Her psychiatrist determines that she has capacity to make decisions about treatment, if she gets advice and support.

Her mother is trying to persuade Sara to agree to electro-convulsive therapy (ECT), which helped her mother when she had clinical depression in the past. However, a friend has told Sara that ECT is 'barbaric'.

The psychiatrist provides factual information about the different types of treatment available and explains their advantages and disadvantages. She also describes how different people experience different reactions or side effects. Sara is then able to consider what treatment is right for her, based on factual information rather than the personal opinions of her mother and friend.

2.9   In some situations treatment cannot be delayed while a person gets support to make a decision. This can happen in emergency situations or when an urgent decision is required (for example, immediate medical treatment). In these situations, the only practical and appropriate steps might be to keep a person informed of what is happening and why.

Principle 3: *'A person is not to be treated as unable to make a decision merely because he makes an unwise decision.' (section 1(4))*

2.10   Everybody has their own values, beliefs, preferences and attitudes. A person should not be assumed to lack the capacity to make a decision just because other people think their decision is unwise. This applies even if family members, friends or healthcare or social care staff are unhappy with a decision.

Scenario: Allowing people to make decisions that others think are unwise

Mr Garvey is a 40-year-old man with a history of mental health problems. He sees a Community Psychiatric Nurse (CPN) regularly. Mr Garvey decides to spend £2,000 of his savings on a camper van to travel around Scotland for six months. His CPN is concerned that it will be difficult to give Mr Garvey continuous support and treatment while travelling, and that his mental health might deteriorate as a result.

However, having talked it through with his CPN, it is clear that Mr Garvey is fully aware of these concerns and has the capacity to make this particular decision. He has decided he would like to have a break and thinks this will be good for him.

Just because, in the CPN's opinion, continuity of care might be a wiser option, it should not be assumed that Mr Garvey lacks the capacity to make this decision for himself.

Chapter 2

What are the statutory principles and how should they be applied?

2.11 There may be cause for concern if somebody:

- repeatedly makes unwise decisions that put them at significant risk of harm or exploitation or

- makes a particular unwise decision that is obviously irrational or out of character.

These things do not necessarily mean that somebody lacks capacity. But there might be need for further investigation, taking into account the person's past decisions and choices. For example, have they developed a medical condition or disorder that is affecting their capacity to make particular decisions? Are they easily influenced by undue pressure? Or do they need more information to help them understand the consequences of the decision they are making?

Scenario: Decisions that cause concern

Cyril, an elderly man with early signs of dementia, spends nearly £300 on fresh fish from a door-to-door salesman. He has always been fond of fish and has previously bought small amounts in this way. Before his dementia, Cyril was always very careful with his money and would never have spent so much on fish in one go.

This decision alone may not automatically mean Cyril now lacks capacity to manage all aspects of his property and affairs. But his daughter makes further enquiries and discovers Cyril has overpaid his cleaner on several occasions – something he has never done in the past. He has also made payments from his savings that he cannot account for.

His daughter decides it is time to use the registered Lasting Power of Attorney her father made in the past. This gives her the authority to manage Cyril's property and affairs whenever he lacks the capacity to manage them himself. She takes control of Cyril's chequebook to protect him from possible exploitation, but she can still ensure he has enough money to spend on his everyday needs.

Principle 4: *'An act done, or decision made, under this Act for or on behalf of a person who lacks capacity must be done, or made, in his best interests.'* *(section 1(5))*

2.12   The principle of acting or making a decision *in the best interests* of a person who lacks capacity to make the decision in question is a well-established principle in the common law.[2] This principle is now set out in the Act, so that a person's best interests must be the basis for all decisions made and actions carried out on their behalf in situations where they lack capacity to make those particular decisions for themselves. The only exceptions to this are around research (see chapter 11) and advance decisions to refuse treatment (see chapter 9) where other safeguards apply.

---

[2]   See for example *Re MB (Medical Treatment)* [1997] 2 FLR 426, CA; *Re A (Male Sterilisation)* [2000] 1 FLR 549; *Re S (Sterilisation: Patient's Best Interests)* [2000] 2 FLR 389; *Re F (Adult Patient: Sterilisation)* [2001] Fam 15

2.13 It is impossible to give a single description of what 'best interests' are, because they depend on individual circumstances. However, section 4 of the Act sets out a checklist of steps to follow in order to determine what is in the best interests of a person who lacks capacity to make the decision in question each time someone acts or makes a decision on that person's behalf. See chapter 5 for detailed guidance and examples.

Chapter 2

What are the statutory principles and how should they be applied?

Principle 5: *'Before the act is done, or the decision is made, regard must be had to whether the purpose for which it is needed can be as effectively achieved in a way that is less restrictive of the person's rights and freedom of action.' (section 1(6))*

2.14 Before somebody makes a decision or acts on behalf of a person who lacks capacity to make that decision or consent to the act, they must always question if they can do something else that would interfere less with the person's basic rights and freedoms. This is called finding the 'less restrictive alternative'. It includes considering whether there is a need to act or make a decision at all.

2.15 Where there is more than one option, it is important to explore ways that would be less restrictive or allow the most freedom for a person who lacks capacity to make the decision in question. However, the final decision must always allow the original purpose of the decision or act to be achieved.

2.16 Any decision or action must still be in the best interests of the person who lacks capacity. So sometimes it may be necessary to choose an option that is not the least restrictive alternative if that option is in the person's best interests. In practice, the process of choosing a less restrictive option and deciding what is in the person's best interests will be combined. But both principles must be applied each time a decision or action may be taken on behalf of a person who lacks capacity to make the relevant decision.

Scenario: Finding a less restrictive option

Sunil, a young man with severe learning disabilities, also has a very severe and unpredictable form of epilepsy that is associated with drop attacks. These can result in serious injury. A neurologist has advised that, to limit the harm that might come from these attacks, Sunil should either be under constant close observation, or wear a protective helmet.

After assessment, it is decided that Sunil lacks capacity to decide on the most appropriate course of action for himself. But through his actions and behaviour, Sunil makes it clear he doesn't like to be too closely observed – even though he likes having company.

The staff of the home where he lives consider various options, such as providing a special room for him with soft furnishings, finding ways to keep him under close observation or getting him to wear a helmet. In discussion with Sunil's parents, they agree that the option that is in his best interests, and is less restrictive, will be the helmet – as it will enable him to go out, and prevent further harm.

3 How should people be helped to make their own decisions?

Before deciding that someone lacks capacity to make a particular decision, it is important to take all practical and appropriate steps to enable them to make that decision themselves (statutory principle 2, see chapter 2). In addition, as section 3(2) of the Act underlines, these steps (such as helping individuals to communicate) must be taken in a way which reflects the person's individual circumstances and meets their particular needs. This chapter provides practical guidance on how to support people to make decisions for themselves, or play as big a role as possible in decision-making.

In this chapter, as throughout the Code, a person's capacity (or lack of capacity) refers specifically to their capacity to make a particular decision at the time it needs to be made.

Quick summary

To help someone make a decision for themselves, check the following points:

Providing relevant information

- Does the person have all the relevant information they need to make a particular decision?
- If they have a choice, have they been given information on all the alternatives?

Communicating in an appropriate way

- Could information be explained or presented in a way that is easier for the person to understand (for example, by using simple language or visual aids)?
- Have different methods of communication been explored if required, including non-verbal communication?
- Could anyone else help with communication (for example, a family member, support worker, interpreter, speech and language therapist or advocate)?

Making the person feel at ease

- Are there particular times of day when the person's understanding is better?
- Are there particular locations where they may feel more at ease?
- Could the decision be put off to see whether the person can make the decision at a later time when circumstances are right for them?

Supporting the person

- Can anyone else help or support the person to make choices or express a view?

How can someone be helped to make a decision?

3.1 There are several ways in which people can be helped and supported to enable them to make a decision for themselves. These will vary depending on the decision to be made, the time-scale for making the decision and the individual circumstances of the person making it.

3.2 The Act applies to a wide range of people with different conditions that may affect their capacity to make particular decisions. So, the appropriate steps to take will depend on:

- a person's individual circumstances (for example, somebody with learning difficulties may need a different approach to somebody with dementia)
- the decision the person has to make and
- the length of time they have to make it.

3.3 Significant, one-off decisions (such as moving house) will require different considerations from day-to-day decisions about a person's care and welfare. However, the same general processes should apply to each decision.

3.4 In most cases, only some of the steps described in this chapter will be relevant or appropriate, and the list included here is not exhaustive. It is up to the people (whether family carers, paid carers, healthcare staff or anyone else) caring for or supporting an individual to consider what is possible and appropriate in individual cases. In all cases it is extremely important to find the most effective way of communicating with the person concerned. Good communication is essential for explaining relevant information in an appropriate way and for ensuring that the steps being taken meet an individual's needs.

3.5 Providing appropriate help with decision-making should form part of care planning processes for people receiving health or social care services. Examples include:

- Person Centred Planning for people with learning disabilities
- the Care Programme Approach for people with mental disorders
- the Single Assessment Process for older people in England, and
- the Unified Assessment Process in Wales.

Chapter 3

How should people be helped to make their own decisions?

What happens in emergency situations?

3.6 Clearly, in emergency medical situations (for example, where a person collapses with a heart attack or for some unknown reason and is brought unconscious into a hospital), urgent decisions will have to be made and immediate action taken in the person's best interests. In these situations, it may not be practical or appropriate to delay the treatment while trying to help the person make their own decisions, or to consult with any known attorneys or deputies. However, even in emergency situations, healthcare staff should try to communicate with the person and keep them informed of what is happening.

What information should be provided to people and how should it be provided?

3.7 Providing relevant information is essential in all decision-making. For example, to make a choice about what they want for breakfast, people need to know what food is available. If the decision concerns medical treatment, the doctor must explain the purpose and effect of the course of treatment and the likely consequences of accepting or refusing treatment.

3.8 All practical and appropriate steps must be taken to help people to make a decision for themselves. Information must be tailored to an individual's needs and abilities. It must also be in the easiest and most appropriate form of communication for the person concerned.

What information is relevant?

3.9 The Act cannot state exactly what information will be relevant in each case. Anyone helping someone to make a decision for themselves should therefore follow these steps.

- Take time to explain anything that might help the person make a decision. It is important that they have access to all the information they need to make an informed decision.

- Try not to give more detail than the person needs – this might confuse them. In some cases, a simple, broad explanation will be enough. But it must not miss out important information.

- What are the risks and benefits? Describe any foreseeable consequences of making the decision, and of not making any decision at all.

- Explain the effects the decision might have on the person and those close to them – including the people involved in their care.

- If they have a choice, give them the same information in a balanced way for all the options.

- For some types of decisions, it may be important to give access to advice from elsewhere. This may be independent or specialist advice (for example, from a medical practitioner or a financial or legal adviser). But it might simply be advice from trusted friends or relatives.

Communication – general guidance

3.10 To help someone make a decision for themselves, all possible and appropriate means of communication should be tried.

- Ask people who know the person well about the best form of communication (try speaking to family members, carers, day centre staff or support workers). They may also know somebody the person can communicate with easily, or the time when it is best to communicate with them.

- Use simple language. Where appropriate, use pictures, objects or illustrations to demonstrate ideas.

- Speak at the right volume and speed, with appropriate words and sentence structure. It may be helpful to pause to check understanding or show that a choice is available.

- Break down difficult information into smaller points that are easy to understand. Allow the person time to consider and understand each point before continuing.

- It may be necessary to repeat information or go back over a point several times.

- Is help available from people the person trusts (relatives, friends, GP, social worker, religious or community leaders)? If so, make sure the person's right to confidentiality is respected.

- Be aware of cultural, ethnic or religious factors that shape a person's way of thinking, behaviour or communication. For example, in some cultures it is important to involve the community in decision-making. Some religious beliefs (for example, those of Jehovah's Witnesses or Christian Scientists) may influence the person's approach to medical treatment and information about treatment decisions.

- If necessary, consider using a professional language interpreter. Even if a person communicated in English or Welsh in the past, they may have lost some verbal skills (for example, because of dementia). They may now prefer to communicate in their first language. It is often more appropriate to use a professional interpreter rather than to use family members.

- If using pictures to help communication, make sure they are relevant and the person can understand them easily. For example, a red bus may represent a form of transport to one person but a day trip to another.

- Would an advocate (someone who can support and represent the person) improve communication in the current situation? (See chapters 10 and 15 for more information about advocates.)

Chapter 3

How should people be helped to make their own decisions?

Scenario: Providing relevant information

Mrs Thomas has Alzheimer's disease and lives in a care home. She enjoys taking part in the activities provided at the home. Today there is a choice between going to a flower show, attending her usual pottery class or watching a DVD. Although she has the capacity to choose, having to decide is making her anxious.

The care assistant carefully explains the different options. She tells Mrs Thomas about the DVD she could watch, but Mrs Thomas doesn't like the sound of it. The care assistant shows her a leaflet about the flower show. She explains the plans for the day, where the show is being held and how long it will take to get there in the mini-van. She has to repeat this information several times, as Mrs Thomas keeps asking whether they will be back in time for supper. She also tells Mrs Thomas that one of her friends is going on the trip.

At first, Mrs Thomas is reluctant to disturb her usual routine. But the care assistant reassures her she will not lose her place at pottery if she misses a class. With this information, Mrs Thomas can therefore choose whether or not to go on the day trip.

Helping people with specific communication or cognitive problems

3.11 Where people have specific communication or cognitive problems, the following steps can help:

- Find out how the person is used to communicating. Do they use picture boards or Makaton (signs and symbols for people with communication or learning difficulties)? Or do they have a way of communicating that is only known to those close to them?

- If the person has hearing difficulties, use their preferred method of communication (for example, visual aids, written messages or sign language). Where possible, use a qualified interpreter.

- Are mechanical devices such as voice synthesisers, keyboards or other computer equipment available to help?

- If the person does not use verbal communication skills, allow more time to learn how to communicate effectively.

- For people who use non-verbal methods of communication, their behaviour (in particular, changes in behaviour) can provide indications of their feelings.

- Some people may prefer to use non-verbal means of communication and can communicate most effectively in written form using computers or other communication technologies. This is particularly true for those with autistic spectrum disorders.

- For people with specific communication difficulties, consider other types of professional help (for example, a speech and language therapist or an expert in clinical neuropsychology).

Scenario: Helping people with specific communication difficulties

David is a deafblind man with learning disabilities who has no formal communication. He lives in a specialist home. He begins to bang his head against the wall and repeats this behaviour throughout the day. He has not done this before.

The staff in the home are worried and discuss ways to reduce the risk of injury. They come up with a range of possible interventions, aimed at engaging him with activities and keeping him away from objects that could injure him. They assess these as less restrictive ways to ensure he is safe. But David lacks the capacity to make a decision about which would the best option.

The staff call in a specialist in challenging behaviour, who says that David's behaviour is communicative. After investigating this further, staff discover he is in pain because of tooth decay. They consult a dentist about how to resolve this, and the dentist decides it is in David's best interests to get treatment for the tooth decay. After treatment, David's head-banging stops.

What steps should be taken to put a person at ease?

3.12   To help put someone at ease and so improve their ability to make a decision, careful consideration should be given to both location and timing.

Location

3.13   In terms of location, consider the following:

- Where possible, choose a location where the person feels most at ease. For example, people are usually more comfortable in their own home than at a doctor's surgery.

- Would the person find it easier to make their decision in a relevant location? For example, could you help them decide about medical treatment by taking them to hospital to see what is involved?

- Choose a quiet location where the discussion can't be easily interrupted.

- Try to eliminate any background noise or distractions (for example, the television or radio, or people talking).

- Choose a location where the person's privacy and dignity can be properly respected.

Timing

3.14   In terms of timing, consider the following:

- Try to choose the time of day when the person is most alert – some people are better in the mornings, others are more lively in the afternoon or early evening. It may be necessary to try several times before a decision can be made.

- If the person's capacity is likely to improve in the foreseeable future, wait until it has done so – if practical and appropriate. For example, this might be the case after treatment for depression or a psychotic episode. Obviously, this may not be practical and appropriate if the decision is urgent.

- Some medication could affect a person's capacity (for example, medication which causes drowsiness or affects memory). Can the decision be delayed until side effects have subsided?

- Take one decision at a time – be careful to avoid making the person tired or confused.

- Don't rush – allow the person time to think things over or ask for clarification, where that is possible and appropriate.

- Avoid or challenge time limits that are unnecessary if the decision is not urgent. Delaying the decision may enable further steps to be taken to assist people to make the decision for themselves.

Scenario: Getting the location and timing right

Luke, a young man, was seriously injured in a road traffic accident and suffered permanent brain damage. He has been in hospital several months, and has made good progress, but he gets very frustrated at his inability to concentrate or do things for himself.

Luke now needs surgical treatment on his leg. During the early morning ward round, the surgeon tries to explain what is involved in the operation. She asks Luke to sign a consent form, but he gets angry and says he doesn't want to talk about it.

His key nurse knows that Luke becomes more alert and capable later in the day. After lunch, she asks him if he would like to discuss the operation again. She also knows that he responds better one-to-one than in a group. So she takes Luke into a private room and repeats the information that the surgeon gave him earlier. He understands why the treatment is needed, what is involved and the likely consequences. Therefore, Luke has the capacity to make a decision about the operation.

Support from other people

3.15   In some circumstances, individuals will be more comfortable making decisions when someone else is there to support them.

- Might the person benefit from having another person present? Sometimes having a relative or friend nearby can provide helpful support and reduce anxiety. However, some people might find this intrusive, and it could increase their anxiety or affect their ability to make a free choice. Find ways of getting the person's views on this, for example, by watching their behaviour towards other people.

- Always respect a person's right to confidentiality.

Scenario: Getting help from other people

Jane has a learning disability. She expresses herself using some words, facial expressions and body language. She has lived in her current community home all her life, but now needs to move to a new group home. She finds it difficult to discuss abstract ideas or things she hasn't experienced. Staff conclude that she lacks the capacity to decide for herself which new group home she should move to.

The staff involve an advocate to help Jane express her views. Jane's advocate spends time with her in different environments. The advocate uses pictures, symbols and Makaton to find out the things that are important to Jane, and speaks to people who know Jane to find out what they think she likes. She then supports Jane to show their work to her care manager, and checks that the new homes suggested for her are able to meet Jane's needs and preferences.

When the care manager has found some suitable places, Jane's advocate visits the homes with Jane. They take photos of the houses to help her distinguish between them. The advocate then uses the photos to help Jane work out which home she prefers. Jane's own feelings can now play an important part in deciding what is in her best interests – and so in the final decision about where she will live.

What other ways are there to enable decision-making?

3.16 There are other ways to help someone make a decision for themselves.

- Many people find it helpful to talk things over with people they trust – or people who have been in a similar situation or faced similar dilemmas. For example, people with learning difficulties may benefit from the help of a designated support worker or being part of a support network.

- If someone is very distressed (for example, following a death of someone close) or where there are long-standing problems that affect someone's ability to understand an issue, it may be possible to delay a decision so that the person can have psychological therapy, if needed.

- Some organisations have produced materials to help people who need support to make decisions and for those who support them. Some of this material is designed to help people with specific conditions, such as Alzheimer's disease or profound learning disability.

- It may be important to provide access to technology. For example, some people who appear not to communicate well verbally can do so very well using computers.

Scenario: Making the most of technology

Ms Patel has an autistic spectrum disorder. Her family and care staff find it difficult to communicate with her. She refuses to make eye contact, and gets very upset and angry when her carers try to encourage her to speak.

One member of staff notices that Ms Patel is interested in the computer equipment. He shows her how to use the keyboard, and they are able to have a conversation using the computer. An IT specialist works with her to make sure she can make the most of her computing skills to communicate her feelings and decisions.

4 How does the Act define a person's capacity to make a decision and how should capacity be assessed?

This chapter explains what the Act means by 'capacity' and 'lack of capacity'. It provides guidance on how to assess whether someone has the capacity to make a decision, and suggests when professionals should be involved in the assessment.

> In this chapter, as throughout the Code, a person's capacity (or lack of capacity) refers specifically to their capacity to make a particular decision at the time it needs to be made.

Quick summary

This checklist is a summary of points to consider when assessing a person's capacity to make a specific decision. Readers should also refer to the more detailed guidance in this chapter and chapters 2 and 3.

Presuming someone has capacity

- The starting assumption must always be that a person has the capacity to make a decision, unless it can be established that they lack capacity.

Understanding what is meant by capacity and lack of capacity

- A person's capacity must be assessed specifically in terms of their capacity to make a particular decision at the time it needs to be made.

Treating everyone equally

- A person's capacity must not be judged simply on the basis of their age, appearance, condition or an aspect of their behaviour.

Supporting the person to make the decision for themselves

- It is important to take all possible steps to try to help people make a decision for themselves (see chapter 2, principle 2, and chapter 3).

Assessing capacity

Anyone assessing someone's capacity to make a decision for themselves should use the two-stage test of capacity.

Chapter 4

How does the Act define a person's capacity to make a decision and how should capacity be assessed?

- Does the person have an impairment of the mind or brain, or is there some sort of disturbance affecting the way their mind or brain works? (It doesn't matter whether the impairment or disturbance is temporary or permanent.)

- If so, does that impairment or disturbance mean that the person is unable to make the decision in question at the time it needs to be made?

Assessing ability to make a decision

- Does the person have a general understanding of what decision they need to make and why they need to make it?

- Does the person have a general understanding of the likely consequences of making, or not making, this decision?

- Is the person able to understand, retain, use and weigh up the information relevant to this decision?

- Can the person communicate their decision (by talking, using sign language or any other means)? Would the services of a professional (such as a speech and language therapist) be helpful?

Assessing capacity to make more complex or serious decisions

- Is there a need for a more thorough assessment (perhaps by involving a doctor or other professional expert)?

What is mental capacity?

4.1   Mental capacity is the ability to make a decision.

- This includes the ability to make a decision that affects daily life – such as when to get up, what to wear or whether to go to the doctor when feeling ill – as well as more serious or significant decisions.

- It also refers to a person's ability to make a decision that may have legal consequences – for them or others. Examples include agreeing to have medical treatment, buying goods or making a will.

4.2   The starting point must always be to assume that a person has the capacity to make a specific decision (see chapter 2, principle 1). Some people may need help to be able to make or communicate a decision (see chapter 3). But this does not necessarily mean that they lack capacity to do so. What matters is their ability to carry out the processes involved in making the decision – and not the outcome.

What does the Act mean by 'lack of capacity'?

4.3   Section 2(1) of the Act states:

'For the purposes of this Act, a person lacks capacity in relation to a matter if at the material time he is unable to make a decision for himself in relation to the matter because of an impairment of, or a disturbance in the functioning of, the mind or brain.'

This means that a person lacks capacity if:

- they have an impairment or disturbance (for example, a disability, condition or trauma) that affects the way their mind or brain works, and

- the impairment or disturbance means that they are unable to make a specific decision at the time it needs to be made.

4.4   An assessment of a person's capacity must be based on their ability to make a specific decision at the time it needs to be made, and not their ability to make decisions in general. Section 3 of the Act defines what it means to be unable to make a decision (this is explained in paragraph 4.14 below).

4.5   Section 2(2) states that the impairment or disturbance does not have to be permanent. A person can lack capacity to make a decision at the time it needs to be made even if:

- the loss of capacity is partial

- the loss of capacity is temporary

- their capacity changes over time.

A person may also lack capacity to make a decision about one issue but not about others.

4.6   The Act generally applies to people who are aged 16 or older. Chapter 12 explains how the Act affects children and young people – in particular those aged 16 and 17 years.

What safeguards does the Act provide around assessing someone's capacity?

Chapter 4

How does the Act define a person's capacity to make a decision and how should capacity be assessed?

4.7 An assessment that a person lacks capacity to make a decision must never be based simply on:

- their age

- their appearance

- assumptions about their condition, or

- any aspect of their behaviour. (section 2(3))

4.8 The Act deliberately uses the word 'appearance', because it covers all aspects of the way people look. So for example, it includes the physical characteristics of certain conditions (for example, scars, features linked to Down's syndrome or muscle spasms caused by cerebral palsy) as well as aspects of appearance like skin colour, tattoos and body piercings, or the way people dress (including religious dress).

4.9 The word 'condition' is also wide-ranging. It includes physical disabilities, learning difficulties and disabilities, illness related to age, and temporary conditions (for example, drunkenness or unconsciousness). Aspects of behaviour might include extrovert (for example, shouting or gesticulating) and withdrawn behaviour (for example, talking to yourself or avoiding eye contact).

Scenario: Treating everybody equally

Tom, a man with cerebral palsy, has slurred speech. Sometimes he also falls over for no obvious reason.

One day Tom falls in the supermarket. Staff call an ambulance, even though he says he is fine. They think he may need treatment after his fall.

When the ambulance comes, the ambulance crew know they must not make assumptions about Tom's capacity to decide about treatment, based simply on his condition and the effects of his disability. They talk to him and find that he is capable of making healthcare decisions for himself.

What proof of lack of capacity does the Act require?

4.10   Anybody who claims that an individual lacks capacity should be able to provide proof. They need to be able to show, *on the balance of probabilities*, that the individual lacks capacity to make a particular decision, at the time it needs to be made (section 2(4)). This means being able to show that it is more likely than not that the person lacks capacity to make the decision in question.

What is the test of capacity?

To help determine if a person lacks capacity to make particular decisions, the Act sets out a two-stage test of capacity.

Stage 1: Does the person have an impairment of, or a disturbance in the functioning of, their mind or brain?

4.11   Stage 1 requires proof that the person has an impairment of the mind or brain, or some sort of or disturbance that affects the way their mind or brain works. If a person does not have such an impairment or disturbance of the mind or brain, they will not lack capacity under the Act.

4.12   Examples of an impairment or disturbance in the functioning of the mind or brain may include the following:

- conditions associated with some forms of mental illness
- dementia
- significant learning disabilities
- the long-term effects of brain damage
- physical or medical conditions that cause confusion, drowsiness or loss of consciousness
- delirium
- concussion following a head injury, and
- the symptoms of alcohol or drug use.

> **Scenario: Assessing whether an impairment or disturbance is affecting someone's ability to make a decision**
>
> Mrs Collins is 82 and has had a stroke. This has weakened the left-hand side of her body. She is living in a house that has been the family home for years. Her son wants her to sell her house and live with him.
>
> Mrs Collins likes the idea, but her daughter does not. She thinks her mother will lose independence and her condition will get worse. She talks to her mother's consultant to get information that will help stop the sale. But he says that although Mrs Collins is anxious about the physical effects the stroke has had on her body, it has not caused any mental impairment or affected her brain, so she still has capacity to make her own decision about selling her house.

Chapter 4

How does the Act define a person's capacity to make a decision and how should capacity be assessed?

Stage 2: Does the impairment or disturbance mean that the person is unable to make a specific decision when they need to?

4.13   For a person to lack capacity to make a decision, the Act says their impairment or disturbance must affect their ability to make the specific decision when they need to. But first people must be given all practical and appropriate support to help them make the decision for themselves (see chapter 2, principle 2). Stage 2 can only apply if all practical and appropriate support to help the person make the decision has failed. See chapter 3 for guidance on ways of helping people to make their own decisions.

What does the Act mean by 'inability to make a decision'?

4.14   A person is unable to make a decision if they cannot:

1.   understand information about the decision to be made (the Act calls this 'relevant information')

2.   retain that information in their mind

3.   use or weigh that information as part of the decision-making process, or

4.   communicate their decision (by talking, using sign language or any other means). See section 3(1).

4.15 These four points are explained in more detail below. The first three should be applied together. If a person cannot do any of these three things, they will be treated as unable to make the decision. The fourth only applies in situations where people cannot communicate their decision in any way.

Understanding information about the decision to be made

4.16 It is important not to assess someone's understanding before they have been given relevant information about a decision. Every effort must be made to provide information in a way that is most appropriate to help the person to understand. Quick or inadequate explanations are not acceptable unless the situation is urgent (see chapter 3 for some practical steps). Relevant information includes:

- the nature of the decision
- the reason why the decision is needed, and
- the likely effects of deciding one way or another, or making no decision at all.

4.17 Section 3(2) outlines the need to present information in a way that is appropriate to meet the individual's needs and circumstances. It also stresses the importance of explaining information using the most effective form of communication for that person (such as simple language, sign language, visual representations, computer support or any other means).

4.18 For example:

- a person with a learning disability may need somebody to read information to them. They might also need illustrations to help them to understand what is happening. Or they might stop the reader to ask what things mean. It might also be helpful for them to discuss information with an advocate.
- a person with anxiety or depression may find it difficult to reach a decision about treatment in a group meeting with professionals. They may prefer to read the relevant documents in private. This way they can come to a conclusion alone, and ask for help if necessary.
- someone who has a brain injury might need to be given information several times. It will be necessary to check that the person understands the information. If they have difficulty understanding, it might be useful to present information in a different way (for example, different forms of words, pictures or diagrams). Written information, audiotapes, videos and posters can help people remember important facts.

4.19 Relevant information must include what the likely consequences of a decision would be (the possible effects of deciding one way or another) – and also the likely consequences of making no decision at all (section 3(4)). In some cases, it may be enough to give a broad explanation using simple language. But a person might need more detailed information or access to advice, depending on the decision that needs to be made. If a decision could have serious or grave consequences, it is even more important that a person understands the information relevant to that decision.

Chapter 4

How does the Act define a person's capacity to make a decision and how should capacity be assessed?

Scenario: Providing relevant information in an appropriate format

Mr Leslie has learning disabilities and has developed an irregular heartbeat. He has been prescribed medication for this, but is anxious about having regular blood tests to check his medication levels. His doctor gives him a leaflet to explain:

- the reason for the tests

- what a blood test involves

- the risks in having or not having the tests, and

- that he has the right to decide whether or not to have the test.

The leaflet uses simple language and photographs to explain these things. Mr Leslie's carer helps him read the leaflet over the next few days, and checks that he understands it.

Mr Leslie goes back to tell the doctor that, even though he is scared of needles, he will agree to the blood tests so that he can get the right medication. He is able to pick out the equipment needed to do the blood test. So the doctor concludes that Mr Leslie can understand, retain and use the relevant information and therefore has the capacity to make the decision to have the test.

Retaining information

4.20 The person must be able to hold the information in their mind long enough to use it to make an effective decision. But section 3(3) states that people who can only retain information for a short while must not automatically be assumed to lack the capacity to decide – it depends on what is necessary for the decision in question. Items such as notebooks, photographs, posters, videos and voice recorders can help people record and retain information.

> **Scenario: Assessing a person's ability to retain information**
>
> Walter, an elderly man, is diagnosed with dementia and has problems remembering things in the short term. He can't always remember his great-grandchildren's names, but he recognises them when they come to visit. He can also pick them out on photographs.
>
> Walter would like to buy premium bonds (a type of financial investment) for each of his great-grandchildren. He asks his solicitor to make the arrangements. After assessing his capacity to make financial decisions, the solicitor is satisfied that Walter has capacity to make this decision, despite his short-term memory problems.

Using or weighing information as part of the decision-making process

4.21   For someone to have capacity, they must have the ability to weigh up information and use it to arrive at a decision. Sometimes people can understand information but an impairment or disturbance stops them using it. In other cases, the impairment or disturbance leads to a person making a specific decision without understanding or using the information they have been given.[3]

4.22   For example, a person with the eating disorder anorexia nervosa may understand information about the consequences of not eating. But their compulsion not to eat might be too strong for them to ignore. Some people who have serious brain damage might make impulsive decisions regardless of information they have been given or their understanding of it.

Inability to communicate a decision in any way

4.23   Sometimes there is no way for a person to communicate. This will apply to very few people, but it does include:

- people who are unconscious or in a coma, or
- those with the very rare condition sometimes known as 'locked-in syndrome', who are conscious but cannot speak or move at all.

---

[3]   This issue has been considered in a number of court cases, including *Re MB* [1997] 2 FLR 426; *R v Collins and Ashworth Hospital Authority ex parte Brady* [2001] 58 BMLR 173

Chapter 4

How does the
Act define a
person's capacity
to make a
decision and how
should capacity
be assessed?

If a person cannot communicate their decision in any way at all, the Act says they should be treated as if they are unable to make that decision.

4.24 Before deciding that someone falls into this category, it is important to make all practical and appropriate efforts to help them communicate. This might call for the involvement of speech and language therapists, specialists in non-verbal communication or other professionals. Chapter 3 gives advice for communicating with people who have specific disabilities or cognitive problems.

4.25 Communication by simple muscle movements can show that somebody can communicate and may have capacity to make a decision.[4] For example, a person might blink an eye or squeeze a hand to say 'yes' or 'no'. In these cases, assessment must use the first three points listed in paragraph 4.14, which are explained in more depth in paragraphs 4.16–4.22.

What other issues might affect capacity?

People with fluctuating or temporary capacity

4.26 Some people have fluctuating capacity – they have a problem or condition that gets worse occasionally and affects their ability to make decisions. For example, someone who has manic depression may have a temporary manic phase which causes them to lack capacity to make financial decisions, leading them to get into debt even though at other times they are perfectly able to manage their money. A person with a psychotic illness may have delusions that affect their capacity to make decisions at certain times but disappear at others. Temporary factors may also affect someone's ability to make decisions. Examples include acute illness, severe pain, the effect of medication, or distress after a death or shock. More guidance on how to support someone with fluctuating or temporary capacity to make a decision can be found in chapter 3, particularly paragraphs 3.12–3.16. More information about factors that may indicate that a person may regain or develop capacity in the future can be found at paragraph 5.28.

4.27 As in any other situation, an assessment must only examine a person's capacity to make a particular decision when it needs to be made. It may be possible to put off the decision until the person has the capacity to make it (see also guidance on best interests in chapter 5).

---

4   This was demonstrated in the case *Re AK (Adult Patient) (Medical Treatment: Consent)* [2001] 1 FLR 129

Ongoing conditions that may affect capacity

4.28   Generally, capacity assessments should be related to a specific
       decision. But there may be people with an ongoing condition that
       affects their ability to make certain decisions or that may affect other
       decisions in their life. One decision on its own may make sense, but
       may give cause for concern when considered alongside others.

4.29   Again, it is important to review capacity from time to time, as people
       can improve their decision-making capabilities. In particular, someone
       with an ongoing condition may become able to make some, if not all,
       decisions. Some people (for example, people with learning disabilities)
       will learn new skills throughout their life, improving their capacity to
       make certain decisions. So assessments should be reviewed from time
       to time. Capacity should always be reviewed:

       • whenever a care plan is being developed or reviewed

       • at other relevant stages of the care planning process, and

       • as particular decisions need to be made.

4.30   It is important to acknowledge the difference between:

       • unwise decisions, which a person has the right to make (chapter 2,
         principle 3), and

       • decisions based on a lack of understanding of risks or inability to
         weigh up the information about a decision.

       Information about decisions the person has made based on a lack of
       understanding of risks or inability to weigh up the information can form
       part of a capacity assessment – particularly if someone repeatedly
       makes decisions that put them at risk or result in harm to them or
       someone else.

Chapter 4

How does the
Act define a
person's capacity
to make a
decision and how
should capacity
be assessed?

Scenario: Ongoing conditions

Paul had an accident at work and suffered severe head injuries. He was awarded compensation to pay for care he will need throughout his life as a result of his head injury. An application was made to the Court of Protection to consider how the award of compensation should be managed, including whether to appoint a deputy to manage Paul's financial affairs. Paul objected as he believed he could manage his life and should be able to spend his money however he liked.

He wrote a list of what he intended to spend his money on. This included fully-staffed luxury properties and holiday villas, cars with chauffeurs, jewellery and various other items for himself and his family. But spending money on all these luxury items would not leave enough money to cover the costs of his care in future years.

The court judged that Paul had capacity to make day-to-day financial decisions, but he did not understand why he had received compensation and what the money was supposed to be used for. Nor did he understand how buying luxuries now could affect his future care. The court therefore decided Paul lacked capacity to manage large amounts of money and appointed a deputy to make ongoing financial decisions relating to his care. But it gave him access to enough funds to cover everyday needs and occasional treats.

What other legal tests of capacity are there?

4.31   The Act makes clear that the definition of 'lack of capacity' and the two-stage test for capacity set out in the Act are 'for the purposes of this Act'. This means that the definition and test are to be used in situations covered by this Act. Schedule 6 of the Act also amends existing laws to ensure that the definition and test are used in other areas of law not covered directly by this Act.

For example, Schedule 6, paragraph 20 allows a person to be disqualified from jury service if they lack the capacity (using this Act's definition) to carry out a juror's tasks.

4.32   There are several tests of capacity that have been produced following judgments in court cases (known as common law tests).[5] These cover:

---

[5]   For details, see British Medical Association & Law Society, *Assessment of Mental Capacity: Guidance for Doctors and Lawyers* (Second edition) (London: BMJ Books, 2004)

- capacity to make a will[6]
- capacity to make a gift[7]
- capacity to enter into a contract[8]
- capacity to litigate (take part in legal cases),[9] and
- capacity to enter into marriage.[10]

4.33 The Act's new definition of capacity is in line with the existing common law tests, and the Act does not replace them. When cases come before the court on the above issues, judges can adopt the new definition if they think it is appropriate. The Act will apply to all other cases relating to financial, healthcare or welfare decisions.

When should capacity be assessed?

4.34 Assessing capacity correctly is vitally important to everyone affected by the Act. Someone who is assessed as lacking capacity may be denied their right to make a specific decision – particularly if others think that the decision would not be in their best interests or could cause harm. Also, if a person lacks capacity to make specific decisions, that person might make decisions they do not really understand. Again, this could cause harm or put the person at risk. So it is important to carry out an assessment when a person's capacity is in doubt. It is also important that the person who does an assessment can justify their conclusions. Many organisations will provide specific professional guidance for members of their profession.[11]

4.35 There are a number of reasons why people may question a person's capacity to make a specific decision:

- the person's behaviour or circumstances cause doubt as to whether they have the capacity to make a decision

---

6 *Banks v Goodfellow* (1870) LR 5 QB 549

7 *Re Beaney (deceased)* [1978] 2 All ER 595

8 *Boughton v Knight* (1873) LR 3 PD 64

9 *Masterman-Lister v Brutton & Co and Jewell & Home Counties Dairies* [2003] 3 All ER 162 (CA)

10 *Sheffield City Council v E & S* [2005] 1 FLR 965

11 See for example, British Medical Association & Law Society, *Assessment of Mental Capacity: Guidance for Doctors and Lawyers* (Second edition) (London: BMJ Books, 2004); the Joint Royal Colleges Ambulance Service Liaison Committee Clinical Practice Guidelines (JRCALC, available online at www2.warwick.ac.uk/fac/med/research/hsri/emergencycare/jrcalc_2006/clinical_guidelines_2006.pdf) and British Psychological Society, *Guidelines on assessing capacity* (BPS, 2006 available online at www.bps.org.uk)

Chapter 4

How does the
Act define a
person's capacity
to make a
decision and how
should capacity
be assessed?

- somebody else says they are concerned about the person's capacity, or

- the person has previously been diagnosed with an impairment or disturbance that affects the way their mind or brain works (see paragraphs 4.11–4.12 above), and it has already been shown they lack capacity to make other decisions in their life.

4.36 The starting assumption must be that the person has the capacity to make the specific decision. If, however, anyone thinks a person lacks capacity, it is important to then ask the following questions:

- Does the person have all the relevant information they need to make the decision?

- If they are making a decision that involves choosing between alternatives, do they have information on all the different options?

- Would the person have a better understanding if information was explained or presented in another way?

- Are there times of day when the person's understanding is better?

- Are there locations where they may feel more at ease?

- Can the decision be put off until the circumstances are different and the person concerned may be able to make the decision?

- Can anyone else help the person to make choices or express a view (for example, a family member or carer, an advocate or someone to help with communication)?

4.37 Chapter 3 describes ways to deal with these questions and suggest steps which may help people make their own decisions. If all practical and appropriate steps fail, an assessment will then be needed of the person's capacity to make the decision that now needs to be made.

Who should assess capacity?

4.38 The person who assesses an individual's capacity to make a decision will usually be the person who is directly concerned with the individual at the time the decision needs to be made. This means that different people will be involved in assessing someone's capacity to make different decisions at different times.

For most day-to-day decisions, this will be the person caring for them at the time a decision must be made. For example, a care worker might need to assess if the person can agree to being bathed. Then a district nurse might assess if the person can consent to have a dressing changed.

4.39 For acts of care or treatment (see chapter 6), the assessor must have a 'reasonable belief' that the person lacks capacity to agree to the action or decision to be taken (see paragraphs 4.44–4.45 for a description of reasonable belief).

4.40 If a doctor or healthcare professional proposes treatment or an examination, they must assess the person's capacity to consent. In settings such as a hospital, this can involve the multi-disciplinary team (a team of people from different professional backgrounds who share responsibility for a patient). But ultimately, it is up to the professional responsible for the person's treatment to make sure that capacity has been assessed.

4.41 For a legal transaction (for example, making a will), a solicitor or legal practitioner must assess the client's capacity to instruct them. They must assess whether the client has the capacity to satisfy any relevant legal test. In cases of doubt, they should get an opinion from a doctor or other professional expert.

4.42 More complex decisions are likely to need more formal assessments (see paragraph 4.54 below). A professional opinion on the person's capacity might be necessary. This could be, for example, from a psychiatrist, psychologist, a speech and language therapist, occupational therapist or social worker. But the final decision about a person's capacity must be made by the person intending to make the decision or carry out the action on behalf of the person who lacks capacity – not the professional, who is there to advise.

4.43 Any assessor should have the skills and ability to communicate effectively with the person (see chapter 3). If necessary, they should get professional help to communicate with the person.

Chapter 4

How does the
Act define a
person's capacity
to make a
decision and how
should capacity
be assessed?

Scenario: Getting help with assessing capacity

Ms Dodd suffered brain damage in a road accident and is unable to
speak. At first, her family thought she was not able to make decisions.
But they soon discovered that she could choose by pointing at things,
such as the clothes she wants to wear or the food she prefers. Her
behaviour also indicates that she enjoys attending a day centre, but
she refuses to go swimming. Her carers have assessed her as having
capacity to make these decisions.

Ms Dodd needs hospital treatment but she gets distressed when away
from home. Her mother feels that Ms Dodd is refusing treatment by her
behaviour, but her father thinks she lacks capacity to say no to treatment
that could improve her condition.

The clinician who is proposing the treatment will have to assess Ms
Dodd's capacity to consent. He gets help from a member of staff at
the day centre who knows Ms Dodd's communication well and also
discusses things with her parents. Over several meetings the clinician
explains the treatment options to Ms Dodd with the help of the staff
member. The final decision about Ms Dodd's capacity rests with the
clinician, but he will need to use information from the staff member and
others who know Ms Dodd well to make this assessment.

What is 'reasonable belief' of lack of capacity?

4.44   Carers (whether family carers or other carers) and care workers do not
have to be experts in assessing capacity. But to have protection from
liability when providing care or treatment (see chapter 6), they must
have a 'reasonable belief' that the person they care for lacks capacity
to make relevant decisions about their care or treatment (section 5 (1)).
To have this reasonable belief, they must have taken 'reasonable' steps
to establish that that the person lacks capacity to make a decision or
consent to an act at the time the decision or consent is needed. They
must also establish that the act or decision is in the person's best
interests (see chapter 5).

They do not usually need to follow formal processes, such as involving
a professional to make an assessment. However, if somebody
challenges their assessment (see paragraph 4.63 below), they must
be able to describe the steps they have taken. They must also have
objective reasons for believing the person lacks capacity to make the
decision in question.

4.45   The steps that are accepted as 'reasonable' will depend on individual circumstances and the urgency of the decision. Professionals, who are qualified in their particular field, are normally expected to undertake a fuller assessment, reflecting their higher degree of knowledge and experience, than family members or other carers who have no formal qualifications. See paragraph 4.36 for a list of points to consider when assessing someone's capacity. The following may also be helpful:

- Start by assuming the person has capacity to make the specific decision. Is there anything to prove otherwise?

- Does the person have a previous diagnosis of disability or mental disorder? Does that condition now affect their capacity to make this decision? If there has been no previous diagnosis, it may be best to get a medical opinion.

- Make every effort to communicate with the person to explain what is happening.

- Make every effort to try to help the person make the decision in question.

- See if there is a way to explain or present information about the decision in a way that makes it easier to understand. If the person has a choice, do they have information about all the options?

- Can the decision be delayed to take time to help the person make the decision, or to give the person time to regain the capacity to make the decision for themselves?

- Does the person understand what decision they need to make and why they need to make it?

- Can they understand information about the decision? Can they retain it, use it and weigh it to make the decision?

- Be aware that the fact that a person agrees with you or assents to what is proposed does not necessarily mean that they have capacity to make the decision.

What other factors might affect an assessment of capacity?

4.46   It is important to assess people when they are in the best state to make the decision, if possible. Whether this is possible will depend on the nature and urgency of the decision to be made. Many of the practical steps suggested in chapter 3 will help to create the best environment for assessing capacity. The assessor must then carry out the two stages of the test of capacity (see paragraphs 4.11–4.25 above).

4.47 In many cases, it may be clear that the person has an impairment or disturbance in the functioning of their mind or brain which could affect their ability to make a decision. For example, there might be a past diagnosis of a disability or mental disorder, or there may be signs that an illness is returning. Old assumptions about an illness or condition should be reviewed. Sometimes an illness develops gradually (for example, dementia), and it is hard to know when it starts to affect capacity. Anyone assessing someone's capacity may need to ask for a medical opinion as to whether a person has an illness or condition that could affect their capacity to make a decision in this specific case.

Chapter 4

How does the Act define a person's capacity to make a decision and how should capacity be assessed?

Scenario: Getting a professional opinion

Mr Elliott is 87 years old and lives alone. He has poor short-term memory, and he often forgets to eat. He also sometimes neglects his personal hygiene. His daughter talks to him about the possibility of moving into residential care. She decides that he understands the reasons for her concerns as well as the risks of continuing to live alone and, having weighed these up, he has the capacity to decide to stay at home and accept the consequences.

Two months later, Mr Elliott has a fall and breaks his leg. While being treated in hospital, he becomes confused and depressed. He says he wants to go home, but the staff think that the deterioration in his mental health has affected his capacity to make this decision at this time. They think he cannot understand the consequences or weigh up the risks he faces if he goes home. They refer him to a specialist in old age psychiatry, who assesses whether his mental health is affecting his capacity to make this decision. The staff will then use the specialist's opinion to help their assessment of Mr Elliott's capacity.

4.48 Anyone assessing someone's capacity must not assume that a person lacks capacity simply because they have a particular diagnosis or condition. There must be proof that the diagnosed illness or condition affects the ability to make a decision when it needs to be made. The person assessing capacity should ask the following questions:

* Does the person have a general understanding of what decision they need to make and why they need to make it?

* Do they understand the likely consequences of making, or not making, this decision?

- Can they understand and process information about the decision? And can they use it to help them make a decision?

In borderline cases, or where there is doubt, the assessor must be able to show that it is more likely than not that the answer to these questions is 'no'.

What practical steps should be taken when assessing capacity?

4.49 Anyone assessing someone's capacity will need to decide which of these steps are relevant to their situation.

- They should make sure that they understand the nature and effect of the decision to be made themselves. They may need access to relevant documents and background information (for example, details of the person's finances if assessing capacity to manage affairs). See chapter 16 for details on access to information.

- They may need other relevant information to support the assessment (for example, healthcare records or the views of staff involved in the person's care).

- Family members and close friends may be able to provide valuable background information (for example, the person's past behaviour and abilities and the types of decisions they can currently make). But their personal views and wishes about what *they* would want for the person must not influence the assessment.

- They should again explain to the person all the information relevant to the decision. The explanation must be in the most appropriate and effective form of communication for that person.

- Check the person's understanding after a few minutes. The person should be able to give a rough explanation of the information that was explained. There are different methods for people who use non-verbal means of communication (for example, observing behaviour or their ability to recognise objects or pictures).

- Avoid questions that need only a 'yes' or 'no' answer (for example, did you understand what I just said?). They are not enough to assess the person's capacity to make a decision. But there may be no alternative in cases where there are major communication difficulties. In these cases, check the response by asking questions again in a different way.

- Skills and behaviour do not necessarily reflect the person's capacity to make specific decisions. The fact that someone has good social or language skills, polite behaviour or good manners doesn't necessarily mean they understand the information or are able to weigh it up.

- Repeating these steps can help confirm the result.

Chapter 4

How does the Act define a person's capacity to make a decision and how should capacity be assessed?

4.50   For certain kinds of complex decisions (for example, making a will), there are specific legal tests (see paragraph 4.32 above) in addition to the two-stage test for capacity. In some cases, medical or psychometric tests may also be helpful tools (for example, for assessing cognitive skills) in assessing a person's capacity to make particular decisions, but the relevant legal test of capacity must still be fulfilled.

When should professionals be involved?

4.51   Anyone assessing someone's capacity may need to get a professional opinion when assessing a person's capacity to make complex or major decisions. In some cases this will simply involve contacting the person's general practitioner (GP) or family doctor. If the person has a particular condition or disorder, it may be appropriate to contact a specialist (for example, consultant psychiatrist, psychologist or other professional with experience of caring for patients with that condition). A speech and language therapist might be able to help if there are communication difficulties. In some cases, a multi-disciplinary approach is best. This means combining the skills and expertise of different professionals.

4.52   Professionals should never express an opinion without carrying out a proper examination and assessment of the person's capacity to make the decision. They must apply the appropriate test of capacity. In some cases, they will need to meet the person more than once – particularly if the person has communication difficulties. Professionals can get background information from a person's family and carers. But the personal views of these people about what they want for the person who lacks capacity must not influence the outcome of that assessment.

4.53   Professional involvement might be needed if:

- the decision that needs to be made is complicated or has serious consequences

- an assessor concludes a person lacks capacity, and the person challenges the finding

- family members, carers and/or professionals disagree about a person's capacity

- there is a conflict of interest between the assessor and the person being assessed

- the person being assessed is expressing different views to different people – they may be trying to please everyone or telling people what they think they want to hear

- somebody might challenge the person's capacity to make the decision – either at the time of the decision or later (for example, a family member might challenge a will after a person has died on the basis that the person lacked capacity when they made the will)

- somebody has been accused of abusing a vulnerable adult who may lack capacity to make decisions that protect them

- a person repeatedly makes decisions that put them at risk or could result in suffering or damage.

Scenario: Involving professional opinion

Ms Ledger is a young woman with learning disabilities and some autistic spectrum disorders. Recently she began a sexual relationship with a much older man, who is trying to persuade her to move in with him and come off the pill. There are rumours that he has been violent towards her and has taken her bankbook.

Ms Ledger boasts about the relationship to her friends. But she has admitted to her key worker that she is sometimes afraid of the man. Staff at her sheltered accommodation decide to make a referral under the local adult protection procedures. They arrange for a clinical psychologist to assess Ms Ledger's understanding of the relationship and her capacity to consent to it.

4.54 In some cases, it may be a legal requirement, or good professional practice, to undertake a formal assessment of capacity. These cases include:

- where a person's capacity to sign a legal document (for example, a will), could later be challenged, in which case an expert should be asked for an opinion[12]

---

[12] *Kenward v Adams*, The Times, 29 November 1975

- to establish whether a person who might be involved in a legal case needs the assistance of the Official Solicitor or other litigation friend (somebody to represent their views to a court and give instructions to their legal representative) and there is doubt about the person's capacity to instruct a solicitor or take part in the case[13]

- whenever the Court of Protection has to decide if a person lacks capacity in a certain matter

- if the courts are required to make a decision about a person's capacity in other legal proceedings[14]

- if there may be legal consequences of a finding of capacity (for example, deciding on financial compensation following a claim for personal injury).

Chapter 4

How does the Act define a person's capacity to make a decision and how should capacity be assessed?

Are assessment processes confidential?

4.55 People involved in assessing capacity will need to share information about a person's circumstances. But there are ethical codes and laws that require professionals to keep personal information confidential. As a general rule, professionals must ask their patients or clients if they can reveal information to somebody else – even close relatives. But sometimes information may be disclosed without the consent of the person who the information concerns (for example, to protect the person or prevent harm to other people).[15]

4.56 Anyone assessing someone's capacity needs accurate information concerning the person being assessed that is relevant to the decision the person has to make. So professionals should, where possible, make relevant information available. They should make every effort to get the person's permission to reveal relevant information. They should give a full explanation of why this is necessary, and they should tell the person about the risks and consequences of revealing, and not revealing information. If the person is unable to give permission, the professional might still be allowed to provide information that will help make an accurate assessment of the person's capacity to make the specific decision. Chapter 16 has more detail on how to access information.

---

[13] Civil Procedure Rules 1998, r 21.1

[14] *Masterman-Lister v Brutton & Co and Jewell & Home Counties Dairies* [2002] EWCA Civ 1889, CA at 54

[15] For example, in the circumstances discussed in *W v Egdell and others* [1990] 1 All ER 835 at 848; *S v Plymouth City Council and C*, [2002] EWCA Civ 388) at 49

What if someone refuses to be assessed?

4.57 There may be circumstances in which a person whose capacity is in doubt refuses to undergo an assessment of capacity or refuses to be examined by a doctor or other professional. In these circumstances, it might help to explain to someone refusing an assessment why it is needed and what the consequences of refusal are. But threats or attempts to force the person to agree to an assessment are not acceptable.

4.58 If the person lacks capacity to agree or refuse, the assessment can normally go ahead, as long as the person does not object to the assessment, and it is in their best interests (see chapter 5).

4.59 Nobody can be forced to undergo an assessment of capacity. If someone refuses to open the door to their home, it cannot be forced. If there are serious worries about the person's mental health, it may be possible to get a warrant to force entry and assess the person for treatment in hospital – but the situation must meet the requirements of the Mental Health Act 1983 (section 135). But simply refusing an assessment of capacity is in no way sufficient grounds for an assessment under the Mental Health Act 1983 (see chapter 13).

Who should keep a record of assessments?

4.60 Assessments of capacity to take day-to-day decisions or consent to care require no formal assessment procedures or recorded documentation. Paragraphs 4.44–4.45 above explain the steps to take to reach a 'reasonable belief' that someone lacks capacity to make a particular decision. It is good practice for paid care workers to keep a record of the steps they take when caring for the person concerned.

Professional records

4.61 It is good practice for professionals to carry out a proper assessment of a person's capacity to make particular decisions and to record the findings in the relevant professional records.

- A doctor or healthcare professional proposing treatment should carry out an assessment of the person's capacity to consent (with a multi-disciplinary team, if appropriate) and record it in the patient's clinical notes.

- Solicitors should assess a client's capacity to give instructions or carry out a legal transaction (obtaining a medical or other professional opinion, if necessary) and record it on the client's file.

- An assessment of a person's capacity to consent or agree to the provision of services will be part of the care planning processes for health and social care needs, and should be recorded in the relevant documentation. This includes:

- Person Centred Planning for people with learning disabilities

- the Care Programme Approach for people with mental illness

- the Single Assessment Process for older people in England, and

- the Unified Assessment Process in Wales.

Chapter 4

How does the Act define a person's capacity to make a decision and how should capacity be assessed?

Formal reports or certificates of capacity

4.62 In some cases, a more detailed report or certificate of capacity may be required, for example,

- for use in court or other legal processes

- as required by Regulations, Rules or Orders made under the Act.

How can someone challenge a finding of lack of capacity?

4.63 There are likely to be occasions when someone may wish to challenge the results of an assessment of capacity. The first step is to raise the matter with the person who carried out the assessment. If the challenge comes from the individual who is said to lack capacity, they might need support from family, friends or an advocate. Ask the assessor to:

- give reasons why they believe the person lacks capacity to make the decision, and

- provide objective evidence to support that belief.

4.64 The assessor must show they have applied the principles of the Mental Capacity Act (see chapter 2). Attorneys, deputies and professionals will need to show that they have also followed guidance in this chapter.

4.65 It might be possible to get a second opinion from an independent professional or another expert in assessing capacity. Chapter 15 has other suggestions for dealing with disagreements. But if a disagreement cannot be resolved, the person who is challenging the assessment may be able to apply to the Court of Protection. The Court of Protection can rule on whether a person has capacity to make the decision covered by the assessment (see chapter 8).

5 What does the Act mean when it talks about 'best interests'?

One of the key principles of the Act is that any act done for, or any decision made on behalf of a person who lacks capacity must be done, or made, in that person's *best interests*. That is the same whether the person making the decision or acting is a family carer, a paid care worker, an attorney, a court-appointed deputy, or a healthcare professional, and whether the decision is a minor issue – like what to wear – or a major issue, like whether to provide particular healthcare.

As long as these acts or decisions are in the best interests of the person who lacks capacity to make the decision for themselves, or to consent to acts concerned with their care or treatment, then the decision-maker or carer will be protected from liability.

There are exceptions to this, including circumstances where a person has made an advance decision to refuse treatment (see chapter 9) and, in specific circumstances, the involvement of a person who lacks capacity in research (see chapter 11). But otherwise the underpinning principle of the Act is that all acts and decisions should be made in the best interests of the person without capacity.

Working out what is in someone else's best interests may be difficult, and the Act requires people to follow certain steps to help them work out whether a particular act or decision is in a person's best interests. In some cases, there may be disagreement about what someone's best interests really are. As long as the person who acts or makes the decision has followed the steps to establish whether a person has capacity, and done everything they reasonably can to work out what someone's best interests are, the law should protect them.

This chapter explains what the Act means by 'best interests' and what things should be considered when trying to work out what is in someone's best interests. It also highlights some of the difficulties that might come up in working out what the best interests of a person who lacks capacity to make the decision actually are.

> In this chapter, as throughout the Code, a person's capacity (or lack of capacity) refers specifically to their capacity to make a particular decision at the time it needs to be made.

Quick summary

Chapter 5

What does the
Act mean when
it talks about
'best interests'?

A person trying to work out the best interests of a person who lacks capacity to make a particular decision ('lacks capacity') should:

Encourage participation

- do whatever is possible to permit and encourage the person to take part, or to improve their ability to take part, in making the decision

Identify all relevant circumstances

- try to identify all the things that the person who lacks capacity would take into account if they were making the decision or acting for themselves

Find out the person's views

- try to find out the views of the person who lacks capacity, including:
  - the person's past and present wishes and feelings – these may have been expressed verbally, in writing or through behaviour or habits.
  - any beliefs and values (e.g. religious, cultural, moral or political) that would be likely to influence the decision in question.
  - any other factors the person themselves would be likely to consider if they were making the decision or acting for themselves.

Avoid discrimination

- not make assumptions about someone's best interests simply on the basis of the person's age, appearance, condition or behaviour.

Assess whether the person might regain capacity

- consider whether the person is likely to regain capacity (e.g. after receiving medical treatment). If so, can the decision wait until then?

If the decision concerns life-sustaining treatment

- not be motivated in any way by a desire to bring about the person's death. They should not make assumptions about the person's quality of life.

Consult others

- if it is practical and appropriate to do so, consult other people for their views about the person's best interests and to see if they have any information about the person's wishes and feelings, beliefs and values. In particular, try to consult:

  - anyone previously named by the person as someone to be consulted on either the decision in question or on similar issues

  - anyone engaged in caring for the person

  - close relatives, friends or others who take an interest in the person's welfare

  - any attorney appointed under a Lasting Power of Attorney or Enduring Power of Attorney made by the person

  - any deputy appointed by the Court of Protection to make decisions for the person.

- For decisions about major medical treatment or where the person should live and where there is no-one who fits into any of the above categories, an Independent Mental Capacity Advocate (IMCA) must be consulted. (See chapter 10 for more information about IMCAs.)

- When consulting, remember that the person who lacks the capacity to make the decision or act for themselves still has a right to keep their affairs private – so it would not be right to share every piece of information with everyone.

Avoid restricting the person's rights

- see if there are other options that may be less restrictive of the person's rights.

Take all of this into account

- weigh up all of these factors in order to work out what is in the person's best interests.

What is the best interests principle and who does it apply to?

5.1   The best interests principle underpins the Mental Capacity Act. It is set out in section 1(5) of the Act.

'An act done, or decision made, under this Act for or on behalf of a person who lacks capacity must be done, or made, in his best interests.'

The concept has been developed by the courts in cases relating to people who lack capacity to make specific decisions for themselves, mainly decisions concerned with the provision of medical treatment or social care.

Chapter 5

What does the Act mean when it talks about 'best interests'?

5.2   This principle covers all aspects of financial, personal welfare and healthcare decision-making and actions. It applies to anyone making decisions or acting under the provisions of the Act, including:

- family carers, other carers and care workers

- healthcare and social care staff

- attorneys appointed under a Lasting Power of Attorney or registered Enduring Power of Attorney

- deputies appointed by the court to make decisions on behalf of someone who lacks capacity, and

- the Court of Protection.

5.3   However, as chapter 2 explained, the Act's first key principle is that people must be assumed to have capacity to make a decision or act for themselves unless it is established that they lack it. That means that working out a person's best interests is only relevant when that person has been assessed as lacking, or is reasonably believed to lack, capacity to make the decision in question or give consent to an act being done.

People with capacity are able to decide for themselves what they want to do. When they do this, they might choose an option that other people don't think is in their best interests. That is their choice and does not, in itself, mean that they lack capacity to make those decisions.

Exceptions to the best interests principle

5.4   There are two circumstances when the best interests principle will not apply. The first is where someone has previously made an advance decision to refuse medical treatment while they had the capacity to do so. Their advance decision should be respected when they lack capacity, even if others think that the decision to refuse treatment is not in their best interests (guidance on advance decisions is given in chapter 9).

The second concerns the involvement in research, in certain circumstances, of someone lacking capacity to consent (see chapter 11).

What does the Act mean by best interests?

5.5   The term 'best interests' is not actually defined in the Act. This is because so many different types of decisions and actions are covered by the Act, and so many different people and circumstances are affected by it.

5.6   Section 4 of the Act explains how to work out the best interests of a person who lacks capacity to make a decision at the time it needs to be made. This section sets out a checklist of common factors that must always be considered by anyone who needs to decide what is in the best interests of a person who lacks capacity in any particular situation. This checklist is only the starting point: in many cases, extra factors will need to be considered.

5.7   When working out what is in the best interests of the person who lacks capacity to make a decision or act for themselves, decision-makers must take into account all relevant factors that it would be reasonable to consider, not just those that they think are important. They must not act or make a decision based on what they would want to do if they were the person who lacked capacity.

Chapter 5

What does the
Act mean when
it talks about
'best interests'?

Scenario: Whose best interests?

Pedro, a young man with a severe learning disability, lives in a care home. He has dental problems which cause him a lot of pain, but refuses to open his mouth for his teeth to be cleaned.

The staff suggest that it would be a good idea to give Pedro an occasional general anaesthetic so that a dentist can clean his teeth and fill any cavities. His mother is worried about the effects of an anaesthetic, but she hates to see him distressed and suggests instead that he should be given strong painkillers when needed.

While the views of Pedro's mother and carers are important in working out what course of action would be in his best interests, the decision must *not* be based on what would be less stressful for them. Instead, it must focus on Pedro's best interests.

Having talked to others, the dentist tries to find ways of involving Pedro in the decision, with the help of his key worker and an advocate, to try to find out the cause and location of the problem and to explain to him that they are trying to stop the pain. The dentist tries to find out if any other forms of dental care would be better, such as a mouthwash or dental gum.

The dentist concludes that it would be in Pedro's best interests for:

- a proper investigation to be carried out under anaesthetic so that immediate treatment can be provided

- options for his future dental care to be reviewed by the care team, involving Pedro as far as possible.

Who can be a decision-maker?

5.8   Under the Act, many different people may be required to make decisions or act on behalf of someone who lacks capacity to make decisions for themselves. The person making the decision is referred to throughout this chapter, and in other parts of the Code, as the 'decision-maker', and it is the decision-maker's responsibility to work out what would be in the best interests of the person who lacks capacity.

- For most day-to-day actions or decisions, the decision-maker will be the carer most directly involved with the person at the time.

- Where the decision involves the provision of medical treatment, the doctor or other member of healthcare staff responsible for carrying out the particular treatment or procedure is the decision-maker.

- Where nursing or paid care is provided, the nurse or paid carer will be the decision-maker.

- If a Lasting Power of Attorney (or Enduring Power of Attorney) has been made and registered, or a deputy has been appointed under a court order, the attorney or deputy will be the decision-maker, for decisions within the scope of their authority.

5.9 What this means is that a range of different decision-makers may be involved with a person who lacks capacity to make different decisions.

5.10 In some cases, the same person may make different types of decision for someone who lacks capacity to make decisions for themselves. For instance, a family carer may carry out certain acts in caring for the person on a day-to-day basis, but if they are also an attorney, appointed under a Lasting Power of Attorney (LPA), they may also make specific decisions concerning the person's property and affairs or their personal welfare (depending on what decisions the LPA has been set up to cover).

5.11 There are also times when a joint decision might be made by a number of people. For example, when a care plan for a person who lacks capacity to make relevant decisions is being put together, different healthcare or social care staff might be involved in making decisions or recommendations about the person's care package. Sometimes these decisions will be made by a team of healthcare or social care staff as a whole. At other times, the decision will be made by a specific individual within the team. A different member of the team may then implement that decision, based on what the team has worked out to be the person's best interests.

5.12 No matter who is making the decision, the most important thing is that the decision-maker tries to work out what would be in the best interests of the person who lacks capacity.

Chapter 5

What does the
Act mean when
it talks about
'best interests'?

Scenario: Coming to a joint decision

Jack, a young man with a brain injury, lacks capacity to agree to a rehabilitation programme designed to improve his condition. But the healthcare and social care staff who are looking after him believe that he clearly needs the programme, and have obtained the necessary funding from the Primary Care Trust.

However, Jack's family want to take him home from hospital as they believe they can provide better care for him at home.

A 'best interests' case conference is held, involving Jack, his parents and other family members and the relevant professionals, in order to decide what course of action would be in the Jack's best interests.

A plan is developed to enable Jack to live at home, but attend the day hospital every weekday. Jack seems happy with the proposals and both the family carers and the healthcare and social care staff are satisfied that the plan is in his best interests.

What must be taken into account when trying to work out someone's best interests?

5.13 Because every case – and every decision – is different, the law can't set out all the factors that will need to be taken into account in working out someone's best interests. But section 4 of the Act sets out some common factors that must always be considered when trying to work out someone's best interests. These factors are summarised in the checklist here:

- Working out what is in someone's best interests cannot be based simply on someone's age, appearance, condition or behaviour. (see paragraphs 5.16–5.17).

- All relevant circumstances should be considered when working out someone's best interests (paragraphs 5.18–5.20).

- Every effort should be made to encourage and enable the person who lacks capacity to take part in making the decision (paragraphs 5.21–5.24).

- If there is a chance that the person will regain the capacity to make a particular decision, then it may be possible to put off the decision until later if it is not urgent (paragraphs 5.25–5.28).

- Special considerations apply to decisions about life-sustaining treatment (paragraphs 5.29–5.36).

- The person's past and present wishes and feelings, beliefs and values should be taken into account (paragraphs 5.37–5.48).

- The views of other people who are close to the person who lacks capacity should be considered, as well as the views of an attorney or deputy (paragraphs 5.49–5.55).

It's important not to take shortcuts in working out best interests, and a proper and objective assessment must be carried out on every occasion. If the decision is urgent, there may not be time to examine all possible factors, but the decision must still be made in the best interests of the person who lacks capacity. Not all the factors in the checklist will be relevant to all types of decisions or actions, and in many cases other factors will have to be considered as well, even though some of them may then not be found to be relevant.

5.14   What is in a person's best interests may well change over time. This means that even where similar actions need to be taken repeatedly in connection with the person's care or treatment, the person's best interests should be regularly reviewed.

5.15   Any staff involved in the care of a person who lacks capacity should make sure a record is kept of the process of working out the best interests of that person for each relevant decision, setting out:

- how the decision about the person's best interests was reached

- what the reasons for reaching the decision were

- who was consulted to help work out best interests, and

- what particular factors were taken into account.

This record should remain on the person's file.

For major decisions based on the best interests of a person who lacks capacity, it may also be useful for family and other carers to keep a similar kind of record.

What safeguards does the Act provide around working out someone's best interests?

Chapter 5

What does the Act mean when it talks about 'best interests'?

5.16 Section 4(1) states that anyone working out someone's best interests must not make unjustified assumptions about what their best interests might be simply on the basis of the person's age, appearance, condition or any aspect of their behaviour. In this way, the Act ensures that people who lack capacity to make decisions for themselves are not subject to discrimination or treated any less favourably than anyone else.

5.17 'Appearance' is a broad term and refers to all aspects of physical appearance, including skin colour, mode of dress and any visible medical problems, disfiguring scars or other disabilities. A person's 'condition' also covers a range of factors including physical disabilities, learning difficulties or disabilities, age-related illness or temporary conditions (such as drunkenness or unconsciousness). 'Behaviour' refers to behaviour that might seem unusual to others, such as talking too loudly or laughing inappropriately.

Scenario: Following the checklist

Martina, an elderly woman with dementia, is beginning to neglect her appearance and personal hygiene and has several times been found wandering in the street unable to find her way home. Her care workers are concerned that Martina no longer has capacity to make appropriate decisions relating to her daily care. Her daughter is her personal welfare attorney and believes the time has come to act under the Lasting Power of Attorney (LPA).

She assumes it would be best for Martina to move into a care home, since the staff would be able to help her wash and dress smartly and prevent her from wandering.

However, it cannot be assumed *simply on the basis of her age, condition, appearance or behaviour* either that Martina lacks capacity to make such a decision or that such a move would be in her best interests.

Instead, steps must be taken to assess her capacity. If it is then agreed that Martina lacks the capacity to make this decision, all the relevant factors in the best interests' checklist must be considered to try to work out what her best interests would be.

Her daughter must therefore consider:

• Martina's past and present wishes and feelings

• the views of the people involved in her care

• any alternative ways of meeting her care needs effectively which might be less restrictive of Martina's rights and freedoms, such as increased provision of home care or attendance at a day centre.

By following this process, Martina's daughter can then take decisions on behalf of her mother and in her best interests, when her mother lacks the capacity to make them herself, on any matters that fall under the authority of the LPA.

How does a decision-maker work out what 'all relevant circumstances' are?

5.18   When trying to work out someone's best interests, the decision-maker should try to identify all the issues that would be most relevant to the individual who lacks capacity and to the particular decision, as well as those in the 'checklist'. Clearly, it is not always possible or practical to investigate in depth every issue which may have some relevance to the person who lacks capacity or the decision in question. So relevant circumstances are defined in section 4(11) of the Act as those:

'(a) of which the person making the determination is aware, and

(b) which it would be reasonable to regard as relevant.'

Chapter 5

What does the Act mean when it talks about 'best interests'?

5.19   The relevant circumstances will of course vary from case to case. For example, when making a decision about major medical treatment, a doctor would need to consider the clinical needs of the patient, the potential benefits and burdens of the treatment on the person's health and life expectancy and any other factors relevant to making a professional judgement.[16] But it would not be reasonable to consider issues such as life expectancy when working out whether it would be in someone's best interests to be given medication for a minor problem.

5.20   Financial decisions are another area where the relevant circumstances will vary. For example, if a person had received a substantial sum of money as compensation for an accident resulting in brain injury, the decision-maker would have to consider a wide range of circumstances when making decisions about how the money is spent or invested, such as:

* whether the person's condition is likely to change

* whether the person needs professional care, and

* whether the person needs to live somewhere else to make it easier for them.

These kinds of issues can only be decided on a case-by-case basis.

How should the person who lacks capacity be involved in working out their best interests?

5.21   Wherever possible, the person who lacks capacity to make a decision should still be involved in the decision-making process (section 4(4)).

5.22   Even if the person lacks capacity to make the decision, they may have views on matters affecting the decision, and on what outcome would be preferred. Their involvement can help work out what would be in their best interests.

---

[16] *An Hospital NHS Trust v S* [2003] EWHC 365 (Fam), paragraph 47

5.23   The decision-maker should make sure that all practical means are used to enable and encourage the person to participate as fully as possible in the decision-making process and any action taken as a result, or to help the person improve their ability to participate.

5.24   Consulting the person who lacks capacity will involve taking time to explain what is happening and why a decision needs to be made. Chapter 3 includes a number of practical steps to assist and enable decision-making which may be also be helpful in encouraging greater participation. These include:

- using simple language and/or illustrations or photographs to help the person understand the options

- asking them about the decision at a time and location where the person feels most relaxed and at ease

- breaking the information down into easy-to-understand points

- using specialist interpreters or signers to communicate with the person.

This may mean that other people are required to communicate with the person to establish their views. For example, a trusted relative or friend, a full-time carer or an advocate may be able to help the person to express wishes or aspirations or to indicate a preference between different options.

More information on all of these steps can be found in chapter 3.

Scenario: Involving someone in working out their best interests

The parents of Amy, a young woman with learning difficulties, are going through a divorce and are arguing about who should continue to care for their daughter. Though she cannot understand what is happening, attempts are made to see if Amy can give some indication of where she would prefer to live.

An advocate is appointed to work with Amy to help her understand the situation and to find out her likes and dislikes and matters which are important to her. With the advocate's help, Amy is able to participate in decisions about her future care.

How do the chances of someone regaining and developing capacity affect working out what is in their best interests?

Chapter 5

What does the Act mean when it talks about 'best interests'?

5.25   There are some situations where decisions may be deferred, if someone who currently lacks capacity may regain the capacity to make the decision for themselves. Section 4(3) of the Act requires the decision-maker to consider:

- whether the individual concerned is likely to regain the capacity to make that particular decision in the future, and

- if so, when that is likely to be.

It may then be possible to put off the decision until the person can make it for themselves.

5.26   In emergency situations – such as when urgent medical treatment is needed – it may *not* be possible to wait to see if the person may regain capacity so they can decide for themselves whether or not to have the urgent treatment.

5.27   Where a person currently lacks capacity to make a decision relating to their day-to-day care, the person may – over time and with the right support – be able to develop the skills to do so. Though others may need to make the decision on the person's behalf at the moment, all possible support should be given to that person to enable them to develop the skills so that they can make the decision for themselves in the future.

Scenario: Taking a short-term decision for someone who may regain capacity

Mr Fowler has suffered a stroke leaving him severely disabled and unable to speak. Within days, he has shown signs of improvement, so with intensive treatment there is hope he will recover over time. But at present both his wife and the hospital staff find it difficult to communicate with him and have been unable to find out his wishes.

He has always looked after the family finances, so Mrs Fowler suddenly discovers she has no access to his personal bank account to provide the family with money to live on or pay the bills. Because the decision can't be put off while efforts are made to find effective means of communicating with Mr Fowler, an application is made to the Court of Protection for an order that allows Mrs Fowler to access Mr Fowler's money.

The decision about longer-term arrangements, on the other hand, can be delayed until alternative methods of communication have been tried and the extent of Mr Fowler's recovery is known.

5.28 Some factors which may indicate that a person may regain or develop capacity in the future are:

- the cause of the lack of capacity can be treated, either by medication or some other form of treatment or therapy

- the lack of capacity is likely to decrease in time (for example, where it is caused by the effects of medication or alcohol, or following a sudden shock)

- a person with learning disabilities may learn new skills or be subject to new experiences which increase their understanding and ability to make certain decisions

- the person may have a condition which causes capacity to come and go at various times (such as some forms of mental illness) so it may be possible to arrange for the decision to be made during a time when they do have capacity

- a person previously unable to communicate may learn a new form of communication (see chapter 3).

How should someone's best interests be worked out when making decisions about life-sustaining treatment?

Chapter 5

What does the Act mean when it talks about 'best interests'?

5.29 A special factor in the checklist applies to decisions about treatment which is necessary to keep the person alive ('life-sustaining treatment') and this is set out in section 4(5) of the Act. The fundamental rule is that anyone who is deciding whether or not life-sustaining treatment is in the best interests of someone who lacks capacity to consent to or refuse such treatment must not be motivated by a desire to bring about the person's death.

5.30 Whether a treatment is 'life-sustaining' depends not only on the type of treatment, but also on the particular circumstances in which it may be prescribed. For example, in some situations giving antibiotics may be life-sustaining, whereas in other circumstances antibiotics are used to treat a non-life-threatening condition. It is up to the doctor or healthcare professional providing treatment to assess whether the treatment is life-sustaining in each particular situation.

5.31 All reasonable steps which are in the person's best interests should be taken to prolong their life. There will be a limited number of cases where treatment is futile, overly burdensome to the patient or where there is no prospect of recovery. In circumstances such as these, it may be that an assessment of best interests leads to the conclusion that it would be in the best interests of the patient to withdraw or withhold life-sustaining treatment, even if this may result in the person's death. The decision-maker must make a decision based on the best interests of the person who lacks capacity. They must not be motivated by a desire to bring about the person's death for whatever reason, even if this is from a sense of compassion. Healthcare and social care staff should also refer to relevant professional guidance when making decisions regarding life-sustaining treatment.

5.32 As with all decisions, before deciding to withdraw or withhold life-sustaining treatment, the decision-maker must consider the range of treatment options available to work out what would be in the person's best interests. All the factors in the best interests checklist should be considered, and in particular, the decision-maker should consider any statements that the person has previously made about their wishes and feelings about life-sustaining treatment.

5.33   Importantly, section 4(5) cannot be interpreted to mean that doctors are under an obligation to provide, or to continue to provide, life-sustaining treatment where that treatment is not in the best interests of the person, even where the person's death is foreseen. Doctors must apply the best interests' checklist and use their professional skills to decide whether life-sustaining treatment is in the person's best interests. If the doctor's assessment is disputed, and there is no other way of resolving the dispute, ultimately the Court of Protection may be asked to decide what is in the person's best interests.

5.34   Where a person has made a written statement in advance that requests particular medical treatments, such as artificial nutrition and hydration (ANH), these requests should be taken into account by the treating doctor in the same way as requests made by a patient who has the capacity to make such decisions. Like anyone else involved in making this decision, the doctor must weigh written statements alongside all other relevant factors to decide whether it is in the best interests of the patient to provide or continue life-sustaining treatment.

5.35   If someone has made an advance decision to refuse life-sustaining treatment, specific rules apply. More information about these can be found in chapter 9 and in paragraph 5.45 below.

5.36   As mentioned in paragraph 5.33 above, where there is any doubt about the patient's best interests, an application should be made to the Court of Protection for a decision as to whether withholding or withdrawing life-sustaining treatment is in the patient's best interests.

How do a person's wishes and feelings, beliefs and values affect working out what is in their best interests?

5.37   Section 4(6) of the Act requires the decision-maker to consider, as far as they are 'reasonably ascertainable':

>   '(a) the person's past and present wishes and feelings (and in particular, any relevant written statements made by him when he had capacity),
>
>   (b) the beliefs and values that would be likely to influence his decision if he had capacity, and
>
>   (c) the other factors that he would be likely to consider if he were able to do so.'
>
>   Paragraphs 5.38–5.48 below give further guidance on each of these factors.

5.38 In setting out the requirements for working out a person's 'best interests', section 4 of the Act puts the person who lacks capacity at the centre of the decision to be made. Even if they cannot make the decision, their wishes and feelings, beliefs and values should be taken fully into account – whether expressed in the past or now. But their wishes and feelings, beliefs and values will not necessarily be the deciding factor in working out their best interests. Any such assessment must consider past and current wishes and feelings, beliefs and values alongside all other factors, but the final decision must be based entirely on what is in the person's best interests.

Chapter 5

What does the Act mean when it talks about 'best interests'?

Scenario: Considering wishes and feelings as part of best interests

Andre, a young man with severe learning disabilities who does not use any formal system of communication, cuts his leg while outdoors. There is some earth in the wound. A doctor wants to give him a tetanus jab, but Andre appears scared of the needle and pushes it away. Assessments have shown that he is unable to understand the risk of infection following his injury, or the consequences of rejecting the injection.

The doctor decides that it is in the Andre's best interests to give the vaccination. She asks a nurse to comfort Andre, and if necessary, restrain him while she gives the injection. She has objective reasons for believing she is acting in Andre's best interests, and for believing that Andre lacks capacity to make the decision for himself. So she should be protected from liability under section 5 of the Act (see chapter 6).

What is 'reasonably ascertainable'?

5.39 How much someone can learn about a person's past and present views will depend on circumstances and the time available. 'Reasonably ascertainable' means considering all possible information in the time available. What is available in an emergency will be different to what is available in a non-emergency. But even in an emergency, there may still be an opportunity to try to communicate with the person or his friends, family or carers (see chapter 3 for guidance on helping communication).

What role do a person's past and present wishes and feelings play?

5.40   People who cannot express their current wishes and feelings in words may express themselves through their behaviour. Expressions of pleasure or distress and emotional responses will also be relevant in working out what is in their best interests. It is also important to be sure that other people have not influenced a person's views. An advocate could help the person make choices and express their views.

5.41   The person may have held strong views in the past which could have a bearing on the decision now to be made. All reasonable efforts must be made to find out whether the person has expressed views in the past that will shape the decision to be made. This could have been through verbal communication, writing, behaviour or habits, or recorded in any other way (for example, home videos or audiotapes).

5.42   Section 4(6)(a) places special emphasis on written statements the person might have made before losing capacity. These could provide a lot of information about a person's wishes. For example, these statements could include information about the type of medical treatment they would want in the case of future illness, where they would prefer to live, or how they wish to be cared for.

5.43   The decision-maker should consider written statements carefully. If their decision does not follow something a person has put in writing, they must record the reasons why. They should be able to justify their reasons if someone challenges their decision.

5.44   A doctor should take written statements made by a person before losing capacity which request specific treatments as seriously as those made by people who currently have capacity to make treatment decisions. But they would not have to follow a written request if they think the specific treatment would be clinically unnecessary or not appropriate for the person's condition, so not in the person's best interests.

5.45   It is important to note the distinction between a written statement expressing treatment preferences and a statement which constitutes an advance decision to refuse treatment. This is covered by section 24 of the Act, and it has a different status in law. Doctors cannot ignore a written statement that is a valid advance decision to refuse treatment. An advance decision to refuse treatment must be followed if it meets the Act's requirements and applies to the person's circumstances. In these cases, the treatment must not be given (see chapter 9 for more information). If there is not a valid and applicable advance decision, treatment should be provided based on the person's best interests.

What role do beliefs and values play?

Chapter 5

What does the Act mean when it talks about 'best interests'?

5.46   Everybody's values and beliefs influence the decisions they make. They may become especially important for someone who lacks capacity to make a decision because of a progressive illness such as dementia, for example. Evidence of a person's beliefs and values can be found in things like their:

- cultural background
- religious beliefs
- political convictions, or
- past behaviour or habits.

Some people set out their values and beliefs in a written statement while they still have capacity.

Scenario: Considering beliefs and values

Anita, a young woman, suffers serious brain damage during a car accident. The court appoints her father as deputy to invest the compensation she received. As the decision-maker he must think about her wishes, beliefs and values before deciding how to invest the money.

Anita had worked for an overseas charity. Her father talks to her former colleagues. They tell him how Anita's political beliefs shaped her work and personal beliefs, so he decides not to invest in the bonds that a financial adviser had recommended, because they are from companies Anita would not have approved of. Instead, he employs an ethical investment adviser to choose appropriate companies in line with her beliefs.

What other factors should a decision-maker consider?

5.47   Section 4(6)(c) of the Act requires decision-makers to consider any other factors the person who lacks capacity would consider if they were able to do so. This might include the effect of the decision on other people, obligations to dependants or the duties of a responsible citizen.

5.48   The Act allows actions that benefit other people, as long as they are in the best interests of the person who lacks capacity to make the decision. For example, having considered all the circumstances of the particular case, a decision might be made to take a blood sample from a person who lacks capacity to consent, to check for a genetic link to cancer within the family, because this might benefit someone else in the family. But it might still be in the best interests of the person who lacks capacity. 'Best interests' goes beyond the person's medical interests.

For example, courts have previously ruled that possible wider benefits to a person who lacks capacity to consent, such as providing or gaining emotional support from close relationships, are important factors in working out the person's own best interests.[17] If it is likely that the person who lacks capacity would have considered these factors themselves, they can be seen as part of the person's best interests.

Who should be consulted when working out someone's best interests?

5.49   The Act places a duty on the decision-maker to consult other people close to a person who lacks capacity, where practical and appropriate, on decisions affecting the person and what might be in the person's best interests. This also applies to those involved in caring for the person and interested in the person's welfare. Under section 4(7), the decision-maker has a duty to take into account the views of the following people, where it is practical and appropriate to do so:

- anyone the person has previously named as someone they want to be consulted

- anyone involved in caring for the person

- anyone interested in their welfare (for example, family carers, other close relatives, or an advocate already working with the person)

- an attorney appointed by the person under a Lasting Power of Attorney, and

- a deputy appointed for that person by the Court of Protection.

5.50   If there is no-one to speak to about the person's best interests, in some circumstances the person may qualify for an Independent Mental Capacity Advocate (IMCA). For more information on IMCAs, see chapter 10.

---

[17] See for example *Re Y (Mental Incapacity: Bone marrow transplant)* [1996] 2 FLR 787; *Re A (Male Sterilisation)* [2000] 1 FLR 549

5.51 Decision-makers must show they have thought carefully about who to speak to. If it is practical and appropriate to speak to the above people, they must do so and must take their views into account. They must be able to explain why they did not speak to a particular person – it is good practice to have a clear record of their reasons. It is also good practice to give careful consideration to the views of family carers, if it is possible to do so.

5.52 It is also good practice for healthcare and social care staff to record at the end of the process why they think a specific decision is in the person's best interests. This is particularly important if healthcare and social care staff go against the views of somebody who has been consulted while working out the person's best interests.

5.53 The decision-maker should try to find out:

- what the people consulted think is in the person's best interests in this matter, and

- if they can give information on the person's wishes and feelings, beliefs and values.

5.54 This information may be available from somebody the person named before they lost capacity as someone they wish to be consulted. People who are close to the person who lacks capacity, such as close family members, are likely to know them best. They may also be able to help with communication or interpret signs that show the person's present wishes and feelings. Everybody's views are equally important – even if they do not agree with each other. They must be considered alongside the views of the person who lacks capacity and other factors. See paragraphs 5.62–5.69 below for guidance on dealing with conflicting views.

Chapter 5

What does the Act mean when it talks about 'best interests'?

Scenario: Considering other people's views

Lucia, a young woman with severe brain damage, is cared for at home by her parents and attends a day centre a couple of days each week. The day centre staff would like to take some of the service users on holiday. They speak to Lucia's parents as part of the process of assessing whether the holiday would be in her best interests.

The parents think that the holiday would be good for her, but they are worried that Lucia gets very anxious if she is surrounded by strangers who don't know how to communicate with her. Having tried to seek Lucia's views and involve her in the decision, the staff and parents agree that a holiday would be in her best interests, as long as her care assistant can go with her to help with communication.

5.55 Where an attorney has been appointed under a Lasting Power of Attorney or Enduring Power of Attorney, or a deputy has been appointed by a court, they must make the decisions on any matters they have been appointed to deal with. Attorneys and deputies should also be consulted, if practical and appropriate, on other issues affecting the person who lacks capacity.

For instance, an attorney who is appointed only to look after the person's property and affairs may have information about the person's beliefs and values, wishes and feelings, that could help work out what would be in the person's best interests regarding healthcare or treatment decisions. (See chapters 7 and 8 for more information about the roles of attorneys and deputies.)

How can decision-makers respect confidentiality?

5.56 Decision-makers must balance the duty to consult other people with the right to confidentiality of the person who lacks capacity. So if confidential information is to be discussed, they should only seek the views of people who it is appropriate to consult, where their views are relevant to the decision to be made and the particular circumstances.

5.57 There may be occasions where it is in the person's best interests for personal information (for example, about their medical condition, if the decision concerns the provision of medical treatment) to be revealed to the people consulted as part of the process of working out their best interests (further guidance on this is given in chapter 16). Healthcare and social care staff who are trying to determine a person's best interests must follow their professional guidance, as well as other relevant guidance, about confidentiality.

When does the best interests principle apply?

5.58 Section 1(5) of the Act confirms that the principle applies to any act done, or any decision made, on behalf of someone where there is reasonable belief that the person lacks capacity under the Act. This covers informal day-to-day decisions and actions as well as decisions made by the courts.

Reasonable belief about a person's best interests

5.59 Section 4(9) confirms that if someone acts or makes a decision in the reasonable belief that what they are doing is in the best interests of the person who lacks capacity, then – provided they have followed the checklist in section 4 – they will have complied with the best interests principle set out in the Act. Coming to an incorrect conclusion about a person's capacity or best interests does not necessarily mean that the decision-maker would not get protection from liability (this is explained in chapter 6). But they must be able to show that it was reasonable for them to think that the person lacked capacity and that they were acting in the person's best interests at the time they made their decision or took action.

Chapter 5

What does the Act mean when it talks about 'best interests'?

5.60   Where there is a need for a court decision, the court is likely to require formal evidence of what might be in the person's best interests. This will include evidence from relevant professionals (for example, psychiatrists or social workers). But in most day-to-day situations, there is no need for such formality. In emergency situations, it may not be practical or possible to gather formal evidence.

5.61   Where the court is not involved, people are still expected to have reasonable grounds for believing that they are acting in somebody's best interests. This does not mean that decision-makers can simply impose their own views. They must have objective reasons for their decisions – and they must be able to demonstrate them. They must be able to show they have considered all relevant circumstances and applied all elements of the best interests checklist.

Scenario: Demonstrating reasonable belief

Mrs Prior is mugged and knocked unconscious. She is brought to hospital without any means of identification. She has head injuries and a stab wound, and has lost a lot of blood. In casualty, a doctor arranges an urgent blood transfusion. Because this is necessary to save her life, the doctor believes this is in her best interests.

When her relatives are contacted, they say that Mrs Prior's beliefs meant that she would have refused all blood products. But since Mrs Prior's handbag had been stolen, the doctor had no idea who the woman was nor what her beliefs her. He needed to make an immediate decision and Mrs Prior lacked capacity to make the decision for herself. Therefore he had reasonable grounds for believing that his action was in his patient's best interests – and so was protected from liability.

Now that the doctor knows Mrs Prior's beliefs, he can take them into account in future decisions about her medical treatment if she lacks capacity to make them for herself. He can also consult her family, now that he knows where they are.

What problems could arise when working out someone's best interests?

5.62   It is important that the best interests principle and the statutory checklist are flexible. Without flexibility, it would be impossible to prioritise factors in different cases – and it would be difficult to ensure that the outcome is the best possible for the person who lacks capacity to make the particular decision. Some cases will be straightforward. Others will require decision-makers to balance the pros and cons of all relevant factors.[18] But this flexibility could lead to problems in reaching a conclusion about a person's best interests.

What happens when there are conflicting concerns?

5.63   A decision-maker may be faced with people who disagree about a person's best interests. Family members, partners and carers may disagree between themselves. Or they might have different memories about what views the person expressed in the past. Carers and family might disagree with a professional's view about the person's care or treatment needs.

5.64   The decision-maker will need to find a way of balancing these concerns or deciding between them. The first approach should be to review all elements of the best interests checklist with everyone involved. They should include the person who lacks capacity (as much as they are able to take part) and anyone who has been involved in earlier discussions. It may be possible to reach an agreement at a meeting to air everyone's concerns. But an agreement in itself might not be in the person's best interests. Ultimate responsibility for working out best interests lies with the decision-maker.

---

18   *Re A (Male Sterilisation)* [2000] 1 FLR 549

Chapter 5

What does the
Act mean when
it talks about
'best interests'?

Scenario: Dealing with disagreement

Some time ago, Mr Graham made a Lasting Power of Attorney (LPA) appointing his son and daughter as joint attorneys to manage his finances and property. He now has Alzheimer's disease and has moved into private residential care. The son and daughter have to decide what to do with Mr Graham's house.

His son thinks it is in their father's best interests to sell it and invest the money for Mr Graham's future care. But his daughter thinks it is in Mr Graham's best interests to keep the property, because he enjoys visiting and spending time in his old home.

After making every effort to get Mr Graham's views, the family meets to discuss all the issues involved. After hearing other family views, the attorneys agree that it would be in their father's best interests to keep the property for so long as he is able to enjoy visiting it.

Family, partners and carers who are consulted

5.65 If disagreement continues, the decision-maker will need to weigh up the views of different parties. This will depend entirely upon the circumstances of each case, the people involved and their relationship with the person who lacks capacity. Sometimes the decision-maker will find that carers have an insight into how to interpret a person's wishes and feelings that can help them reach a decision.

5.66 At the same time, paid care workers and voluntary sector support workers may have specialist knowledge about up-to-date care options or treatments. Some may also have known the person for many years.

5.67 People with conflicting interests should not be cut out of the process (for example, those who stand to inherit from the person's will may still have a right to be consulted about the person's care or medical treatment). But decision-makers must always ensure that the interests of those consulted do not overly influence the process of working out a person's best interests. In weighing up different contributions, the decision-maker should consider:

  * how long an individual has known the person who lacks capacity, and

  * what their relationship is.

Scenario: Settling disagreements

Robert is 19 and has learning disabilities and autism. He is about to leave his residential special school. His parents want Robert to go to a specialist unit run by a charitable organisation, but he has been offered a place in a local supported living scheme. The parents don't think Robert will get appropriate care there.

The school sets up a 'best interests' meeting. People who attend include Robert, his parents, teachers from his school and professionals involved in preparing Robert's care plan. Robert's parents and teachers know him best. They set out their views and help Robert to communicate where he would like to live.

Social care staff identify some different placements within the county. Robert visits these with his parents. After further discussion, everyone agrees that a community placement near his family home would be in Robert's best interests.

Settling disputes about best interests

5.68 If someone wants to challenge a decision-maker's conclusions, there are several options:

- Involve an advocate to act on behalf of the person who lacks capacity to make the decision (see paragraph 5.69 below).
- Get a second opinion.
- Hold a formal or informal 'best interests' case conference.
- Attempt some form of mediation (see chapter 15).
- Pursue a complaint through the organisation's formal procedures.

Ultimately, if all other attempts to resolve the dispute have failed, the court might need to decide what is in the person's best interests. Chapter 8 provides more information about the Court of Protection.

Advocacy

5.69 An advocate might be useful in providing support for the person who lacks capacity to make a decision in the process of working out their best interests, if:

- the person who lacks capacity has no close family or friends to take an interest in their welfare, and they do not qualify for an Independent Mental Capacity Advocate (see chapter 10)

- family members disagree about the person's best interests

- family members and professionals disagree about the person's best interests

- there is a conflict of interest for people who have been consulted in the best interests assessment (for example, the sale of a family property where the person lives)

- the person who lacks capacity is already in contact with an advocate

- the proposed course of action may lead to the use of restraint or other restrictions on the person who lacks capacity

- there is a concern about the protection of a vulnerable adult.

Chapter 5

What does the Act mean when it talks about 'best interests'?

6 What protection does the Act offer for people providing care or treatment?

Section 5 of the Act allows carers, healthcare and social care staff to carry out certain tasks without fear of liability. These tasks involve the personal care, healthcare or treatment of people who lack capacity to consent to them. The aim is to give legal backing for acts that need to be carried out in the best interests of the person who lacks capacity to consent.[19]

This chapter explains:

- how the Act provides protection from liability
- how that protection works in practice
- where protection is restricted or limited, and
- when a carer can use a person's money to buy goods or services without formal permission.

> In this chapter, as throughout the Code, a person's capacity (or lack of capacity) refers specifically to their capacity to make a particular decision at the time it needs to be made.

Quick summary

The following steps list all the things that people providing care or treatment should bear in mind to ensure they are protected by the Act.

Acting in connection with the care or treatment of someone who lacks capacity to consent

- Is the action to be carried out in connection with the care or treatment of a person who lacks capacity to give consent to that act?
- Does it involve major life changes for the person concerned? If so, it will need special consideration.
- Who is carrying out the action? Is it appropriate for that person to do so at the relevant time?

---

[19] The provisions of section 5 are based on the common law 'doctrine of necessity' as set out in *Re F (Mental Patient: Sterilisation)* [1990] 2 AC 1

Checking whether the person has capacity to consent

- Have all possible steps been taken to try to help the person make a decision for themselves about the action?
- Has the two-stage test of capacity been applied?
- Are there reasonable grounds for believing the person lacks capacity to give permission?

Chapter 6

What protection does the Act offer for people providing care or treatment?

Acting in the person's best interests

- Has the best interests checklist been applied and all relevant circumstances considered?
- Is a less restrictive option available?
- Is it reasonable to believe that the proposed act is in the person's best interests?

Understanding possible limitations on protection from liability

- If restraint is being considered, is it necessary to prevent harm to the person who lacks capacity, and is it a proportionate response to the likelihood of the person suffering harm – and to the seriousness of that harm?
- Could the restraint be classed as a 'deprivation of the person's liberty'?
- Does the action conflict with a decision that has been made by an attorney or deputy under their powers?

Paying for necessary goods and services

- If someone wishes to use the person's money to buy goods or pay for services for someone who lacks capacity to do so themselves, are those goods or services necessary and in the person's best interests?
- Is it necessary to take money from the person's bank or building society account or to sell the person's property to pay for goods or services? If so, formal authority will be required.

What protection do people have when caring for those who lack capacity to consent?

6.1 Every day, millions of acts are done to and for people who lack capacity either to:

- take decisions about their own care or treatment, or

- consent to someone else caring for them.

Such acts range from everyday tasks of caring (for example, helping someone to wash) to life-changing events (for example, serious medical treatment or arranging for someone to go into a care home).

In theory, many of these actions could be against the law. Legally, people have the right to stop others from interfering with their body or property unless they give permission. But what happens if someone lacks capacity to give permission? Carers who dress people who cannot dress themselves are potentially interfering with someone's body without their consent, so could theoretically be prosecuted for assault. A neighbour who enters and cleans the house of a person who lacks capacity could be trespassing on the person's property.

6.2   Section 5 of the Act provides 'protection from liability'. In other words, it protects people who carry out these actions. It stops them being prosecuted for acts that could otherwise be classed as civil wrongs or crimes. By protecting family and other carers from liability, the Act allows necessary caring acts or treatment to take place as if a person who lacks capacity to consent had consented to them. People providing care of this sort do not therefore need to get formal authority to act.

6.3   Importantly, section 5 does not give people caring for or treating someone the power to make any other decisions on behalf of those who lack capacity to make their own decisions. Instead, it offers protection from liability so that they can act in connection with the person's care or treatment. The power to make decisions on behalf of someone who lacks capacity can be granted through other parts of the Act (such as the powers granted to attorneys and deputies, which are explained in chapters 7 and 8).

What type of actions might have protection from liability?

6.4   Section 5(1) provides possible protection for actions carried out *in connection with care or treatment*. The action may be carried out on behalf of someone who is believed to lack capacity to give permission for the action, so long as it is in that person's best interests (see chapter 5). The Act does not define 'care' or 'treatment'. They should be given their normal meaning. However, section 64(1) makes clear that treatment includes diagnostic or other procedures.

6.5   Actions that might be covered by section 5 include:

Personal care

Chapter 6

What protection does the Act offer for people providing care or treatment?

- helping with washing, dressing or personal hygiene
- helping with eating and drinking
- helping with communication
- helping with mobility (moving around)
- helping someone take part in education, social or leisure activities
- going into a person's home to drop off shopping or to see if they are alright
- doing the shopping or buying necessary goods with the person's money
- arranging household services (for example, arranging repairs or maintenance for gas and electricity supplies)
- providing services that help around the home (such as homecare or meals on wheels)
- undertaking actions related to community care services (for example, day care, residential accommodation or nursing care) – but see also paragraphs 6.7–6.14 below
- helping someone to move home (including moving property and clearing the former home).

Healthcare and treatment

- carrying out diagnostic examinations and tests (to identify an illness, condition or other problem)
- providing professional medical, dental and similar treatment
- giving medication
- taking someone to hospital for assessment or treatment
- providing nursing care (whether in hospital or in the community)
- carrying out any other necessary medical procedures (for example, taking a blood sample) or therapies (for example, physiotherapy or chiropody)
- providing care in an emergency.

6.6 These actions only receive protection from liability if the person is reasonably believed to lack capacity to give permission for the action. The action must also be in the person's best interests and follow the Act's principles (see paragraph 6.26 onwards).

6.7 Some acts in connection with care or treatment may cause major life changes with significant consequences for the person concerned. Those requiring particularly careful consideration include a change of residence, perhaps into a care home or nursing home, or major decisions about healthcare and medical treatment. These are described in the following paragraphs.

A change of residence

6.8 Sometimes a person cannot get sufficient or appropriate care in their own home, and they may have to move – perhaps to live with relatives or to go into a care home or nursing home. If the person lacks capacity to consent to a move, the decision-maker(s) must consider whether the move is in the person's best interests (by referring to the best interests checklist in chapter 5 and in particular the person's past and present wishes and feelings, as well as the views of other relevant people). The decision-maker(s) must also consider whether there is a less restrictive option (see chapter 2, principle 5).

This may involve speaking to:

- anyone currently involved in the person's care
- family carers and other family members close to the person and interested in their welfare
- others who have an interest in the person's welfare
- anyone the person has previously named as someone to be consulted, and
- an attorney or deputy who has been legally appointed to make particular decisions on their behalf.

6.9 Some cases will require an Independent Mental Capacity Advocate (IMCA). The IMCA represents and supports the person who lacks capacity and they will provide information to make sure the final decision is in the person's best interests (see chapter 10). An IMCA is needed when there is no-one close to the person who lacks capacity to give an opinion about what is best for them, and:

- an NHS body is proposing to provide serious medical treatment or
- an NHS body or local authority is proposing to arrange accommodation in hospital or a care home or other longer-term accommodation and
  - the person will stay in hospital longer than 28 days, or
  - they will stay in a care home for more than eight weeks.

There are also some circumstances where an IMCA may be appointed on a discretionary basis. More guidance is available in chapter 10.

Chapter 6

What protection does the Act offer for people providing care or treatment?

6.10   Sometimes the final outcome may not be what the person who lacks capacity wanted. For example, they might want to stay at home, but those caring for them might decide a move is in their best interests. In all cases, those making the decision must first consider other options that might restrict the person's rights and freedom of action less (see chapter 2, principle 5).

6.11   In some cases, there may be no alternative but to move the person. Such a move would normally require the person's formal consent if they had capacity to give, or refuse, it. In cases where a person lacks capacity to consent, section 5 of the Act allows carers to carry out actions relating to the move – as long as the Act's principles and the requirements for working out best interests have been followed. This applies even if the person continues to object to the move.

However, section 6 places clear limits on the use of force or restraint by only permitting restraint to be used (for example, to transport the person to their new home) where this is necessary to protect the person from harm and is a proportionate response to the risk of harm (see paragraphs 6.40–6.53). Any action taken to move the person concerned or their property could incur liability unless protected under section 5.

6.12   If there is a serious disagreement about the need to move the person that cannot be settled in any other way, the Court of Protection can be asked to decide what the person's best interests are and where they should live. For example, this could happen if members of a family disagree over what is best for a relative who lacks capacity to give or deny permission for a move.

6.13   In some circumstances, being placed in a hospital or care home may deprive the person of their liberty (see paragraphs 6.49–6.53). If this is the case, there is no protection from liability – even if the placement was considered to be in the best interests of the person (section 6(5)). It is up to the decision-maker to first look at a range of alternative and less restrictive options to see if there is any way of avoiding taking away the person's liberty.

6.14   If there is no alternative way of caring for the person, specific authority will be required to keep the person in a situation which deprives them of their liberty. For instance, sometimes the Court of Protection might be prepared to grant an order of which a consequence is the deprivation of a person's liberty – if it is satisfied that this is in the person's best interests. In other cases, if the person needs treatment for a mental disorder and meets the criteria for detention under the Mental Health Act 1983, this may be used to admit or keep the person in hospital (see chapter 13).

Healthcare and treatment decisions

6.15 Section 5 also allows actions to be taken to ensure a person who lacks capacity to consent receives necessary medical treatment. This could involve taking the person to hospital for out-patient treatment or arranging for admission to hospital. Even if a person who lacks capacity to consent objects to the proposed treatment or admission to hospital, the action might still be allowed under section 5 (but see paragraphs 6.20 and 6.22 below). But there are limits about whether force or restraint can be used to impose treatment (see paragraphs 6.40–6.53).

6.16 Major healthcare and treatment decisions – for example, major surgery or a decision that no attempt is to be made to resuscitate the patient (known as 'DNR' decisions) – will also need special consideration. Unless there is a valid and applicable advance decision to refuse the specific treatment, healthcare staff must carefully work out what would be in the person's best interests (see chapter 5). As part of the process of working this out, they will need to consider (where practical and appropriate):

- the past and present wishes and feelings, beliefs and values of the person who lacks capacity to make the treatment decision, including any advance statement the person wrote setting out their wishes when they had capacity

- the views of anyone previously named by the person as someone to be consulted

- the views of anyone engaged in caring for the person

- the views of anyone interested in their welfare, and

- the views of any attorney or deputy appointed for the person.

In specific cases where there is no-one else available to consult about the person's best interests, an IMCA must be appointed to support and represent the person (see paragraph 6.9 above and chapter 10).

Healthcare staff must also consider whether there are alternative treatment options that might be less intrusive or restrictive (see chapter

2, principle 5). When deciding about the provision or withdrawal of life-sustaining treatment, anyone working out what is in the best interests of a person who lacks capacity must not be motivated by a desire to bring about the person's death (see chapter 5).

Chapter 6

What protection does the Act offer for people providing care or treatment?

6.17 Multi-disciplinary meetings are often the best way to decide on a person's best interests. They bring together healthcare and social care staff with different skills to discuss the person's options and may involve those who are closest to the person concerned. But final responsibility for deciding what is in a person's best interest lies with the member of healthcare staff responsible for the person's treatment. They should record their decision, how they reached it and the reasons for it in the person's clinical notes. As long as they have recorded objective reasons to show that the decision is in the person's best interests, and the other requirements of section 5 of the Act are met, all healthcare staff taking actions in connection with the particular treatment will be protected from liability.

6.18 Some treatment decisions are so serious that the court has to make them – unless the person has previously made a Lasting Power of Attorney appointing an attorney to make such healthcare decisions for them (see chapter 7) or they have made a valid advance decision to refuse the proposed treatment (see chapter 9). The Court of Protection must be asked to make decisions relating to:[20]

- the proposed withholding or withdrawal of artificial nutrition and hydration (ANH) from a patient in a permanent vegetative state (PVS)

- cases where it is proposed that a person who lacks capacity to consent should donate an organ or bone marrow to another person

- the proposed non-therapeutic sterilisation of a person who lacks capacity to consent (for example, for contraceptive purposes)

- cases where there is a dispute about whether a particular treatment will be in a person's best interests.

See paragraphs 8.18–8.24 for more details on these types of cases.

6.19 This last category may include cases that introduce ethical dilemmas concerning untested or innovative treatments (for example, new treatments for variant Creutzfeldt-Jakob Disease (CDJ)) where it is not known if the treatment will be effective, or certain cases involving a termination of pregnancy. It may also include cases where there is conflict between professionals or between professionals and family members which cannot be resolved in any other way.

---

[20] The procedures resulting from those court judgements are set out in a Practice Note from the Official Solicitor (available at www.officialsolicitor.gov.uk) and will be set out in a Practice Direction from the new Court of Protection.

Where there is conflict, it is advisable for parties to get legal advice, though they may not necessarily be able to get legal aid to pay for this advice. Chapter 8 gives more information about the need to refer cases to court for a decision.

Who is protected from liability by section 5?

6.20 Section 5 of the Act is most likely to affect:

- family carers and other kinds of carers
- care workers
- healthcare and social care staff, and
- others who may occasionally be involved in the care or treatment of a person who lacks capacity to consent (for example, ambulance staff, housing workers, police officers and volunteer support workers).

6.21 At any time, it is likely that several people will be carrying out tasks that are covered by section 5 of the Act. Section 5 does not:

- give one person more rights than another to carry out tasks
- specify who has the authority to act in a specific instance
- allow somebody to make decisions relating to subjects other than the care or treatment of the person who lacks capacity, or
- allow somebody to give consent on behalf of a person who lacks capacity to do so.

6.22 To receive protection from liability under section 5, all actions must be related to the care or treatment of the person who lacks capacity to consent. Before taking action, carers must first reasonably believe that:

- the person lacks the capacity to make that particular decision at the time it needs to be made, and
- the action is in the person's best interests.

This is explained further in paragraphs 6.26–6.34 below.

Scenario: Protecting multiple carers

Mr Rose, an older man with dementia, gets help from several people. His sister sometimes cooks meals for him. A district nurse visits him to change the dressing on a pressure sore, and a friend often takes Mr Rose to the park, guiding him when they cross the road. Each of these individuals would be protected from liability under section 5 of the Act – but only if they take reasonable steps to check that he lacks capacity to consent to the actions they take and hold a reasonable belief that the actions are in Mr Rose's best interests.

Chapter 6

What protection does the Act offer for people providing care or treatment?

6.23 Section 5 may also protect carers who need to use the person's money to pay for goods or services that the person needs but lacks the capacity to purchase for themselves. However, there are strict controls over who may have access to another person's money. See paragraphs 6.56–6.66 for more information.

6.24 Carers who provide personal care services must not carry out specialist procedures that are normally done by trained healthcare staff. If the action involves medical treatment, the doctor or other member of healthcare staff with responsibility for the patient will be the decision-maker who has to decide whether the proposed treatment is in the person's best interests (see chapter 5). A doctor can delegate responsibility for giving the treatment to other people in the clinical team who have the appropriate skills or expertise. People who do more than their experience or qualifications allow may not be protected from liability.

Care planning

6.25 Decisions about a person's care or treatment are often made by a multi-disciplinary team (a team of professionals with different skills that contribute to a person's care), by drawing up a care plan for the person. The preparation of a care plan should always include an assessment of the person's capacity to consent to the actions covered by the care plan, and confirm that those actions are agreed to be in the person's best interests. Healthcare and social care staff may then be able to assume that any actions they take under the care plan are in the person's best interests, and therefore receive protection from liability under section 5. But a person's capacity and best interests must still be reviewed regularly.

What steps should people take to be protected from liability?

6.26   As well as taking the following steps, somebody who wants to be protected from liability should bear in mind the statutory principles set out in section 1 of the Act (see chapter 2).

6.27   First, reasonable steps must be taken to find out whether a person has the capacity to make a decision about the proposed action (section 5(1)(a)). If the person has capacity, they must give their consent for anyone to take an action on their behalf, so that the person taking the action is protected from liability. For guidance on what is classed as 'reasonable steps', see paragraphs 6.29–6.34. But reasonable steps must always include:

- taking all practical and appropriate steps to help people to make a decision about an action themselves, and

- applying the two-stage test of capacity (see chapter 4).

The person who is going to take the action must have a 'reasonable belief' that the individual lacks capacity to give consent for the action at the time it needs to be taken.

6.28   Secondly, the person proposing to take action must have reasonable grounds for believing that the action is in the best interests of the person who lacks capacity. They should apply all elements of the best interests checklist (see chapter 5), and in particular

- consider whether the person is likely to regain capacity to make this decision in the future. Can the action wait until then?

- consider whether a less restrictive option is available (chapter 2, principle 5), and

- have objective reasons for thinking an action is in the best interests of the person who lacks capacity to consent to it.

What is 'reasonable'?

6.29   As explained in chapter 4, anyone assessing a person's capacity to make decisions for themselves or give consent must focus wholly on whether the person has capacity to make a specific decision at the time it needs to be made and not the person's capacity to make decisions generally. For example, a carer helping a person to dress can assess a person's capacity to agree to their help by explaining the different options (getting dressed or staying in nightclothes), and the consequences (being able to go out, or staying in all day).

6.30 Carers do not have to be experts in assessing capacity. But they must be able to show that they have taken *reasonable steps* to find out if the person has the capacity to make the specific decision. Only then will they have *reasonable grounds for believing* the person lacks capacity in relation to that particular matter. See paragraphs 4.44–4.45 for guidance on what is classed as 'reasonable' – although this will vary, depending on circumstances.

Chapter 6

What protection does the Act offer for people providing care or treatment?

6.31 For the majority of decisions, formal assessment processes are unlikely to be required. But in some circumstances, professional practice requires some formal procedures to be carried out (for example, where consent to medical treatment is required, the doctor will need to assess – and record the person's capacity to consent). Under section 5, carers and professionals will be protected from liability as long as they are able to provide some objective reasons that explain why they believe that the person lacks capacity to consent to the action. If somebody challenges their belief, both carers and professionals will be protected from liability as long as they can show that they took steps to find out whether the person has capacity and that they have a reasonable belief that the person lacks capacity.

6.32 Similarly, carers, relatives and others involved in caring for someone who lacks capacity must have *reasonable grounds for believing* that their action is in the person's best interests. They must not simply impose their own views. They must be able to show that they considered all relevant circumstances and applied the best interests checklist. This includes showing that they have tried to involve the person who lacks capacity, and find out their wishes and feelings, beliefs and values. They must also have asked other people's opinions, where practical and appropriate. If somebody challenges their decision, they will be protected from liability if they can show that it was reasonable for them to believe that their action was in the person's best interests – in all the circumstances of that particular case.

6.33 If healthcare and social care staff are involved, their skills and knowledge will affect what is classed as 'reasonable'. For example, a doctor assessing somebody's capacity to consent to treatment must demonstrate more skill than someone without medical training. They should also record in the person's healthcare record the steps they took and the reasons for the finding. Healthcare and social care staff should apply normal clinical and professional standards when deciding what treatments to offer. They must then decide whether the proposed treatment is in the best interests of the person who lacks capacity to consent. This includes considering all relevant circumstances and applying the best interests checklist (see chapter 5).

6.34 Healthcare and social care staff can be said to have 'reasonable grounds for believing' that a person lacks capacity if:

- they are working to a person's care plan, and

- the care planning process involved an assessment of the person's capacity to make a decision about actions in the care plan.

It is also reasonable for them to assume that the care planning process assessed a person's best interests. But they should still make every effort to communicate with the person to find out if they still lack capacity and the action is still in their best interests.

Scenario: Working with a care plan

Margaret, an elderly woman, has serious mental health and physical problems. She lives in a nursing home and a care plan has been prepared by the multi-disciplinary team, in consultation with her relatives in deciding what course of action would be in Margaret's best interests. The care plan covers the medication she has been prescribed, the physiotherapy she needs, help with her personal care and other therapeutic activities such as art therapy.

Although attempts were made to involve Margaret in the care planning process, she has been assessed by the doctor responsible for her care as lacking capacity to consent to most aspects of her care plan. The care plan can be relied on by the nurse or care assistant who administers the medication, by the physiotherapist and art therapist, and also by the care assistant who helps with Margaret's personal care, providing them with reasonable grounds for believing that they are acting in her best interests.

However, as each act is performed, they must all take reasonable steps to communicate with Margaret to explain what they are doing and to ascertain whether she has the capacity to consent to the act in question. If they think she does, they must stop the treatment unless or until Margaret agrees that it should continue.

What happens in emergency situations?

6.35 Sometimes people who lack capacity to consent will require emergency medical treatment to save their life or prevent them from serious harm. In these situations, what steps are 'reasonable' will differ to those in non-urgent cases. In emergencies, it will almost always be in the person's best interests to give urgent treatment without delay. One exception to this is when the healthcare staff giving treatment are satisfied that an advance decision to refuse treatment exists (see paragraph 6.37).

Chapter 6

What protection does the Act offer for people providing care or treatment?

What happens in cases of negligence?

6.36 Section 5 does not provide a defence in cases of negligence – either in carrying out a particular act or by failing to act where necessary. For example, a doctor may be protected against a claim of battery for carrying out an operation that is in a person's best interests. But if they perform the operation negligently, they are not protected from a charge of negligence. So the person who lacks capacity has the same rights in cases of negligence as someone who has consented to the operation.

What is the effect of an advance decision to refuse treatment?

6.37 Sometimes people will make an advance decision to refuse treatment while they still have capacity to do so and before they need that particular treatment. Healthcare staff must respect this decision if it is valid and applies to the proposed treatment.

6.38 If healthcare staff are satisfied that an advance decision is valid and applies to the proposed treatment, they are not protected from liability if they give any treatment that goes against it. But they are protected from liability if they did not know about an advance decision or they are not satisfied that the advance decision is valid and applies in the current circumstances (section 26(2)). See chapter 9 for further guidance.

What limits are there on protection from liability?

6.39 Section 6 imposes some important limitations on acts which can be carried out with protection from liability under section 5 (as described in the first part of this chapter). The key areas where acts might not be protected from liability are where there is inappropriate use of restraint or where a person who lacks capacity is deprived of their liberty.

Using restraint

6.40 Section 6(4) of the Act states that someone is using restraint if they:

- use force – or threaten to use force – to make someone do something that they are resisting, or

- restrict a person's freedom of movement, whether they are resisting or not.

6.41 Any action intended to restrain a person who lacks capacity will not attract protection from liability unless the following two conditions are met:

- the person taking action must reasonably believe that restraint is *necessary* to prevent *harm* to the person who lacks capacity, and

- the amount or type of restraint used and the amount of time it lasts must be a *proportionate response* to the likelihood and seriousness of harm.

See paragraphs 6.44–6.48 for more explanation of the terms *necessary, harm* and a *proportionate response*.

6.42 Healthcare and social care staff should also refer to:

- professional and other guidance on restraint or physical intervention, such as that issued by the Department of Health[21] or Welsh Assembly Government,[22] and

- limitations imposed by regulations and standards, such as the national minimum standards for care services (see chapter 14).

6.43 In addition to the requirements of the Act, the common law imposes a duty of care on healthcare and social care staff in respect of all people to whom they provide services. Therefore if a person who lacks capacity to consent has challenging behaviour, or is in the acute stages of illness causing them to act in way which may cause harm to others, staff may, under the common law, take appropriate and necessary action to restrain or remove the person, in order to prevent harm, both to the person concerned and to anyone else.

However, within this context, the common law would not provide sufficient grounds for an action that would have the effect of depriving someone of their liberty (see paragraphs 6.49–6.53).

---

[21] For guidance on using restraint with people with learning disabilities and autistic spectrum disorder, see *Guidance for restrictive physical interventions* (published by the Department of Health and Department for Education and Skills and available at www.dh.gov.uk/ assetRoot/04/06/84/61/04068461.pdf).

[22] In Wales, the relevant guidance is the Welsh Assembly Government's *Framework for restrictive physical intervention policy and practice* (available at www.childrenfirst.wales. gov.uk/content/framework/phys-int-e.pdf).

When might restraint be 'necessary'?

Chapter 6

What protection does the Act offer for people providing care or treatment?

6.44 Anybody considering using restraint must have objective reasons to justify that restraint is necessary. They must be able to show that the person being cared for is likely to suffer harm unless proportionate restraint is used. A carer or professional must not use restraint just so that they can do something more easily. If restraint is necessary to prevent harm to the person who lacks capacity, it must be the minimum amount of force for the shortest time possible.

Scenario: Appropriate use of restraint

Derek, a man with learning disabilities, has begun to behave in a challenging way. Staff at his care home think he might have a medical condition that is causing him distress. They take him to the doctor, who thinks that Derek might have a hormone imbalance. But the doctor needs to take a blood test to confirm this, and when he tries to take the test Derek attempts to fight him off.

The results might be negative – so the test might not be necessary. But the doctor decides that a test is in Derek's best interests, because failing to treat a problem like a hormone imbalance might make it worse. It is therefore in Derek's best interests to restrain him to take the blood test. The temporary restraint is in proportion to the likely harm caused by failing to treat a possible medical condition.

What is 'harm'?

6.45 The Act does not define 'harm', because it will vary depending on the situation. For example,

- a person with learning disabilities might run into a busy road without warning, if they do not understand the dangers of cars

- a person with dementia may wander away from home and get lost, if they cannot remember where they live

- a person with manic depression might engage in excessive spending during a manic phase, causing them to get into debt

- a person may also be at risk of harm if they behave in a way that encourages others to assault or exploit them (for example, by behaving in a dangerously provocative way).

6.46 Common sense measures can often help remove the risk of harm (for example, by locking away poisonous chemicals or removing obstacles). Also, care planning should include risk assessments and set out appropriate actions to try to prevent possible risks. But it is impossible to remove all risk, and a proportionate response is needed when the risk of harm does arise.

What is a 'proportionate response'?

6.47 A 'proportionate response' means using the least intrusive type and minimum amount of restraint to achieve a specific outcome in the best interests of the person who lacks capacity. On occasions when the use of force may be necessary, carers and healthcare and social care staff should use the minimum amount of force for the shortest possible time.

For example, a carer may need to hold a person's arm while they cross the road, if the person does not understand the dangers of roads. But it would not be a proportionate response to stop the person going outdoors at all. It may be appropriate to have a secure lock on a door that faces a busy road, but it would not be a proportionate response to lock someone in a bedroom all the time to prevent them from attempting to cross the road.

6.48 Carers and healthcare and social care staff should consider less restrictive options before using restraint. Where possible, they should ask other people involved in the person's care what action they think is necessary to protect the person from harm. For example, it may be appropriate to get an advocate to work with the person to see if they can avoid or minimise the need for restraint to be used.

Scenario: Avoiding restraint

Oscar has learning disabilities. People at the college he attends sometimes cannot understand him, and he gets frustrated. Sometimes he hits the wall and hurts himself.

Staff don't want to take Oscar out of class, because he says he enjoys college and is learning new skills. They have allowed his support worker to sit with him, but he still gets upset. The support worker could try to hold Oscar back. But she thinks this is too forceful, even though it would stop him hurting himself.

Instead, she gets expert advice from members of the local community team. Observation helps them understand Oscar's behaviour better. They come up with a support strategy that reduces the risk of harmful behaviour and is less restrictive of his freedom.

When are acts seen as depriving a person of their liberty?

6.49 Although section 5 of the Act permits the use of restraint where it is necessary under the above conditions, section 6(5) confirms that there is no protection under the Act for actions that result in someone being deprived of their liberty (as defined by Article 5(1) of the European Convention on Human Rights). This applies not only to public authorities covered by the Human Rights Act 1998 but to everyone who might otherwise get protection under section 5 of the Act. It also applies to attorneys or deputies – they cannot give permission for an action that takes away a person's liberty.

6.50 Sometimes there is no alternative way to provide care or treatment other than depriving the person of their liberty. In this situation, some people may be detained in hospital under the Mental Health Act 1983 – but this only applies to people who require hospital treatment for a mental disorder (see chapter 13). Otherwise, actions that amount to a deprivation of liberty will not be lawful unless formal authorisation is obtained.

6.51 In some cases, the Court of Protection might grant an order that permits the deprivation of a person's liberty, if it is satisfied that this is in a person's best interests.

6.52 It is difficult to define the difference between actions that amount to a restriction of someone's liberty and those that result in a deprivation of liberty. In recent legal cases, the European Court of Human Rights said that the difference was 'one of degree or intensity, not one of nature or substance'.[23] There must therefore be particular factors in the specific situation of the person concerned which provide the 'degree' or 'intensity' to result in a deprivation of liberty. In practice, this can relate to:

- the type of care being provided
- how long the situation lasts
- its effects, or
- the way in a particular situation came about.[24]

Chapter 6

What protection does the Act offer for people providing care or treatment?

---

[23] *HL v The United Kingdom* (Application no, 45508/99). Judgement 5 October 2004, paragraph 89

[24] In *HL v UK* (also known as the 'Bournewood' case), the European Court said that "the key factor in the present case [is] that the health care professionals treating and managing the applicant exercised complete and effective control over his care and movements". They found "the concrete situation was that the applicant was under continuous supervision and control and was not free to leave."

The European Court of Human Rights has identified the following as factors contributing to deprivation of liberty in its judgments on cases to date:

* restraint was used, including sedation, to admit a person who is resisting

* professionals exercised complete and effective control over care and movement for a significant period

* professionals exercised control over assessments, treatment, contacts and residence

* the person would be prevented from leaving if they made a meaningful attempt to do so

* a request by carers for the person to be discharged to their care was refused

* the person was unable to maintain social contacts because of restrictions placed on access to other people

* the person lost autonomy because they were under continuous supervision and control.[25]

6.53   The Government has announced that it intends to amend the Act to introduce new procedures and provisions for people who lack capacity to make relevant decisions but who need to be deprived of their liberty, in their best interests, otherwise than under the Mental Health Act 1983 (the so-called 'Bournewood provisions'). This chapter will be fully revised in due course to reflect those changes. Information about the Government's current proposals in respect of the Bournewood safeguards is available on the Department of Health website. This information includes draft illustrative Code of Practice guidance about the proposed safeguards. See paragraphs 13.52–13.55 for more details.

How does section 5 apply to attorneys and deputies?

6.54   Section 5 does not provide protection for actions that go against the decision of someone who has been authorised to make decisions for a person who lacks capacity to make such decision for themselves. For instance, if someone goes against the decision of an attorney acting under a Lasting Power of Attorney (LPA) (see chapter 7) or a deputy appointed by the Court of Protection (see chapter 8), they will not be protected under section 5.

---

[25]   These are listed in the Department of Health's draft illustrative Code of Practice guidance about the proposed safeguards. www.dh.gov.uk/assetRoot/04/14/17/64/04141764.pdf

6.55 Attorneys and deputies must only make decisions within the scope of the authority of the LPA or court order. Sometimes carers or healthcare and social care staff might feel that an attorney or deputy is making decisions they should not be making, or that are not in a person's best interests. If this is the case, and the disagreement cannot be settled any other way, either the carers, the staff or the attorney or deputy can apply to the Court of Protection. If the dispute concerns the provision of medical treatment, medical staff can still give life-sustaining treatment, or treatment which stops a person's condition getting seriously worse, while the court is coming to a decision (section 6(6)).

Chapter 6

What protection does the Act offer for people providing care or treatment?

Who can pay for goods or services?

6.56 Carers may have to spend money on behalf of someone who lacks capacity to purchase necessary goods or services. For example, they may need to pay for a milk delivery or for a chiropodist to provide a service at the person's home. In some cases, they might have to pay for more costly arrangements such as house repairs or organising a holiday. Carers are likely to be protected from liability if their actions are properly taken under section 5, and in the best interests of the person who lacks capacity.

6.57 In general, a contract entered into by a person who lacks capacity to make the contract cannot be enforced if the other person knows, or must be taken to have known, of the lack of capacity. Section 7 of the Act modifies this rule and states that where the contract is for 'necessary' goods or services for a person who lacks capacity to make the arrangements for themselves, that person must pay a reasonable price for them.

What are necessary goods and services?

6.58 'Necessary' means something that is suitable to the person's condition in life (their place in society, rather than any mental or physical condition) and their actual requirements when the goods or services are provided (section 7(2)). The aim is to make sure that people can enjoy a similar standard of living and way of life to those they had before lacking capacity. For example, if a person who now lacks capacity previously chose to buy expensive designer clothes, these are still necessary goods – as long as they can still afford them. But they would not be necessary for a person who always wore cheap clothes, no matter how wealthy they were.

6.59 Goods are not necessary if the person already has a sufficient supply of them. For example, buying one or two new pairs of shoes for a person who lacks capacity could be necessary. But a dozen pairs would probably not be necessary.

How should payments be arranged?

6.60 If a person lacks capacity to arrange for payment for necessary goods and services, sections 5 and 8 allow a carer to arrange payment on their behalf.

6.61 The carer must first take reasonable steps to check whether a person can arrange for payment themselves, or has the capacity to consent to the carer doing it for them. If the person lacks the capacity to consent or pay themselves, the carer must decide what goods or services would be necessary for the person and in their best interests. The carer can then lawfully deal with payment for those goods and services in one of three ways:

- If neither the carer nor the person who lacks capacity can produce the necessary funds, the carer may promise that the person who lacks capacity will pay. A supplier may not be happy with this, or the carer may be worried that they will be held responsible for any debt. In such cases, the carer must follow the formal steps in paragraphs 6.62–6.66 below.

- If the person who lacks capacity has cash, the carer may use that money to pay for goods or services (for example, to pay the milkman or the hairdresser).

- The carer may choose to pay for the goods or services with their own money. The person who lacks capacity must pay them back. This may involve using cash in the person's possession or running up an IOU. (This is not appropriate for paid care workers, whose contracts might stop them handling their clients' money.) The carer must follow formal steps to get money held in a bank or building society account (see paragraphs 6.63–6.66 below).

6.62 Carers should keep bills, receipts and other proof of payment when paying for goods and services. They will need these documents when asking to get money back. Keeping appropriate financial records and documentation is a requirement of the national minimum standards for care homes or domiciliary care agencies.

Access to a person's assets

6.63 The Act does not give a carer or care worker access to a person's income or assets. Nor does it allow them to sell the person's property.

Chapter 6

What protection does the Act offer for people providing care or treatment?

6.64 Anyone wanting access to money in a person's bank or building society will need formal legal authority. They will also need legal authority to sell a person's property. Such authority could be given in a Lasting Power of Attorney (LPA) appointing an attorney to deal with property and affairs, or in an order of the Court of Protection (either a single decision of the court or an order appointing a deputy to make financial decisions for the person who lacks capacity to make such decisions).

Scenario: Being granted access to a person's assets

A storm blew some tiles off the roof of a house owned by Gordon, a man with Alzheimer's disease. He lacks capacity to arrange for repairs and claim on his insurance. The repairs are likely to be costly.

Gordon's son decides to organise the repairs, and he agrees to pay because his father doesn't have enough cash available. The son could then apply to the Court of Protection for authority to claim insurance on his father's behalf and for him to be reimbursed from his father's bank account to cover the cost of the repairs once the insurance payment had been received.

6.65 Sometimes another person will already have legal control of the finances and property of a person who lacks capacity to manage their own affairs. This could be an attorney acting under a registered EPA or an appropriate LPA (see chapter 7) or a deputy appointed by the Court of Protection (see chapter 8). Or it could be someone (usually a carer) that has the right to act as an 'appointee' (under Social Security Regulations) and claim benefits for a person who lacks capacity to make their own claim and use the money on the person's behalf. But an appointee cannot deal with other assets or savings from sources other than benefits.

6.66 Section 6(6) makes clear that a family carer or other carer cannot make arrangements for goods or services to be supplied to a person who lacks capacity if this conflicts with a decision made by someone who has formal powers over the person's money and property, such as an attorney or deputy acting within the scope of their authority. Where there is no conflict and the carer has paid for necessary goods and services the carer may ask for money back from an attorney, a deputy or where relevant, an appointee.

7 What does the Act say about Lasting Powers of Attorney?

This chapter explains what Lasting Powers of Attorney (LPAs) are and how they should be used. It also sets out:

- how LPAs differ from Enduring Powers of Attorney (EPAs)
- the types of decisions that people can appoint attorneys to make (attorneys are also called 'donees' in the Act)
- situations in which an LPA can and cannot be used
- the duties and responsibilities of attorneys
- the standards required of attorneys, and
- measures for dealing with attorneys who don't meet appropriate standards.

This chapter also explains what should happen to EPAs that were made before the Act comes into force.

> In this chapter, as throughout the Code, a person's capacity (or lack of capacity) refers specifically to their capacity to make a particular decision at the time it needs to be made.

Quick summary

Anyone asked to be an attorney should:

- consider whether they have the skills and ability to act as an attorney (especially if it is for a property and affairs LPA)
- ask themselves whether they actually want to be an attorney and take on the duties and responsibilities of the role.

Before acting under an LPA, attorneys must:

- make sure the LPA has been registered with the Public Guardian
- take all practical and appropriate steps to help the donor make the particular decision for themselves.

When acting under an LPA:

- make sure that the Act's statutory principles are followed
- check whether the person has the capacity to make that particular decision for themselves. If they do:
  - a personal welfare LPA cannot be used – the person must make the decision
  - a property and affairs LPA can be used even if the person has capacity to make the decision, unless they have stated in the LPA that they should make decisions for themselves when they have capacity to do so.

At all times, remember:

- anything done under the authority of the LPA must be in the person's best interests
- anyone acting as an attorney must have regard to guidance in this Code of Practice that is relevant to the decision that is to be made
- attorneys must fulfil their responsibilities and duties to the person who lacks capacity.

What is a Lasting Power of Attorney (LPA)?

7.1 Sometimes one person will want to give another person authority to make a decision on their behalf. A power of attorney is a legal document that allows them to do so. Under a power of attorney, the chosen person (the attorney or donee) can make decisions that are as valid as one made by the person (the donor).

7.2 Before the Enduring Powers of Attorney Act 1985, every power of attorney automatically became invalid as soon as the donor lacked the capacity to make their own decision. But that Act introduced the Enduring Power of Attorney (EPA). An EPA allows an attorney to make decisions about property and financial affairs even if the donor lacks capacity to manage their own affairs.

7.3 The Mental Capacity Act replaces the EPA with the Lasting Power of Attorney (LPA). It also increases the range of different types of decisions that people can authorise others to make on their behalf. As well as property and affairs (including financial matters), LPAs can also cover personal welfare (including healthcare and consent to medical treatment) for people who lack capacity to make such decisions for themselves.

7.4 The donor can choose one person or several to make different kinds of decisions. See paragraphs 7.21–7.31 for more information about personal welfare LPAs. See paragraphs 7.32–7.42 for more information about LPAs on property and affairs.

How do LPAs compare to EPAs?

7.5 There are a number of differences between LPAs and EPAs. These are summarised as follows:

- EPAs only cover property and affairs. LPAs can also cover personal welfare.

- Donors must use the relevant specific form (prescribed in regulations) to make EPAs and LPAs. There are different forms for EPAs, personal welfare LPAs and property and affairs LPAs.

- EPAs must be registered with the Public Guardian when the donor can no longer manage their own affairs (or when they start to lose capacity). But LPAs can be registered at any time before they are used – before or after the donor lacks capacity to make particular decisions that the LPA covers. If the LPA is not registered, it can't be used.

- EPAs can be used while the donor still has capacity to manage their own property and affairs, as can property and affairs LPAs, so long as the donor does not say otherwise in the LPA. But personal welfare LPAs can only be used once the donor lacks capacity to make the welfare decision in question.

- Once the Act comes into force, only LPAs can be made but existing EPAs will continue to be valid. There will be different laws and procedures for EPAs and LPAs.

- Attorneys making decisions under a registered EPA or LPA must follow the Act's principles and act in the best interests of the donor.

- The duties under the law of agency apply to attorneys of both EPAs and LPAs (see paragraphs 7.58–7.68 below).

- Decisions that the courts have made about EPAs may also affect how people use LPAs.

- Attorneys acting under an LPA have a legal duty to have regard to the guidance in this Code of Practice. EPA attorneys do not. But the Code's guidance will still be helpful to them.

How does a donor create an LPA?

Chapter 7

What does the
Act say about
Lasting Powers
of Attorney?

7.6   The donor must also follow the right procedures for creating and registering an LPA, as set out below. Otherwise the LPA might not be valid. It is not always necessary to get legal advice. But it is a good idea for certain cases (for example, if the donor's circumstances are complicated).

7.7   Only adults aged 18 or over can make an LPA, and they can only make an LPA if they have the capacity to do so. For an LPA to be valid:

- the LPA must be a written document set out in the statutory form prescribed by regulations[26]

- the document must include prescribed information about the nature and effect of the LPA (as set out in the regulations)

- the donor must sign a statement saying that they have read the prescribed information (or somebody has read it to them) and that they want the LPA to apply when they no longer have capacity

- the document must name people (not any of the attorneys) who should be told about an application to register the LPA, or it should say that there is no-one they wish to be told

- the attorneys must sign a statement saying that they have read the prescribed information and that they understand their duties – in particular the duty to act in the donor's best interests

- the document must include a certificate completed by an independent third party,[27] confirming that:

  - in their opinion, the donor understands the LPA's purpose

  - nobody used fraud or undue pressure to trick or force the donor into making the LPA and

  - there is nothing to stop the LPA being created.

Who can be an attorney?

7.8   A donor should think carefully before choosing someone to be their attorney. An attorney should be someone who is trustworthy, competent and reliable. They should have the skills and ability to carry out the necessary tasks.

---

[26] The prescribed forms will be available from the Office of the Public Guardian (OPG) or from legal stationers.

[27] Details of who may and who may not be a certificate provider will be available in regulations. The OPG will produce guidance for certificate providers on their role.

7.9 Attorneys must be at least 18 years of age. For property and affairs LPAs, the attorney could be either:

- an individual (as long as they are not bankrupt at the time the LPA is made), or

- a trust corporation (often parts of banks or other financial institutions).

If an attorney nominated under a property and affairs LPA becomes bankrupt at any point, they will no longer be allowed to act as an attorney for property and affairs. People who are bankrupt can still act as an attorney for personal welfare LPAs.

7.10 The donor must name an individual rather than a job title in a company or organisation, (for example, 'The Director of Adult Services' or 'my solicitor' would not be sufficient). A paid care worker (such as a care home manager) should not agree to act as an attorney, apart from in unusual circumstances (for example, if they are the only close relative of the donor).

7.11 Section 10(4) of the Act allows the donor to appoint two or more attorneys and to specify whether they should act 'jointly', 'jointly and severally', or 'jointly in respect of some matters and jointly and severally in respect of others'.

- Joint attorneys must always act together. All attorneys must agree decisions and sign any relevant documents.

- Joint and several attorneys can act together but may also act independently if they wish. Any action taken by any attorney alone is as valid as if they were the only attorney.

7.12 The donor may want to appoint attorneys to act jointly in some matters but jointly and severally in others. For example, a donor could choose to appoint two or more financial attorneys jointly and severally. But they might say then when selling the donor's house, the attorneys must act jointly. The donor may appoint welfare attorneys to act jointly and severally but specify that they must act jointly in relation to giving consent to surgery. If a donor who has appointed two or more attorneys does not specify how they should act, they must always act jointly (section 10(5)).

7.13 Section 10(8) says that donors may choose to name replacement attorneys to take over the duties in certain circumstances (for example, in the event of an attorney's death). The donor may name a specific attorney to be replaced, or the replacements can take over from any attorney, if necessary. Donors cannot give their attorneys the right to appoint a substitute or successor.

How should somebody register and use an LPA?

7.14 An LPA must be registered with the Office of the Public Guardian (OPG) before it can be used. An unregistered LPA will not give the attorney any legal powers to make a decision for the donor. The donor can register the LPA while they are still capable, or the attorney can apply to register the LPA at any time.

7.15 There are advantages in registering the LPA soon after the donor makes it (for example, to ensure that there is no delay when the LPA needs to be used). But if this has not been done, an LPA can be registered after the donor lacks the capacity to make a decision covered by the LPA.

7.16 If an LPA is unregistered, attorneys must register it before making any decisions under the LPA. If the LPA has been registered but not used for some time, the attorney should tell the OPG when they begin to act under it – so that the attorney can be sent relevant, up-to-date information about the rules governing LPAs.

7.17 While they still have capacity, donors should let the OPG know of permanent changes of address for the donor or the attorney or any other changes in circumstances. If the donor no longer has capacity to do this, attorneys should report any such changes to the OPG. Examples include an attorney of a property and affairs LPA becoming bankrupt or the ending of a marriage between the donor and their attorney. This will help keep OPG records up to date, and will make sure that attorneys do not make decisions that they no longer have the authority to make.

What guidance should an attorney follow?

7.18 Section 9(4) states that attorneys must meet the requirements set out in the Act. Most importantly, they have to follow the statutory principles (section 1) and make decisions in the best interests of the person who lacks capacity (section 4). They must also respect any conditions or restrictions that the LPA document contains. See chapter 2 for guidance on how to apply the Act's principles.

7.19 Chapter 3 gives suggestions of ways to help people make their own decisions in accordance with the Act's second principle. Attorneys should also refer to the guidance in chapter 4 when assessing the donor's capacity to make particular decisions, and in particular, should follow the steps suggested for establishing a 'reasonable belief' that the donor lacks capacity (see paragraphs 4.44–4.45). Assessments of capacity or best interests must not be based merely on:

- a donor's age or appearance, or
- unjustified assumptions about any condition they might have or their behaviour.

7.20 When deciding what is in the donor's best interests, attorneys should refer to the guidance in chapter 5. In particular, they must consider the donor's past and present wishes and feelings, beliefs and values. Where practical and appropriate, they should consult with:

- anyone involved in caring for the donor
- close relatives and anyone else with an interest in their welfare
- other attorneys appointed by the donor.

See paragraphs 7.52–7.68 for a description of an attorney's duties.

Scenario: Making decisions in a donor's best interests

Mr Young has been a member of the Green Party for a long time. He has appointed his solicitor as his attorney under a property and affairs LPA. But Mr Young did not state in the LPA that investments made on his behalf must be ethical investments. When the attorney assesses his client's best interests, however, the attorney considers the donor's past wishes, values and beliefs. He makes sure that he only invests in companies that are socially and environmentally responsible.

What decisions can an LPA attorney make?

Personal welfare LPAs

7.21 LPAs can be used to appoint attorneys to make decisions about personal welfare, which can include healthcare and medical treatment decisions. Personal welfare LPAs might include decisions about:

- where the donor should live and who they should live with

Chapter 7

What does the
Act say about
Lasting Powers
of Attorney?

- the donor's day-to-day care, including diet and dress

- who the donor may have contact with

- consenting to or refusing medical examination and treatment on the donor's behalf

- arrangements needed for the donor to be given medical, dental or optical treatment

- assessments for and provision of community care services

- whether the donor should take part in social activities, leisure activities, education or training

- the donor's personal correspondence and papers

- rights of access to personal information about the donor, or

- complaints about the donor's care or treatment.

7.22 The standard form for personal welfare LPAs allows attorneys to make decisions about anything that relates to the donor's personal welfare. But donors can add restrictions or conditions to areas where they would not wish the attorney to have the power to act. For example, a donor might only want an attorney to make decisions about their social care and not their healthcare. There are particular rules for LPAs authorising an attorney to make decisions about life-sustaining treatment (see paragraphs 7.30–7.31 below).

7.23 A general personal welfare LPA gives the attorney the right to make all of the decisions set out above although this is not a full list of the actions they can take or decisions they can make. However, a personal welfare LPA can only be used at a time when the donor lacks capacity to make a specific welfare decision.

Scenario: Denying attorneys the right to make certain decisions

Mrs Hutchison is in the early stages of Alzheimer's disease. She is anxious to get all her affairs in order while she still has capacity to do so. She makes a personal welfare LPA, appointing her daughter as attorney. But Mrs Hutchison knows that her daughter doesn't always get on with some members of the family – and she wouldn't want her daughter to stop those relatives from seeing her.

She states in the LPA that her attorney does not have the authority to decide who can contact her or visit her. If her daughter wants to prevent anyone having contact with Mrs Hutchison, she must ask the Court of Protection to decide.

7.24 Before making a decision under a personal welfare LPA, the attorney must be sure that:

- the LPA has been registered with the OPG

- the donor lacks the capacity to make the particular decision or the attorney reasonably believes that the donor lacks capacity to take the decisions covered by the LPA (having applied the Act's principles), and

- they are making the decision in the donor's best interests.

7.25 When healthcare or social care staff are involved in preparing a care plan for someone who has appointed a personal welfare attorney, they must first assess whether the donor has capacity to agree to the care plan or to parts of it. If the donor lacks capacity, professionals must then consult the attorney and get their agreement to the care plan. They will also need to consult the attorney when considering what action is in the person's best interests.

Personal welfare LPAs that authorise an attorney to make healthcare decisions

7.26 A personal welfare LPA allows attorneys to make decisions to accept or refuse healthcare or treatment unless the donor has stated clearly in the LPA that they do not want the attorney to make these decisions.

7.27 Even where the LPA includes healthcare decisions, attorneys do not have the right to consent to or refuse treatment in situations where:

- **the donor has capacity to make the particular healthcare decision (section 11(7)(a))**
  An attorney has no decision-making power if the donor can make their own treatment decisions.

- **the donor has made an advance decision to refuse the proposed treatment (section 11(7)(b))**
  An attorney cannot consent to treatment if the donor has made a valid and applicable advance decision to refuse a specific treatment (see chapter 9). But if the donor made an LPA after the advance decision, and gave the attorney the right to consent to or refuse the treatment, the attorney can choose not to follow the advance decision.

- **a decision relates to life-sustaining treatment (section 11(7)(c))**
  An attorney has no power to consent to or refuse life-sustaining treatment, unless the LPA document expressly authorises this (See paragraphs 7.30–7.31 below.)

- **the donor is detained under the Mental Health Act (section 28)**
An attorney cannot consent to or refuse treatment for a mental disorder for a patient detained under the Mental Health Act 1983 (see also chapter 13).

7.28　LPAs cannot give attorneys the power to demand specific forms of medical treatment that healthcare staff do not believe are necessary or appropriate for the donor's particular condition.

7.29　Attorneys must always follow the Act's principles and make decisions in the donor's best interests. If healthcare staff disagree with the attorney's assessment of best interests, they should discuss the case with other medical experts and/or get a formal second opinion. Then they should discuss the matter further with the attorney. If they cannot settle the disagreement, they can apply to the Court of Protection (see paragraphs 7.45–7.49 below). While the court is coming to a decision, healthcare staff can give life-sustaining treatment to prolong the donor's life or stop their condition getting worse.

Personal welfare LPAs that authorise an attorney to make decisions about life-sustaining treatment

7.30　An attorney can only consent to or refuse life-sustaining treatment on behalf of the donor if, when making the LPA, the donor has specifically stated in the LPA document that they want the attorney to have this authority.

7.31　As with all decisions, an attorney must act in the donor's best interests when making decisions about such treatment. This will involve applying the best interests checklist (see chapter 5) and consulting with carers, family members and others interested in the donor's welfare. In particular, the attorney must not be motivated in any way by the desire to bring about the donor's death (see paragraphs 5.29–5.36). Anyone who doubts that the attorney is acting in the donor's best interests can apply to the Court of Protection for a decision.

> ### Scenario: Making decisions about life-sustaining treatment
>
> Mrs Joshi has never trusted doctors. She prefers to rely on alternative therapies. Because she saw her father suffer after invasive treatment for cancer, she is clear that she would refuse such treatment herself.
>
> She is diagnosed with cancer and discusses her wishes with her husband. Mrs Joshi knows that he would respect her wishes if he ever had to make a decision about her treatment. She makes a personal welfare LPA appointing him as her attorney with authority to make all her welfare and healthcare decisions. She includes a specific statement authorising him to consent to or refuse life-sustaining treatment.
>
> He will then be able to consider her views and make decisions about treatment in her best interests if she later lacks capacity to make those decisions herself.

Property and affairs LPAs

7.32   A donor can make an LPA giving an attorney the right to make decisions about property and affairs (including financial matters). Unless the donor states otherwise, once the LPA is registered, the attorney is allowed to make all decisions about the donor's property and affairs even if the donor still has capacity to make the decisions for themselves. In this situation, the LPA will continue to apply when the donor no longer has capacity.

7.33   Alternatively a donor can state in the LPA document that the LPA should only apply when they lack capacity to make a relevant decision. It is the donor's responsibility to decide how their capacity should then be assessed. For example, the donor may trust the attorney to carry out an assessment, or they may say that the LPA only applies if their GP or another doctor confirms in writing that they lack capacity to make specific decisions about property or finances. Financial institutions may wish to see the written confirmation before recognising the attorney's authority to act under the LPA.

7.34   The fact that someone has made a property and affairs LPA does not mean that they cannot continue to carry out financial transactions for themselves. The donor may have full capacity, but perhaps anticipates that they may lack capacity at some future time. Or they may have fluctuating or partial capacity and therefore be able to make some decisions (or at some times), but need an attorney to make others (or at other times). The attorney should allow and encourage the donor to do as much as possible, and should only act when the donor asks them to or to make those decisions the donor lacks capacity to make. However, in other cases, the donor may wish to hand over responsibility for all decisions to the attorney, even those they still have capacity to make.

7.35 If the donor restricts the decisions an attorney can make, banks may ask the attorney to sign a declaration that protects the bank from liability if the attorney misuses the account.[28]

7.36 If a donor does not restrict decisions the attorney can make, the attorney will be able to decide on any or all of the person's property and financial affairs. This might include:

- buying or selling property

- opening, closing or operating any bank, building society or other account

- giving access to the donor's financial information

- claiming, receiving and using (on the donor's behalf) all benefits, pensions, allowances and rebates (unless the Department for Work and Pensions has already appointed someone and everyone is happy for this to continue)

- receiving any income, inheritance or other entitlement on behalf of the donor

- dealing with the donor's tax affairs

- paying the donor's mortgage, rent and household expenses

- insuring, maintaining and repairing the donor's property

- investing the donor's savings

- making limited gifts on the donor's behalf (but see paragraphs 7.40–7.42 below)

- paying for private medical care and residential care or nursing home fees

- applying for any entitlement to funding for NHS care, social care or adaptations

- using the donor's money to buy a vehicle or any equipment or other help they need

- repaying interest and capital on any loan taken out by the donor.

---

[28] See British Banking Association's guidance for bank staff on *'Banking for mentally incapacitated and learning disabled customers'*.

7.37 A general property and affairs LPA will allow the attorney to carry out any or all of the actions above (although this is not a full list of the actions they can take). However, the donor may want to specify the types of powers they wish the attorney to have, or to exclude particular types of decisions. If the donor holds any assets as trustee, they should get legal advice about how the LPA may affect this.

7.38 The attorney must make these decisions personally and cannot generally give someone else authority to carry out their duties (see paragraphs 7.61–7.62 below). But if the donor wants the attorney to be able to give authority to a specialist to make specific decisions, they need to state this clearly in the LPA document (for example, appointing an investment manager to make particular investment decisions).

7.39 Donors may like to appoint someone (perhaps a family member or a professional) to go through their accounts with the attorney from time to time. This might help to reassure donors that somebody will check their financial affairs when they lack capacity to do so. It may also be helpful for attorneys to arrange a regular check that everything is being done properly. The donor should ensure that the person is willing to carry out this role and is prepared to ask for the accounts if the attorney does not provide them. They should include this arrangement in the signed LPA document. The LPA should also say whether the person can charge a fee for this service.

What gifts can an attorney make under a property and affairs LPA?

7.40 An attorney can only make gifts of the donor's money or belongings to people who are related to or connected with the donor (including the attorney) on specific occasions, including:

- births or birthdays

- weddings or wedding anniversaries

- civil partnership ceremonies or anniversaries, or

- any other occasion when families, friends or associates usually give presents (section 12(3)(b)).

7.41 If the donor previously made donations to any charity regularly or from time to time, the attorney can make donations from the person's funds. This also applies if the donor could have been expected to make such payments (section 12(2)(b)). But the value of any gift or donation must be reasonable and take into account the size of the donor's estate. For example, it would not be reasonable to buy expensive gifts at Christmas if the donor was living on modest means and had to do without essential items in order to pay for them.

7.42   The donor cannot use the LPA to make more extensive gifts than those allowed under section 12 of the Act. But they can impose stricter conditions or restrictions on the attorney's powers to make gifts. They should state these restrictions clearly in the LPA document when they are creating it. When deciding on appropriate gifts, the attorney should consider the donor's wishes and feelings to work out what would be in the donor's best interests. The attorney can apply to the Court of Protection for permission to make gifts that are not included in the LPA (for example, for tax planning purposes).

Are there any other restrictions on attorneys' powers?

7.43   Attorneys are not protected from liability if they do something that is intended to restrain the donor, unless:

- the attorney reasonably believes that the donor lacks capacity to make the decision in question, *and*

- the attorney reasonably believes that restraint is necessary to prevent harm to the donor, *and*

- the type of restraint used is in proportion to the likelihood and the seriousness of the harm.

If an attorney needs to make a decision or take action which may involve the use of restraint, they should take account of the guidance set out in chapter 6.

7.44   Attorneys have no authority to take actions that result in the donor being deprived of their liberty. Any deprivation of liberty will only be lawful if this has been properly authorised and there is other protection available for the person who lacks capacity. An example would be the protection around detention under the Mental Health Act 1983 (see chapter 13) or a court ruling. Chapter 6 gives more guidance on working out whether an action is restraint or a deprivation of liberty.

What powers does the Court of Protection have over LPAs?

7.45   The Court of Protection has a range of powers to:

- determine whether an LPA is valid

- give directions about using the LPA, and

- to remove an attorney (for example, if the attorney does not act in the best interests of the donor).

Chapter 8 gives more information about the Court of Protection's powers.

7.46 If somebody has doubts over whether an LPA is valid, they can ask the court to decide whether the LPA:

- meets the Act's requirements

- has been revoked (cancelled) by the donor, or

- has come to an end for any other reason.

7.47 The court can also stop somebody registering an LPA or rule that an LPA is invalid if:

- the donor made the LPA as a result of undue pressure or fraud, or

- the attorney behaves, has behaved or is planning to behave in a way that goes against their duties or is not in the donor's best interests.

7.48 The court can also clarify an LPA's meaning, if it is not clear, and it can tell attorneys how they should use an LPA. If an attorney thinks that an LPA does not give them enough powers, they can ask the court to extend their powers – if the donor no longer has capacity to authorise this. The court can also authorise an attorney to give a gift that the Act does not normally allow (section 12(2)), if it is in the donor's best interests.

7.49 All attorneys should keep records of their dealings with the donor's affairs (see also paragraph 7.67 below). The court can order attorneys to produce records (for example, financial accounts) and to provide specific reports, information or documentation. If somebody has concerns about an attorney's payment or expenses, the court could resolve the matter.

What responsibilities do attorneys have?

7.50 A donor cannot insist on somebody agreeing to become an attorney. It is down to the proposed attorney to decide whether to take on this responsibility. When an attorney accepts the role by signing the LPA document, this is confirmation that they are willing to act under the LPA once it is registered. An attorney can withdraw from the appointment if they ever become unable or unwilling to act, but if the LPA has been registered they must follow the correct procedures for withdrawing. (see paragraph 7.66 below).

7.51 Once the attorney starts to act under an LPA, they must meet certain standards. If they don't carry out the duties below, they could be removed from the role. In some circumstances they could face charges of fraud or negligence.

What duties does the Act impose?

Chapter 7

What does the
Act say about
Lasting Powers
of Attorney?

7.52   Attorneys acting under an LPA have a duty to:

- follow the Act's statutory principles (see chapter 2)

- make decisions in the donor's best interests

- have regard to the guidance in the Code of Practice

- only make those decisions the LPA gives them authority to make.

Principles and best interests

7.53   Attorneys must act in accordance with the Act's statutory principles
(section 1) and in the best interests of the donor (the steps for working
out best interests are set out in section 4). In particular, attorneys must
consider whether the donor has capacity to make the decision for
themselves. If not, they should consider whether the donor is likely
to regain capacity to make the decision in the future. If so, it may be
possible to delay the decision until the donor can make it.

The Code of Practice

7.54   As well as this chapter, attorneys should pay special attention to the
following guidance set out in the Code:

- chapter 2, which sets out how the Act's principles should be applied

- chapter 3, which describes the steps which can be taken to try to
help the person make decisions for themselves

- chapter 4, which describes the Act's definition of lack of capacity
and gives guidance on assessing capacity, and

- chapter 5, which gives guidance on working out the donor's
best interests.

7.55   In some circumstances, attorneys might also find it useful to refer to
guidance in:

- chapter 6, which explains when attorneys who have caring
responsibilities may have protection from liability and gives
guidance on the few circumstances when the Act allows restraint in
connection with care and treatment

- chapter 8, which gives a summary of the Court of Protection's
powers relating to LPAs

- chapter 9, which explains how LPAs may be affected if the donor
has made an advance decision to refuse treatment, and

- chapter 15, which describes ways to settle disagreements.

Only making decisions covered by an LPA

7.56   A personal welfare attorney has no authority to make decisions about a donor's property and affairs (such as their finances). A property and affairs attorney has no authority in decisions about a donor's personal care. (But the same person could be appointed in separate LPAs to carry out both these roles.) Under any LPA, the attorney will have authority in a wide range of decisions. But if a donor includes restrictions in the LPA document, this will limit the attorney's authority (section 9(4)(b)). If the attorney thinks that they need greater powers, they can apply to the Court of Protection which may decide to give the attorney the authority required or alternatively to appoint the attorney as a deputy with the necessary powers (see chapter 8).

7.57   It is good practice for decision-makers to consult attorneys about any decision or action, whether or not it is covered by the LPA. This is because an attorney is likely to have known the donor for some time and may have important information about their wishes and feelings. Researchers can also consult attorneys if they are thinking about involving the donor in research (see chapter 11).

Scenario: Consulting attorneys

Mr Varadi makes a personal welfare LPA appointing his son and daughter as his joint attorneys. He also makes a property and affairs LPA, appointing his son and his solicitor to act jointly and severally. He registers the property and affairs LPA straight away, so his attorneys can help with financial decisions.

Two years later, Mr Varadi has a stroke, is unable to speak and has difficulty communicating his wishes. He also lacks the capacity to make decisions about treatment. The attorneys apply to register the personal welfare LPA. Both feel that they should delay decisions about Mr Varadi's future care, because he might regain capacity to make the decisions himself. But they agree that some decisions cannot wait.

Although the solicitor has no authority to make welfare decisions, the welfare attorneys consult him about their father's best interests. They speak to him about immediate treatment decisions and their suggestion to delay making decisions about his future care. Similarly, the property and affairs attorneys consult the daughter about the financial decisions that Mr Varadi does not have the capacity to make himself.

What are an attorney's other duties?

7.58 An attorney appointed under an LPA is acting as the chosen agent of the donor and therefore, under the law of agency, the attorney has certain duties towards the donor. An attorney takes on a role which carries a great deal of power, which they must use carefully and responsibly. They have a duty to:

- apply certain standards of care and skill (duty of care) when making decisions
- carry out the donor's instructions
- not take advantage of their position and not benefit themselves, but benefit the donor (fiduciary duty)
- not delegate decisions, unless authorised to do so
- act in good faith
- respect confidentiality
- comply with the directions of the Court of Protection
- not give up the role without telling the donor and the court.

In relation to property and affairs LPAs, they have a duty to:

- keep accounts
- keep the donor's money and property separate from their own.

Duty of care

7.59 'Duty of care' means applying a certain standard of care and skill – depending on whether the attorney is paid for their services or holds relevant professional qualifications.

- Attorneys who are not being paid must apply the same care, skill and diligence they would use to make decisions about their own life. An attorney who claims to have particular skills or qualifications must show greater skill in those particular areas than someone who does not make such claims.
- If attorneys are being paid for their services, they should demonstrate a higher degree of care and skill.
- Attorneys who undertake their duties in the course of their professional work (such as solicitors or corporate trustees) must display professional competence and follow their profession's rules and standards.

Fiduciary duty

7.60 A fiduciary duty means attorneys must not take advantage of their position. Nor should they put themselves in a position where their personal interests conflict with their duties. They also must not allow any other influences to affect the way in which they act as an attorney. Decisions should always benefit the donor, and not the attorney. Attorneys must not profit or get any personal benefit from their position, apart from receiving gifts where the Act allows it, whether or not it is at the donor's expense.

Duty not to delegate

7.61 Attorneys cannot usually delegate their authority to someone else. They must carry out their duties personally. The attorney may seek professional or expert advice (for example, investment advice from a financial adviser or advice on medical treatment from a doctor). But they cannot, as a general rule, allow someone else to make a decision that they have been appointed to make, unless this has been specifically authorised by the donor in the LPA.

7.62 In certain circumstances, attorneys may have limited powers to delegate (for example, through necessity or unforeseen circumstances, or for specific tasks which the donor would not have expected the attorney to attend to personally). But attorneys cannot usually delegate any decisions that rely on their discretion.

Duty of good faith

7.63 Acting in good faith means acting with honesty and integrity. For example, an attorney must try to make sure that their decisions do not go against a decision the donor made while they still had capacity (unless it would be in the donor's best interests to do so).

Duty of confidentiality

7.64 Attorneys have a duty to keep the donor's affairs confidential, unless:

- before they lost capacity to do so, the donor agreed that some personal or financial information may be revealed for a particular purpose (for example, they have named someone they want to check their financial accounts), or

- there is some other good reason to release it (for example, it is in the public interest or the best interests of the person who lacks capacity, or there is a risk of harm to the donor or others).

In the latter circumstances, it may be advisable for the attorney to get legal advice. Chapter 16 gives more information about confidentiality.

Duty to comply with the directions of the Court of Protection

7.65   Under sections 22 and 23 of the Act, the Court of Protection has wide-ranging powers to decide on issues relating to the operation or validity of an LPA. It can also:

- give extra authority to attorneys

- order them to produce records (for example, financial accounts), or

- order them to provide specific information or documentation to the court.

Attorneys must comply with any decision or order that the court makes.

Duty not to disclaim without notifying the donor and the OPG

7.66   Once someone becomes an attorney, they cannot give up that role without notifying the donor and the OPG. If they decide to give up their role, they must follow the relevant guidance available from the OPG.

Duty to keep accounts

7.67   Property and affairs attorneys must keep accounts of transactions carried out on the donor's behalf. Sometimes the Court of Protection will ask to see accounts. If the attorney is not a financial expert and the donor's affairs are relatively straightforward, a record of the donor's income and expenditure (for example, through bank statements) may be enough. The more complicated the donor's affairs, the more detailed the accounts may need to be.

Duty to keep the donor's money and property separate

7.68   Property and affairs attorneys should usually keep the donor's money and property separate from their own or anyone else's. There may be occasions where donors and attorneys have agreed in the past to keep their money in a joint bank account (for example, if a husband is acting as his wife's attorney). It might be possible to continue this under the LPA. But in most circumstances, attorneys must keep finances separate to avoid any possibility of mistakes or confusion.

How does the Act protect donors from abuse?

What should someone do if they think an attorney is abusing their position?

7.69 Attorneys are in a position of trust, so there is always a risk of them abusing their position. Donors can help prevent abuse by carefully choosing a suitable and trustworthy attorney. But others have a role to play in looking out for possible signs of abuse or exploitation, and reporting any concerns to the OPG. The OPG will then follow this up in co-operation with relevant agencies.

7.70 Signs that an attorney may be exploiting the donor (or failing to act in the donor's best interests) include:

- stopping relatives or friends contacting the donor – for example, the attorney may prevent contact or the donor may suddenly refuse visits or telephone calls from family and friends for no reason

- sudden unexplained changes in living arrangements (for example, someone moves in to care for a donor they've had little contact with)

- not allowing healthcare or social care staff to see the donor

- taking the donor out of hospital against medical advice, while the donor is having necessary medical treatment

- unpaid bills (for example, residential care or nursing home fees)

- an attorney opening a credit card account for the donor

- spending money on things that are not obviously related to the donor's needs

- the attorney spending money in an unusual or extravagant way

- transferring financial assets to another country.

7.71 Somebody who suspects abuse should contact the OPG immediately. The OPG may direct a Court of Protection Visitor to visit an attorney to investigate. In cases of suspected physical or sexual abuse, theft or serious fraud, the person should contact the police. They might also be able to refer the matter to the relevant local adult protection authorities.

7.72 In serious cases, the OPG will refer the matter to the Court of Protection. The court may revoke (cancel) the LPA or (through the OPG) prevent it being registered, if it decides that:

- the LPA does not meet the legal requirements for creating an LPA

- the LPA has been revoked or come to an end for any other reason
- somebody used fraud or undue pressure to get the donor to make the LPA
- the attorney has done something that they do not have authority to do, or
- the attorney has behaved or is planning to behave in a way that is not in the donor's best interests.

The court might then consider whether the authority previously given to an attorney can be managed by:

- the court making a single decision, or
- appointing a deputy.

What should an attorney do if they think someone else is abusing the donor?

7.73 An attorney who thinks someone else is abusing or exploiting the donor should report it to the OPG and ask for advice on what action they should take. They should contact the police if they suspect physical or sexual abuse, theft or serious fraud. They might also be able to refer the matter to local adult protection authorities.

7.74 Chapter 13 gives more information about protecting vulnerable people from abuse, ill treatment or neglect. It also discusses the duties and responsibilities of the various agencies involved, including the OPG and local authorities. In particular, it is a criminal offence (with a maximum penalty of five years' imprisonment, a fine, or both) for anyone (including attorneys) to wilfully neglect or ill-treat a person in their care who lacks capacity to make decisions for themselves (section 44).

What happens to existing EPAs once the Act comes into force?

7.75 Once the Act comes into force, it will not be possible to make new EPAs. Only LPAs can then be made.

7.76 Some donors will have created EPAs before the Act came into force with the expectation that their chosen attorneys will manage their property and affairs in the future, whether or not they have capacity to do so themselves.

7.77 If donors still have capacity after the Act comes into force, they can cancel the EPA and make an LPA covering their property and affairs. They should also notify attorneys and anyone else aware of the EPA (for example, a bank) that they have cancelled it.

7.78 Some donors will choose not to cancel their EPA or they may already lack the capacity to do so. In such cases, the Act allows existing EPAs, whether registered or not, to continue to be valid so that attorneys can meet the donor's expectations (Schedule 4). An EPA must be registered with the OPG when the attorney thinks the donor lacks capacity to manage their own affairs, or is beginning to lack capacity to do so.

7.79 EPA attorneys may find guidance in this chapter helpful. In particular, all attorneys must comply with the duties described in paragraphs 7.58–7.68 above. EPA attorneys can also be found liable under section 44 of the new Act, which sets out the new criminal offences of ill treatment and wilful neglect. The OPG has produced guidance on EPAs (see Annex A for details of publications and contact information).

8 What is the role of the Court of Protection and court-appointed deputies?

This chapter describes the role of the Court of Protection and the role of court-appointed deputies. It explains the powers that the court has and how to make an application to the court. It also looks at how the court appoints a deputy to act and make decisions on behalf of someone who lacks capacity to make those decisions. In particular, it gives guidance on a deputy's duties and the consequences of not carrying them out responsibly.

The Office of the Public Guardian (OPG) produces detailed guidance for deputies. See the Annex for more details of the publications and how to get them. Further details on the court's procedures are given in the Court of Protection Rules and Practice Directions issued by the court.

> In this chapter, as throughout the Code, a person's capacity (or lack of capacity) refers specifically to their capacity to make a particular decision at the time it needs to be made.

Quick summary

The Court of Protection has powers to:

- decide whether a person has capacity to make a particular decision for themselves
- make declarations, decisions or orders on financial or welfare matters affecting people who lack capacity to make such decisions
- appoint deputies to make decisions for people lacking capacity to make those decisions
- decide whether an LPA or EPA is valid, and
- remove deputies or attorneys who fail to carry out their duties.

Before accepting an appointment as a deputy, a person the court nominates should consider whether:

- they have the skills and ability to carry out a deputy's duties (especially in relation to property and affairs)
- they actually want to take on the duties and responsibilities.

Anyone acting as a deputy must:

- make sure that they only make those decisions that they are authorised to make by the order of the court
- make sure that they follow the Act's statutory principles, including:
  - considering whether the person has capacity to make a particular decision for themselves. If they do, the deputy should allow them to do so unless the person agrees that the deputy should make the decision
  - taking all possible steps to try to help a person make the particular decision
- always make decisions in the person's best interests
- have regard to guidance in the Code of Practice that is relevant to the situation
- fulfil their duties towards the person concerned (in particular the duty of care and fiduciary duties to respect the degree of trust placed in them by the court).

What is the Court of Protection?

8.1 Section 45 of the Act sets up a specialist court, the Court of Protection, to deal with decision-making for adults (and children in a few cases) who may lack capacity to make specific decisions for themselves. The new Court of Protection replaces the old court of the same name, which only dealt with decisions about the property and financial affairs of people lacking capacity to manage their own affairs. As well as property and affairs, the new court also deals with serious decisions affecting healthcare and personal welfare matters. These were previously dealt with by the High Court under its inherent jurisdiction.

8.2 The new Court of Protection is a superior court of record and is able to establish precedent (it can set examples for future cases) and build up expertise in all issues related to lack of capacity. It has the same powers, rights, privileges and authority as the High Court. When reaching any decision, the court must apply all the statutory principles set out in section 1 of the Act. In particular, it must make a decision in the best interests of the person who lacks capacity to make the specific decision. There will usually be a fee for applications to the court.[29]

---

[29] Details of the fees charged by the court, and the circumstances in which the fees may be waived or remitted, are available from the Office of the Public Guardian (OPG).

How can somebody make an application to the Court of Protection?

Chapter 8

What is the role of the Court of Protection and court-appointed deputies?

8.3 In most cases concerning personal welfare matters, the core principles of the Act and the processes set out in chapters 5 and 6 will be enough to:

- help people take action or make decisions in the best interests of someone who lacks capacity to make decisions about their own care or treatment, or

- find ways of settling disagreements about such actions or decisions.

But an application to the Court of Protection may be necessary for:

- particularly difficult decisions

- disagreements that cannot be resolved in any other way (see chapter 15), or

- situations where ongoing decisions may need to be made about the personal welfare of a person who lacks capacity to make decisions for themselves.

8.4 An order of the court will usually be necessary for matters relating to the property and affairs (including financial matters) of people who lack capacity to make specific financial decisions for themselves, unless:

- their only income is state benefits (see paragraph 8.36 below), or

- they have previously made an Enduring Power of Attorney (EPA) or a Lasting Power of Attorney (LPA) to give somebody authority to manage their property and affairs (see chapter 7).

8.5 Receivers appointed by the court before the Act commences will be treated as deputies. But they will keep their existing powers and duties. They must meet the requirements set out in the Act and, in particular, follow the statutory principles and act in the best interests of the person for whom they have been appointed. They must also have regard to guidance in this chapter and other parts of the Code of Practice. Further guidance for receivers is available from the OPG.

Cases involving young people aged 16 or 17

8.6 Either a court dealing with family proceedings or the Court of Protection can hear cases involving people aged 16 or 17 who lack capacity. In some cases, the Court of Protection can hear cases involving people younger than 16 (for example, when somebody needs to be appointed to make longer-term decisions about their financial affairs). Under section 21 of the Mental Capacity Act, the Court of Protection can transfer cases concerning children to a court that has powers under the Children Act 1989. Such a court can also transfer cases to the Court of Protection, if necessary. Chapter 12 gives more detail on cases where this might apply.

Who should make the application?

8.7 The person making the application will vary, depending on the circumstances. For example, a person wishing to challenge a finding that they lack capacity may apply to the court, supported by others where necessary. Where there is a disagreement among family members, for example, a family member may wish to apply to the court to settle the disagreement – bearing in mind the need, in most cases, to get permission beforehand (see paragraphs 8.11–8.12 below).

8.8 For cases about serious or major decisions concerning medical treatment (see paragraphs 8.18–8.24 below), the NHS Trust or other organisation responsible for the patient's care will usually make the application. If social care staff are concerned about a decision that affects the welfare of a person who lacks capacity, the relevant local authority should make the application.

8.9 For decisions about the property and affairs of someone who lacks capacity to manage their own affairs, the applicant will usually be the person (for example, family carer) who needs specific authority from the court to deal with the individual's money or property.

8.10 If the applicant is the person who is alleged to lack capacity, they will always be a party to the court proceedings. In all other cases, the court will decide whether the person who lacks, or is alleged to lack, capacity should be involved as a party to the case. Where the person is a party to the case, the court may appoint the Official Solicitor to act for them.

Who must ask the court for permission to make an application?

8.11 As a general rule, potential applicants must get the permission of the Court of Protection before making an application (section 50). People who the Act says do not need to ask for permission include:

- a person who lacks, or is alleged to lack, capacity in relation to a specific decision or action (or anyone with parental responsibility, if the person is under 18 years)

Chapter 8

What is the role of the Court of Protection and court-appointed deputies?

- the donor of the LPA an application relates to – or their attorney

- a deputy who has been appointed by the court to act for the person concerned, and

- a person named in an existing court order relating to the application.

The Court of Protection Rules also set out specific types of cases where permission is not required.

8.12   When deciding whether to give permission for an application, the court must consider:

- the applicant's connection to the person the application is about

- the reasons for the application

- whether a proposed order or direction of the court will benefit the person the application is about, and

- whether it is possible to get that benefit another way.

Scenario: Considering whether to give permission for an application

Sunita, a young Asian woman, has always been close to her older brother, who has severe learning disabilities and lives in a care home. Two years ago, Sunita married a non-Asian man, and her family cut off contact with her. She still wants to visit her brother and to be consulted about his care and what is in his best interests. But the family is not letting her. The Court of Protection gives Sunita permission to apply to the court for an order allowing her contact with her brother.

What powers does the Court of Protection have?

8.13   The Court of Protection may:

- make declarations, decisions and orders on financial and welfare matters affecting people who lack, or are alleged to lack, capacity (the lack of capacity must relate to the particular issue being presented to the court)

- appoint deputies to make decisions for people who lack capacity to make those decisions

- remove deputies or attorneys who act inappropriately.

The Court can also hear cases about LPAs and EPAs. The court's powers concerning EPAs are set out in Schedule 4 of the Act.

8.14 The court must always follow the statutory principles set out in section 1 of the Act (see chapter 2) and make the decision in the best interests of the person concerned (see chapter 5).

What declarations can the court make?

8.15 Section 15 of the Act provides the court with powers to make a declaration (a ruling) on specific issues. For example, it can make a declaration as to whether a person has capacity to make a particular decision or give consent for or take a particular action. The court will require evidence of any assessment of the person's capacity and may wish to see relevant written evidence (for example, a diary, letters or other papers). If the court decides the person has capacity to make that decision, they will not take the case further. The person can now make the decision for themselves.

8.16 Applications concerning a person's capacity are likely to be rare – people can usually settle doubts and disagreements informally (see chapters 4 and 15). But an application may be relevant if:

- a person wants to challenge a decision that they lack capacity

- professionals disagree about a person's capacity to make a specific (usually serious) decision

- there is a dispute over whether the person has capacity (for example, between family members).

8.17 The court can also make a declaration as to whether a specific act relating to a person's care or treatment is lawful (either where somebody has carried out the action or is proposing to). Under section 15, this can include an omission or failure to provide care or treatment that the person needs.

This power to decide on the lawfulness of an act is particularly relevant for major medical treatment cases where there is doubt or disagreement over whether the treatment would be in the person's best interests. Healthcare staff can still give life-sustaining treatment, or treatment which stops a person's condition getting seriously worse, while the court is coming to a decision.

Serious healthcare and treatment decisions

8.18 Prior to the Act coming into force, the courts decided that some decisions relating to the provision of medical treatment were so serious that in each case, an application should be made to the court for a declaration that the proposed action was lawful before that action was taken. Cases involving any of the following decisions should therefore be brought before a court:

Chapter 8

What is the role of the Court of Protection and court-appointed deputies?

- decisions about the proposed withholding or withdrawal of artificial nutrition and hydration (ANH) from patients in a permanent vegetative state (PVS)

- cases involving organ or bone marrow donation by a person who lacks capacity to consent

- cases involving the proposed non-therapeutic sterilisation of a person who lacks capacity to consent to this (e.g. for contraceptive purposes) and

- all other cases where there is a doubt or dispute about whether a particular treatment will be in a person's best interests.

8.19 The case law requirement to seek a declaration in cases involving the withholding or withdrawing of artificial nutrition and hydration to people in a permanent vegetative state is unaffected by the Act[30] and as a matter of practice, these cases should be put to the Court of Protection for approval.

8.20 Cases involving organ or bone marrow donation by a person who lacks capacity to consent should also be referred to the Court of Protection. Such cases involve medical procedures being performed on a person who lacks capacity to consent but which would benefit a third party (though would not necessarily directly or physically benefit the person who lacks capacity). However, sometimes such procedures may be in the person's overall best interests (see chapter 5). For example, the person might receive emotional, social and psychological benefits as a result of the help they have given, and in some cases the person may experience only minimal physical discomfort.

8.21 A prime example of this is the case of *Re Y*[31] where it was found to be in Y's best interests for her to donate bone marrow to her sister. The court decided that it was in Y's best interests to continue to receive strong emotional support from her mother, which might be diminished if her sister's health were to deteriorate further, or she were to die.

---

30 *Airedale NHS Trust v Bland* [1993] AC 789

31 *Re Y (Mental incapacity: Bone marrow transplant)* [1996] 2 FLR 787

Further details on this area are available in Department of Health or Welsh Assembly guidance.[32]

8.22 Non-therapeutic sterilisation is the sterilisation for contraceptive purposes of a person who cannot consent. Such cases will require a careful assessment of whether such sterilisation would be in the best interests of the person who lacks capacity and such cases should continue to be referred to the court.[33] The court has also given guidance on when certain termination of pregnancy cases should be brought before the court.[34]

8.23 Other cases likely to be referred to the court include those involving ethical dilemmas in untested areas (such as innovative treatments for variant CJD), or where there are otherwise irresolvable conflicts between healthcare staff, or between staff and family members.

8.24 There are also a few types of cases that should generally be dealt with by the court, since other dispute resolution methods are unlikely to be appropriate (see chapter 15). This includes, for example, cases where it is unclear whether proposed serious and/or invasive medical treatment is likely to be in the best interests of the person who lacks capacity to consent.

What powers does the court have to make decisions and appoint deputies?

8.25 In cases of serious dispute, where there is no other way of finding a solution or when the authority of the court is needed in order to make a particular decision or take a particular action, the court can be asked to make a decision to settle the matter using its powers under section 16.

However, if there is a need for ongoing decision-making powers and there is no relevant EPA or LPA, the court may appoint a deputy to make future decisions. It will also state what decisions the deputy has the authority to make on the person's behalf.

---

[32] Reference Guide to Consent for Examination or Treatment, Department of Health, March 2001 www.dh.gov.uk/PublicationsAndStatistics/Publications/PublicationsPolicyAndGuidance/PublicationsPolicyAndGuidanceArticle/fs/en?CONTENT_ID=4006757&chk=snmdw8

[33] See e.g. *Re A (medical treatment: male sterilisation)* (1999) 53 BMLR 66 where a mother applied for a declaration that a vasectomy was in the best interests of A, her son, (who had Down's syndrome and was borderline between significant and severe impairment of intelligence), in the absence of his consent. After balancing the burdens and benefits of the proposed vasectomy to A, the Court of Appeal held that the vasectomy would not be in A's best interests.

[34] *D v An NHS Trust (Medical Treatment: Consent: Termination)* [2004] 1 FLR 1110

8.26 In deciding what type of order to make, the court must apply the Act's principles and the best interests checklist. In addition, it must follow two further principles, intended to make any intervention as limited as possible:

Chapter 8

What is the role of the Court of Protection and court-appointed deputies?

- Where possible, the court should make the decision itself in preference to appointing a deputy.

- If a deputy needs to be appointed, their appointment should be as limited in scope and for as short a time as possible.

What decisions can the court make?

8.27 In some cases, the court must make a decision, because someone needs specific authority to act and there is no other route for getting it. These include cases where:

- there is no EPA or property and affairs LPA in place and someone needs to make a financial decision for a person who lacks capacity to make that decision (for example, the decision to terminate a tenancy agreement), or

- it is necessary to make a will, or to amend an existing will, on behalf of a person who lacks capacity to do so.

8.28 Examples of other types of cases where a court decision might be appropriate include cases where:

- there is genuine doubt or disagreement about the existence, validity or applicability of an advance decision to refuse treatment (see chapter 9)

- there is a major disagreement regarding a serious decision (for example, about where a person who lacks capacity to decide for themselves should live)

- a family carer or a solicitor asks for personal information about someone who lacks capacity to consent to that information being revealed (for example, where there have been allegations of abuse of a person living in a care home)

- someone suspects that a person who lacks capacity to make decisions to protect themselves is at risk of harm or abuse from a named individual (the court could stop that individual contacting the person who lacks capacity).

8.29 Anyone carrying out actions under a decision or order of the court must still also follow the Act's principles.

> **Scenario: Making a decision to settle disagreements**
>
> Mrs Worrell has Alzheimer's disease. Her son and daughter argue over which care home their mother should move to. Although Mrs Worrell lacks the capacity to make this decision herself, she has enough money to pay the fees of a care home.
>
> Her solicitor acts as attorney in relation to her financial affairs under a registered EPA. But he has no power to get involved in this family dispute – nor does he want to get involved.
>
> The Court of Protection makes a decision in Mrs Worrell's best interests, and decides which care home can best meet her needs. Once this matter is resolved, there is no need to appoint a deputy.

What powers does the court have in relation to LPAs?

8.30   The Court of Protection can determine the validity of an LPA or EPA and can give directions as to how an attorney should use their powers under an LPA (see chapter 7). In particular, the court can cancel an LPA and end the attorney's appointment. The court might do this if the attorney was not carrying out their duties properly or acting in the best interests of the donor. The court must then decide whether it is necessary to appoint a deputy to take over the attorney's role.

What are the rules for appointing deputies?

8.31   Sometimes it is not practical or appropriate for the court to make a single declaration or decision. In such cases, if the court thinks that somebody needs to make future or ongoing decisions for someone whose condition makes it likely they will lack capacity to make some further decisions in the future, it can appoint a deputy to act for and make decisions for that person. A deputy's authority should be as limited in scope and duration as possible (see paragraphs 8.35–8.39 below).

How does the court appoint deputies?

8.32   It is for the court to decide who to appoint as a deputy. Different skills may be required depending on whether the deputy's decisions will be about a person's welfare (including healthcare), their finances or both. The court will decide whether the proposed deputy is reliable and trustworthy and has an appropriate level of skill and competence to carry out the necessary tasks.

8.33 In the majority of cases, the deputy is likely to be a family member or someone who knows the person well. But in some cases the court may decide to appoint a deputy who is independent of the family (for example, where the person's affairs or care needs are particularly complicated). This could be, for example, the Director of Adult Services in the relevant local authority (but see paragraph 8.60 below) or a professional deputy. The OPG has a panel of professional deputies (mainly solicitors who specialise in this area of law) who may be appointed to deal with property and affairs if the court decides that would be in the person's best interests.

Chapter 8

What is the role of the Court of Protection and court-appointed deputies?

When might a deputy need to be appointed?

8.34 Whether a person who lacks capacity to make specific decisions needs a deputy will depend on:

- the individual circumstances of the person concerned

- whether future or ongoing decisions are likely to be necessary, and

- whether the appointment is for decisions about property and affairs or personal welfare.

Property and affairs

8.35 The court will appoint a deputy to manage a person's property and affairs (including financial matters) in similar circumstances to those in which they would have appointed a receiver in the past. If a person who lacks capacity to make decisions about property and affairs has not made an EPA or LPA, applications to the court are necessary:

- for dealing with cash assets over a specified amount that remain after any debts have been paid

- for selling a person's property, or

- where the person has a level of income or capital that the court thinks a deputy needs to manage.

8.36 If the only income of a person who lacks capacity is social security benefits and they have no property or savings, there will usually be no need for a deputy to be appointed. This is because the person's benefits can be managed by an *appointee,* appointed by the Department for Work and Pensions to receive and deal with the benefits of a person who lacks capacity to do this for themselves. Although appointees are not covered by the Act, they will be expected to act in the person's best interests and must do so if they are involved in caring for the person. If the court does appoint a property and affairs deputy for someone who has an appointee, it is likely that the deputy would take over the appointee's role.

8.37 Anybody considered for appointment as a property and affairs deputy will need to sign a declaration giving details of their circumstances and ability to manage financial affairs. The declaration will include details of the tasks and duties the deputy must carry out. The deputy must assure the court that they have the skills, knowledge and commitment to carry them out.

Personal welfare (including healthcare)

8.38 Deputies for personal welfare decisions will only be required in the most difficult cases where:

- important and necessary actions cannot be carried out without the court's authority, or
- there is no other way of settling the matter in the best interests of the person who lacks capacity to make particular welfare decisions.

8.39 Examples include when:

- someone needs to make a series of linked welfare decisions over time and it would not be beneficial or appropriate to require all of those decisions to be made by the court. For example, someone (such as a family carer) who is close to a person with profound and multiple learning disabilities might apply to be appointed as a deputy with authority to make such decisions
- the most appropriate way to act in the person's best interests is to have a deputy, who will consult relevant people but have the final authority to make decisions
- there is a history of serious family disputes that could have a detrimental effect on the person's future care unless a deputy is appointed to make necessary decisions
- the person who lacks capacity is felt to be at risk of serious harm if left in the care of family members. In these rare cases, welfare decisions may need to be made by someone independent of the family, such as a local authority officer. There may even be a need for an additional court order prohibiting those family members from having contact with the person.

Who can be a deputy?

Chapter 8

What is the role of the Court of Protection and court-appointed deputies?

8.40 Section 19(1) states that deputies must be at least 18 years of age. Deputies with responsibility for property and affairs can be either an individual or a trust corporation (often parts of banks or other financial institutions). No-one can be appointed as a deputy without their consent.

8.41 Paid care workers (for example, care home managers) should not agree to act as a deputy because of the possible conflict of interest – unless there are exceptional circumstances (for example, if the care worker is the only close relative of the person who lacks capacity). But the court can appoint someone who is an office-holder or in a specified position (for example, the Director of Adult Services of the relevant local authority). In this situation, the court will need to be satisfied that there is no conflict of interest before making such an appointment (see paragraphs 8.58–8.60).

8.42 The court can appoint two or more deputies and state whether they should act 'jointly', 'jointly and severally' or 'jointly in respect of some matters and jointly and severally in respect of others' (section 19 (4)(c)).

- Joint deputies must always act together. They must all agree decisions or actions, and all sign any relevant documents.

- Joint and several deputies can act together, but they may also act independently if they wish. Any action taken by any deputy alone is as valid as if that person were the only deputy.

8.43 Deputies may be appointed jointly for some issues and jointly and severally for others. For example, two deputies could be appointed jointly and severally for most decisions, but the court might rule that they act jointly when selling property.

Scenario: Acting jointly and severally

Toby had a road accident and suffered brain damage and other disabilities. He gets financial compensation but lacks capacity to manage this amount of money or make decisions about his future care. His divorced parents are arguing about where their son should live and how his compensation money should be used. Toby has always been close to his sister, who is keen to be involved but is anxious about dealing with such a large amount of money.

The court decides where Toby will live. It also appoints his sister and a solicitor as joint and several deputies to manage his property and affairs. His sister can deal with any day-to-day decisions that Toby lacks capacity to make, and the solicitor can deal with more complicated matters.

What happens if a deputy can no longer carry out their duties?

8.44   When appointing a deputy, the court can also appoint someone to be a successor deputy (someone who can take over the deputy's duties in certain situations). The court will state the circumstances under which this could occur. In some cases it will also state a period of time in which the successor deputy can act. Appointment of a successor deputy might be useful if the person appointed as deputy is already elderly and wants to be sure that somebody will take over their duties in the future, if necessary.

Scenario: Appointing a successor deputy

Neil, a man with Down's syndrome, inherits a lot of money and property. His parents were already retired when the court appointed them as joint deputies to manage Neil's property and affairs. They are worried about what will happen to Neil when they cannot carry out their duties as deputies any more. The court agrees to appoint other relatives as successor deputies. They will then be able to take over as deputies after the parents' death or if his parents are no longer able to carry out the deputy's role.

Can the court protect people lacking capacity from financial loss?

Chapter 8

What is the role of the Court of Protection and court-appointed deputies?

8.45   Under section 19(9)(a) of the Act the court can ask a property and affairs deputy to provide some form of security (for example, a guarantee bond) to the Public Guardian to cover any loss as a result of the deputy's behaviour in carrying out their role. The court can also ask a deputy to provide reports and accounts to the Public Guardian, as it sees fit.

Are there any restrictions on a deputy's powers?

8.46   Section 20 sets out some specific restrictions on a deputy's powers. In particular, a deputy has no authority to make decisions or take action:

- if they do something that is intended to restrain the person who lacks capacity – apart from under certain circumstances (guidance on the circumstances when restraint might be permitted is given in chapter 6)[35]

- if they think that the person concerned has capacity to make the particular decision for themselves

- if their decision goes against a decision made by an attorney acting under a Lasting Power of Attorney granted by the person before they lost capacity, or

- to refuse the provision or continuation of life-sustaining treatment for a person who lacks capacity to consent – such decisions must be taken by the court.

If a deputy thinks their powers are not enough for them to carry out their duties effectively, they can apply to the court to change their powers. See paragraph 8.54 below.

What responsibilities do deputies have?

8.47   Once a deputy has been appointed by the court, the order of appointment will set out their specific powers and the scope of their authority. On taking up the appointment, the deputy will assume a number of duties and responsibilities and will be required to act in accordance with certain standards. Failure to comply with the duties

---

[35] It is worth noting that there is a drafting error in section 20 of the Act. The word 'or' in section 20(11)(a) should have been 'and' in order to be consistent with sections 6(3)(a) and 11(4)(a). The Government will make the necessary amendment to correct this error at the earliest available legislative opportunity.

set out below could result in the Court of Protection revoking the order appointing the deputy and, in some circumstances, the deputy could be personally liable to claims for negligence or criminal charges of fraud.

8.48 Deputies should always inform any third party they are dealing with that the court has appointed them as deputy. The court will give the deputy official documents to prove their appointment and the extent of their authority.

8.49 A deputy must act whenever a decision or action is needed and it falls within their duties as set out in the court order appointing them. A deputy who fails to act at all in such situations could be in breach of duty.

What duties does the Act impose?

8.50 Deputies must:

- follow the Act's statutory principles (see chapter 2)
- make decisions or act in the best interests of the person who lacks capacity
- have regard to the guidance in this Code of Practice
- only make decisions the Court has given them authority to make.

Principles and best interests

8.51 Deputies must act in accordance with the Act's statutory principles (section 1) and in particular the best interests of the person who lacks capacity (the steps for working out best interests are set out in section 4). In particular, deputies must consider whether the person has capacity to make the decision for themselves. If not, they should consider whether the person is likely to regain capacity to make the decision in the future. If so, it may be possible to delay the decision until the person can make it.

The Code of Practice

8.52 As well as this chapter, deputies should pay special attention to the following guidance set out in the Code:

- chapter 2, which sets out how the Act's principles should be applied
- chapter 3, which describes the steps which can be taken to try to help the person make decisions for themselves

- chapter 4, which describes the Act's definition of lack of capacity and gives guidance on assessing capacity, and

- chapter 5, which gives guidance on working out someone's best interests.

Chapter 8

What is the role of the Court of Protection and court-appointed deputies?

8.53 In some situations, deputies might also find it useful to refer to guidance in:

- chapter 6, which explains when deputies who have caring responsibilities may have protection from liability and gives guidance on the few circumstances when the Act allows restraint in connection with care and treatment, and

- chapter 15, which describes ways to settle disagreements.

Only making decisions the court authorises a deputy to make

8.54 A deputy has a duty to act only within the scope of the actual powers given by the court, which are set out in the order of appointment. It is possible that a deputy will think their powers are not enough for them to carry out their duties effectively. In this situation, they must apply to the court either to:

- ask the court to make the decision in question, or

- ask the court to change the deputy's powers.

What are a deputy's other duties?

8.55 Section 19(6) states that a deputy is to be treated as 'the agent' of the person who lacks capacity when they act on their behalf. Being an agent means that the deputy has legal duties (under the law of agency) to the person they are representing. It also means that when they carry out tasks within their powers, they are not personally liable to third parties.

8.56 Deputies must carry out their duties carefully and responsibly. They have a duty to:

- act with due care and skill (duty of care)

- not take advantage of their situation (fiduciary duty)

- indemnify the person against liability to third parties caused by the deputy's negligence

- not delegate duties unless authorised to do so

- act in good faith
- respect the person's confidentiality, and
- comply with the directions of the Court of Protection.

Property and affairs deputies also have a duty to:

- keep accounts, and
- keep the person's money and property separate from own finances.

Duty of care

8.57 'Duty of care' means applying a certain standard of care and skill – depending on whether the deputy is paid for their services or holds relevant professional qualifications.

- Deputies who are not being paid must use the same care, skill and diligence they would use when making decisions for themselves or managing their own affairs. If they do not, they could be held liable for acting negligently. A deputy who claims to have particular skills or qualifications must show greater skill in those particular areas than a person who does not make such claims.

- If deputies are being paid for their services, they are expected to demonstrate a higher degree of care or skill when carrying out their duties.

- Deputies whose duties form part of their professional work (for example, solicitors or accountants) must display normal professional competence and follow their profession's rules and standards.

Fiduciary duty

8.58 A fiduciary duty means deputies must not take advantage of their position. Nor should they put themselves in a position where their personal interests conflict with their duties. For example, deputies should not buy property that they are selling for the person they have been appointed to represent. They should also not accept a third party commission in any transactions. Deputies must not allow anything else to influence their duties. They cannot use their position for any personal benefit, whether or not it is at the person's expense.

8.59 In many cases, the deputy will be a family member. In rare situations, this could lead to potential conflicts of interests. When making decisions, deputies should follow the Act's statutory principles and apply the best interests checklist and not allow their own personal interests to influence the decision.

8.60 Sometimes the court will consider appointing the Director of Adult Services in England or Director of Social Services in Wales of the relevant local authority as a deputy. The court will need to be satisfied that the authority has arrangements to avoid possible conflicts of interest. For example where the person for whom a financial deputy is required receives community care services from the local authority, the court will wish to be satisfied that decisions about the person's finances will be made in the best interests of that person, regardless of any implications for the services provided.

Chapter 8

What is the role of the Court of Protection and court-appointed deputies?

Duty not to delegate

8.61 A deputy may seek professional or expert advice (for example, investment advice from a financial adviser or a second medical opinion from a doctor). But they cannot give their decision-making responsibilities to someone else. In certain circumstances, the court will authorise the delegation of specific tasks (for example, appointing a discretionary investment manager for the conduct of investment business).

8.62 In certain circumstances, deputies may have limited powers to delegate (for example, through necessity or unforeseen circumstances, or for specific tasks which the court would not have expected the deputy to attend to personally). But deputies cannot usually delegate any decisions that rely on their discretion. If the deputy is the Director of Adult Services in England or Director of Social Services in Wales, or a solicitor, they can delegate specific tasks to other staff. But the deputy is still responsible for any actions or decisions taken, and can therefore be held accountable for any errors that are made.

Duty of good faith

8.63 Acting in good faith means acting with honesty and integrity. For example, a deputy must try to make sure that their decisions do not go against a decision the person made while they still had capacity (unless it would be in the person's best interests to do so).

Duty of confidentiality

8.64 Deputies have a duty to keep the person's affairs confidential, unless:

- before they lost capacity to do so, the person agreed that information could be revealed where necessary

- there is some other good reason to release information (for example, it is in the public interest or in the best interests of the person who lacks capacity, or where there is a risk of harm to the person concerned or to other people).

In the latter circumstances, it is advisable for the deputy to contact the OPG for guidance or get legal advice. See chapter 16 for more information about revealing personal information.

Duty to comply with the directions of the Court of Protection

8.65 The Court of Protection may give specific directions to deputies about how they should use their powers. It can also order deputies to provide reports (for example, financial accounts or reports on the welfare of the person who lacks capacity) to the Public Guardian at any time or at such intervals as the court directs. Deputies must comply with any direction of the court or request from the Public Guardian.

Duty to keep accounts

8.66 A deputy appointed to manage property and affairs is expected to keep, and periodically submit to the Public Guardian, correct accounts of all their dealings and transactions on the person's behalf.

Duty to keep the person's money and property separate

8.67 Property and affairs deputies should usually keep the person's money and property separate from their own or anyone else's. This is to avoid any possibility of mistakes or confusion in handling the person's affairs. Sometimes there may be good reason not to do so (for example, a husband might be his wife's deputy and they might have had a joint account for many years).

Changes of contact details

8.68 A deputy should inform the OPG of any changes of contact details or circumstances (for the deputy or the person they are acting for). This will help make sure that the OPG has up-to-date records. It will also allow the court to discharge people who are no longer eligible to act as deputies.

Who is responsible for supervising deputies?

8.69 Deputies are accountable to the Court of Protection. The court can cancel a deputy's appointment at any time if it decides the appointment is no longer in the best interests of the person who lacks capacity.

8.70   The OPG is responsible for supervising and supporting deputies. But it must also protect people lacking capacity from possible abuse or exploitation. Anybody who suspects that a deputy is abusing their position should contact the OPG immediately. The OPG may instruct a Court of Protection Visitor to visit a deputy to investigate any matter of concern. It can also apply to the court to cancel a deputy's appointment.

8.71   The OPG will consider carefully any concerns or complaints against deputies. But if somebody suspects physical or sexual abuse or serious fraud, they should contact the police and/or social services immediately, as well as informing the OPG. Chapter 14 gives more information about the role of the OPG. It also discusses the protection of vulnerable people from abuse, ill treatment or wilful neglect and the responsibilities of various relevant agencies.

Chapter 8

What is the role of the Court of Protection and court-appointed deputies?

9 What does the Act say about advance decisions to refuse treatment?

This chapter explains what to do when somebody has made an advance decision to refuse treatment. It sets out:

- what the Act means by an 'advance decision'
- guidance on making, updating and cancelling advance decisions
- how to check whether an advance decision exists
- how to check that an advance decision is valid and that it applies to current circumstances
- the responsibilities of healthcare professionals when an advance decision exists
- how to handle disagreements about advance decisions.

> In this chapter, as throughout the Code, a person's capacity (or lack of capacity) refers specifically to their capacity to make a particular decision at the time it needs to be made.

Quick summary

- An advance decision enables someone aged 18 and over, while still capable, to refuse specified medical treatment for a time in the future when they may lack the capacity to consent to or refuse that treatment.
- An advance decision to refuse treatment must be valid and applicable to current circumstances. If it is, it has the same effect as a decision that is made by a person with capacity: healthcare professionals must follow the decision.
- Healthcare professionals will be protected from liability if they:
  - stop or withhold treatment because they reasonably believe that an advance decision exists, and that it is valid and applicable
  - treat a person because, having taken all practical and appropriate steps to find out if the person has made an advance decision to refuse treatment, they do not know or are not satisfied that a valid and applicable advance decision exists.

- People can only make an advance decision under the Act if they are 18 or over and have the capacity to make the decision. They must say what treatment they want to refuse, and they can cancel their decision – or part of it – at any time.

- If the advance decision refuses life-sustaining treatment, it must:

  – be in writing (it can be written by a someone else or recorded in healthcare notes)

  – be signed and witnessed, and

  – state clearly that the decision applies even if life is at risk.

- To establish whether an advance decision is valid and applicable, healthcare professionals must try to find out if the person:

  – has done anything that clearly goes against their advance decision

  – has withdrawn their decision

  – has subsequently conferred the power to make that decision on an attorney, or

  – would have changed their decision if they had known more about the current circumstances.

- Sometimes healthcare professionals will conclude that an advance decision does not exist, is not valid and/or applicable – but that it is an expression of the person's wishes. The healthcare professional must then consider what is set out in the advance decision as an expression of previous wishes when working out the person's best interests (see chapter 5).

- Some healthcare professionals may disagree in principle with patients' decisions to refuse life-sustaining treatment. They do not have to act against their beliefs. But they must not simply abandon patients or act in a way that that affects their care.

- Advance decisions to refuse treatment for mental disorder may not apply if the person who made the advance decision is or is liable to be detained under the Mental Health Act 1983.

Chapter 9

What does the Act say about advance decisions to refuse treatment?

How can someone make an advance decision to refuse treatment?

What is an advance decision to refuse treatment?

9.1   It is a general principle of law and medical practice that people have a right to consent to or refuse treatment. The courts have recognised that adults have the right to say in advance that they want to refuse treatment if they lose capacity in the future – even if this results in their death. A valid and applicable advance decision to refuse treatment has the same force as a contemporaneous decision. This has been a fundamental principle of the common law for many years and it is now set out in the Act. Sections 24–26 of the Act set out the when a person can make an advance decision to refuse treatment. This applies if:

- the person is 18 or older, and

- they have the capacity to make an advance decision about treatment.

Information on advance decisions to refuse treatment made by young people (under the age of 18) will be available at www.dh.gov.uk/consent

9.2   Healthcare professionals must follow an advance decision if it is valid and applies to the particular circumstances. If they do not, they could face criminal prosecution (they could be charged for committing a crime) or civil liability (somebody could sue them).

9.3   Advance decisions can have serious consequences for the people who make them. They can also have an important impact on family and friends, and professionals involved in their care. Before healthcare professionals can apply an advance decision, there must be proof that the decision:

- exists

- is valid, and

- is applicable in the current circumstances.

These tests are legal requirements under section 25(1). Paragraphs 9.38–9.44 explain the standard of proof the Act requires.

Who can make an advance decision to refuse treatment?

9.4   It is up to individuals to decide whether they want to refuse treatment in advance. They are entitled to do so if they want, but there is no obligation to do so. Some people choose to make advance decisions while they are still healthy, even if there is no prospect of illness. This might be because they want to keep some control over what might happen to them in the future. Others may think of an advance decision as part of their preparations for growing older (similar to making a will). Or they might make an advance decision after they have been told they have a specific disease or condition.

Many people prefer not to make an advance decision, and instead leave healthcare professionals to make decisions in their best interests at the time a decision needs to be made. Another option is to make a Lasting Power of Attorney. This allows a trusted family member or friend to make personal welfare decisions, such as those around treatment, on someone's behalf, and in their best interests if they ever lose capacity to make those decisions themselves (see paragraph 9.33 below and chapter 7).

Chapter 9

What does
the Act say
about advance
decisions to
refuse treatment?

9.5   People can only make advance decisions to *refuse* treatment. Nobody has the legal right to demand specific treatment, either at the time or in advance. So no-one can insist (either at the time or in advance) on being given treatments that healthcare professionals consider to be clinically unnecessary, futile or inappropriate. But people can make a request or state their wishes and preferences in advance. Healthcare professionals should then consider the request when deciding what is in a patient's best interests (see chapter 5) if the patient lacks capacity.

9.6   Nobody can ask for and receive procedures that are against the law (for example, help with committing suicide). As section 62 sets out, the Act does not change any of the laws relating to murder, manslaughter or helping someone to commit suicide.

Capacity to make an advance decision

9.7   For most people, there will be no doubt about their capacity to make an advance decision. Even those who lack capacity to make some decisions may have the capacity to make an advance decision. In some cases it may be helpful to get evidence of a person's capacity to make the advance decision (for example, if there is a possibility that the advance decision may be challenged in the future). It is also important to remember that capacity can change over time, and a person who lacks capacity to make a decision now might be able to make it in the future.

Chapter 3 explains how to assess a person's capacity to make a decision.

Scenario: Respecting capacity to make an advance decision

Mrs Long's family has a history of polycystic ovary syndrome. She has made a written advance decision refusing any treatment or procedures that might affect her fertility. The document states that her ovaries and uterus must not be removed. She is having surgery to treat a blocked fallopian tube and, during the consent process, she told her doctor about her advance decision.

During surgery the doctor discovers a solid mass that he thinks might be cancerous. In his clinical judgement, he thinks it would be in Mrs Long's best interests for him to remove the ovary. But he knows that Mrs Long had capacity when she made her valid and applicable advance decision, so he must respect her rights and follow her decision. After surgery, he can discuss the matter with Mrs Long and advise her about treatment options.

9.8   In line with principle 1 of the Act, that 'a person must be assumed to have capacity unless it is established that he lacks capacity', healthcare professionals should always start from the assumption that a person who has made an advance decision had capacity to make it, *unless* they are aware of reasonable grounds to doubt the person had the capacity to make the advance decision at the time they made it. If a healthcare professional is not satisfied that the person had capacity at the time they made the advance decision, or if there are doubts about its existence, validity or applicability, they can treat the person without fear of liability. It is good practice to record their decisions and the reasons for them. The Act does not require them to record their assessment of the person's capacity at the time the decision was made, but it would be good practice to do so.

9.9   Healthcare professionals may have particular concerns about the capacity of someone with a history of suicide attempts or suicidal thoughts who has made an advance decision. It is important to remember that making an advance decision which, if followed, may result in death does not necessarily mean a person is or feels suicidal. Nor does it necessarily mean the person lacks capacity to make the advance decision. If the person is clearly suicidal, this may raise questions about their capacity to make an advance decision at the time they made it.

What should people include in an advance decision?

Chapter 9

What does
the Act say
about advance
decisions to
refuse treatment?

9.10　There are no particular formalities about the format of an advance
decision. It can be written or verbal, unless it deals with life-sustaining
treatment, in which case it must be written and specific rules apply (see
paragraphs 9.24–9.28 below).

9.11　An advance decision to refuse treatment:

- must state precisely what treatment is to be refused – a statement
giving a general desire not to be treated is not enough

- may set out the circumstances when the refusal should apply – it is
helpful to include as much detail as possible

- will only apply at a time when the person lacks capacity to consent
to or refuse the specific treatment.

Specific rules apply to life-sustaining treatment.

9.12　People can use medical language or everyday language in their
advance decision. But they must make clear what their wishes are and
what treatment they would like to refuse.

9.13　An advance decision refusing all treatment in any situation (for
example, where a person explains that their decision is based on their
religion or personal beliefs) may be valid and applicable.

9.14　It is recommended that people who are thinking about making an
advance decision get advice from:

- healthcare professionals (for example, their GP or the person most
closely involved with current healthcare or treatment), or

- an organisation that can provide advice on specific conditions
or situations (they might have their own format for recording an
advance decision).

But it is up to the person whether they want to do this or not.
Healthcare professionals should record details of any discussion on
healthcare records.

9.15　Some people may also want to get legal advice. This will help them
make sure that they express their decision clearly and accurately. It will
also help to make sure that people understand their advance decision
in the future.

9.16 It is a good idea to try to include possible future circumstances in the advance decision. For example, a woman may want to state in the advance decision whether or not it should still apply if she later becomes pregnant. If the document does not anticipate a change in circumstance, healthcare professionals may decide that it is not applicable if those particular circumstances arise.

9.17 If an advance decision is recorded on a patient's healthcare records, it is confidential. Some patients will tell others about their advance decision (for example, they might tell healthcare professionals, friends or family). Others will not. People who do not ask for their advance decision to be recorded on their healthcare record will need to think about where it should be kept and how they are going to let people know about their decision.

Written advance decisions

9.18 A written document can be evidence of an advance decision. It is helpful to tell others that the document exists and where it is. A person may want to carry it with them in case of emergency, or carry a card, bracelet or other indication that they have made an advance decision and explaining where it is kept.

9.19 There is no set form for written advance decisions, because contents will vary depending on a person's wishes and situation. But it is helpful to include the following information:

- full details of the person making the advance decision, including date of birth, home address and any distinguishing features (in case healthcare professionals need to identify an unconscious person, for example)

- the name and address of the person's GP and whether they have a copy of the document

- a statement that the document should be used if the person ever lacks capacity to make treatment decisions

- a clear statement of the decision, the treatment to be refused and the circumstances in which the decision will apply

- the date the document was written (or reviewed)

- the person's signature (or the signature of someone the person has asked to sign on their behalf and in their presence)

- the signature of the person witnessing the signature, if there is one (or a statement directing somebody to sign on the person's behalf).

See paragraphs 9.24–9.28 below if the advance decision deals with life-sustaining treatment.

Chapter 9

What does the Act say about advance decisions to refuse treatment?

9.20 Witnessing the person's signature is not essential, except in cases where the person is making an advance decision to refuse life-sustaining treatment. But if there is a witness, they are witnessing the signature and the fact that it confirms the wishes set out in the advance decision. It may be helpful to give a description of the relationship between the witness and person making the advance decision. The role of the witness is to witness the person's signature, it is not to certify that the person has the capacity to make the advance decision – even if the witness is a healthcare professional or knows the person.

9.21 It is possible that a professional acting as a witness will also be the person who assesses the person's capacity. If so, the professional should also make a record of the assessment, because acting as a witness does not prove that there has been an assessment.

Verbal advance decisions

9.22 There is no set format for verbal advance decisions. This is because they will vary depending on a person's wishes and situation. Healthcare professionals will need to consider whether a verbal advance decision exists and whether it is valid and applicable (see paragraphs 9.38–9.44).

9.23 Where possible, healthcare professionals should record a verbal advance decision to refuse treatment in a person's healthcare record. This will produce a written record that could prevent confusion about the decision in the future. The record should include:

• a note that the decision should apply if the person lacks capacity to make treatment decisions in the future

• a clear note of the decision, the treatment to be refused and the circumstances in which the decision will apply

• details of someone who was present when the oral advance decision was recorded and the role in which they were present (for example, healthcare professional or family member), and

• whether they heard the decision, took part in it or are just aware that it exists.

What rules apply to advance decisions to refuse life-sustaining treatment?

9.24　The Act imposes particular legal requirements and safeguards on the making of advance decisions to refuse life-sustaining treatment. Advance decisions to refuse life-sustaining treatment *must* meet specific requirements:

- They must be put in writing. If the person is unable to write, someone else should write it down for them. For example, a family member can write down the decision on their behalf, or a healthcare professional can record it in the person's healthcare notes.

- The person must sign the advance decision. If they are unable to sign, they can direct someone to sign on their behalf in their presence.

- The person making the decision must sign in the presence of a witness to the signature. The witness must then sign the document in the presence of the person making the advance decision. If the person making the advance decision is unable to sign, the witness can witness them directing someone else to sign on their behalf. The witness must then sign to indicate that they have witnessed the nominated person signing the document in front of the person making the advance decision.

- The advance decision must include a clear, specific written statement from the person making the advance decision that the advance decision is to apply to the specific treatment even if life is at risk.

- If this statement is made at a different time or in a separate document to the advance decision, the person making the advance decision (or someone they have directed to sign) must sign it in the presence of a witness, who must also sign it.

9.25　Section 4(10) states that life-sustaining treatment is treatment which a healthcare professional who is providing care to the person regards as necessary to sustain life. This decision will not just depend on the type of treatment. It will also depend on the circumstances in which the healthcare professional is giving it. For example, in some situations antibiotics may be life-sustaining, but in others they can be used to treat conditions that do not threaten life.

9.26　Artificial nutrition and hydration (ANH) has been recognised as a form of medical treatment. ANH involves using tubes to provide nutrition and fluids to someone who cannot take them by mouth. It bypasses the natural mechanisms that control hunger and thirst and requires clinical monitoring. An advance decision can refuse ANH. Refusing ANH in an advance decision is likely to result in the person's death, if the advance decision is followed.

Chapter 9

What does the Act say about advance decisions to refuse treatment?

9.27   It is very important to discuss advance decisions to refuse life-sustaining treatment with a healthcare professional. But it is not compulsory. A healthcare professional will be able to explain:

- what types of treatment may be life-sustaining treatment, and in what circumstances

- the implications and consequences of refusing such treatment (see also paragraph 9.14).

9.28   An advance decision cannot refuse actions that are needed to keep a person comfortable (sometimes called basic or essential care). Examples include warmth, shelter, actions to keep a person clean and the offer of food and water by mouth. Section 5 of the Act allows healthcare professionals to carry out these actions in the best interests of a person who lacks capacity to consent (see chapter 6). An advance decision can refuse artificial nutrition and hydration.

When should someone review or update an advance decision?

9.29   Anyone who has made an advance decision is advised to regularly review and update it as necessary. Decisions made a long time in advance are not automatically invalid or inapplicable, but they may raise doubts when deciding whether they are valid and applicable. A written decision that is regularly reviewed is more likely to be valid and applicable to current circumstances – particularly for progressive illnesses. This is because it is more likely to have taken on board changes that have occurred in a person's life since they made their decision.

9.30   Views and circumstances may change over time. A new stage in a person's illness, the development of new treatments or a major change in personal circumstances may be appropriate times to review and update an advance decision.

How can someone withdraw an advance decision?

9.31   Section 24(3) allows people to cancel or alter an advance decision at any time while they still have capacity to do so. There are no formal processes to follow. People can cancel their decision verbally or in writing, and they can destroy any original written document. Where possible, the person who made the advance decision should tell anybody who knew about their advance decision that it has been cancelled. They can do this at any time. For example, they can do this on their way to the operating theatre or immediately before being given an anaesthetic. Healthcare professionals should record a verbal cancellation in healthcare records. This then forms a written record for future reference.

How can someone make changes to an advance decision?

9.32   People can makes changes to an advance decision verbally or in writing (section 24(3)) whether or not the advance decision was made in writing. It is good practice for healthcare professionals to record a change of decision in the person's healthcare notes. But if the person wants to change an advance decision to include a refusal of life-sustaining treatment, they must follow the procedures described in paragraphs 9.24–9.28.

How do advance decisions relate to other rules about decision-making?

9.33   A valid and applicable advance decision to refuse treatment is as effective as a refusal made when a person has capacity. Therefore, an advance decision overrules:

- the decision of any personal welfare Lasting Power of Attorney (LPA) made before the advance decision was made. So an attorney cannot give consent to treatment that has been refused in an advance decision made after the LPA was signed

- the decision of any court-appointed deputy (so a deputy cannot give consent to treatment that has been refused in an advance decision which is valid and applicable)

- the provisions of section 5 of the Act, which would otherwise allow healthcare professionals to give treatment that they believe is in a person's best interests.

9.34   An LPA made after an advance decision will make the advance decision invalid, if the LPA gives the attorney the authority to make decisions about the same treatment (see paragraph 9.40).

9.35   The Court of Protection may make declarations as to the existence, validity and applicability of an advance decision, but it has no power to overrule a valid and applicable advance decision to refuse treatment.

9.36 Where an advance decision is being followed, the best interests principle (see chapter 5) does not apply. This is because an advance decision reflects the decision of an adult with capacity who has made the decision for themselves. Healthcare professionals must follow a valid and applicable advance decision, even if they think it goes against a person's best interests.

Chapter 9

What does the Act say about advance decisions to refuse treatment?

Advance decisions regarding treatment for mental disorder

9.37 Advance decisions can refuse any kind of treatment, whether for a physical or mental disorder. But generally an advance decision to refuse treatment for mental disorder can be overruled if the person is detained in hospital under the Mental Health Act 1983, when treatment could be given compulsorily under Part 4 of that Act. Advance decisions to refuse treatment for other illnesses or conditions are not affected by the fact that the person is detained in hospital under the Mental Health Act. For further information see chapter 13.

How can somebody decide on the existence, validity and applicability of advance decisions?

Deciding whether an advance decision exists

9.38 It is the responsibility of the person making the advance decision to make sure their decision will be drawn to the attention of healthcare professionals when it is needed. Some people will want their decision to be recorded on their healthcare records. Those who do not will need to find other ways of alerting people that they have made an advance decision and where somebody will find any written document and supporting evidence. Some people carry a card or wear a bracelet. It is also useful to share this information with family and friends, who may alert healthcare professionals to the existence of an advance decision. But it is not compulsory. Providing their GP with a copy of the written document will allow them to record the decision in the person's healthcare records.

9.39 It is important to be able to establish that the person making the advance decision was 18 or over when they made their decision, and that they had the capacity to make that decision when they made it, in line with the two-stage test for capacity set out in chapter 3. But as explained in paragraphs 9.7–9.9 above, healthcare professionals should always start from the assumption that the person had the capacity to make the advance decision.

Deciding whether an advance decision is valid

9.40   An existing advance decision must still be valid at the time it needs to be put into effect. Healthcare professionals must consider the factors in section 25 of the Act before concluding that an advance decision is valid. Events that would make an advance decision invalid include those where:

- the person withdrew the decision while they still had capacity to do so

- after making the advance decision, the person made a Lasting Power of Attorney (LPA) giving an attorney authority to make treatment decisions that are the same as those covered by the advance decision (see also paragraph 9.33)

- the person has done something that clearly goes against the advance decision which suggests that they have changed their mind.

Scenario: Assessing whether an advance decision is valid

A young man, Angus, sees a friend die after prolonged hospital treatment. Angus makes a signed and witnessed advance decision to refuse treatment to keep him alive if he is ever injured in this way. The advance decision includes a statement that this will apply even if his life is at risk.

A few years later, Angus is seriously injured in a road traffic accident. He is paralysed from the neck down and cannot breathe without the help of a machine. At first he stays conscious and gives permission to be treated. He takes part in a rehabilitation programme. Some months later he loses consciousness.

At this point somebody finds his written advance decision, even though Angus has not mentioned it during his treatment. His actions before his lack of capacity obviously go against the advance decision. Anyone assessing the advance decision needs to consider very carefully the doubt this has created about the validity of the advance decision, and whether the advance decision is valid and applicable as a result.

Deciding whether an advance decision is applicable

9.41 To be applicable, an advance decision must apply to the situation in question and in the current circumstances. Healthcare professionals must first determine if the person still has capacity to accept or refuse treatment at the relevant time (section 25(3)). If the person has capacity, they can refuse treatment there and then. Or they can change their decision and accept treatment. The advance decision is not applicable in such situations.

Chapter 9

What does the Act say about advance decisions to refuse treatment?

9.42 The advance decision must also apply to the proposed treatment. It is not applicable to the treatment in question if (section 25(4)):

- the proposed treatment is not the treatment specified in the advance decision

- the circumstances are different from those that may have been set out in the advance decision, or

- there are reasonable grounds for believing that there have been changes in circumstance, which would have affected the decision if the person had known about them at the time they made the advance decision.

9.43 So when deciding whether an advance decision applies to the proposed treatment, healthcare professionals must consider:

- how long ago the advance decision was made, and

- whether there have been changes in the patient's personal life (for example, the person is pregnant, and this was not anticipated when they made the advance decision) that might affect the validity of the advance decision, and

- whether there have been developments in medical treatment that the person did not foresee (for example, new medications, treatment or therapies).

9.44 For an advance decision to apply to life-sustaining treatment, it must meet the requirements set out in paragraphs 9.24–9.28.

> **Scenario: Assessing if an advance decision is applicable**
>
> Mr Moss is HIV positive. Several years ago he began to have AIDS-related symptoms. He has accepted general treatment, but made an advance decision to refuse specific retro-viral treatments, saying he didn't want to be a 'guinea pig' for the medical profession. Five years later, he is admitted to hospital seriously ill and keeps falling unconscious.
>
> The doctors treating Mr Moss examine his advance decision. They are aware that there have been major developments in retro-viral treatment recently. They discuss this with Mr Moss's partner and both agree that there are reasonable grounds to believe that Mr Moss may have changed his advance decision if he had known about newer treatment options. So the doctors decide the advance decision does not apply to the new retro-virals and give him treatment.
>
> If Mr Moss regains his capacity, he can change his advance decision and accept or refuse future treatment.

What should healthcare professionals do if an advance decision is not valid or applicable?

9.45 If an advance decision is not valid or applicable to current circumstances:

- healthcare professionals must consider the advance decision as part of their assessment of the person's best interests (see chapter 5) if they have reasonable grounds to think it is a true expression of the person's wishes, and

- they must not assume that because an advance decision is either invalid or not applicable, they should always provide the specified treatment (including life-sustaining treatment) – they must base this decision on what is in the person's best interests.

What happens to decisions made before the Act comes into force?

9.46 Advance decisions made before the Act comes into force may still be valid and applicable. Healthcare professionals should apply the rules in the Act to advance decisions made before the Act comes into force, subject to the transitional protections that will apply to advance decisions that refuse life-sustaining treatment. Further guidance will be available at www.dh.gov.uk/consent.

What implications do advance decisions have for healthcare professionals?

What are healthcare professionals' responsibilities?

9.47   Healthcare professionals should be aware that:

- a patient they propose to treat may have refused treatment in advance, and

- valid and applicable advance decisions to refuse treatment have the same legal status as decisions made by people with capacity at the time of treatment.

9.48   Where appropriate, when discussing treatment options with people who have capacity, healthcare professionals should ask if there are any specific types of treatment they do not wish to receive if they ever lack capacity to consent in the future.

9.49   If somebody tells a healthcare professional that an advance decision exists for a patient who now lacks capacity to consent, they should make reasonable efforts to find out what the decision is. Reasonable efforts might include having discussions with relatives of the patient, looking in the patient's clinical notes held in the hospital or contacting the patient's GP.

9.50   Once they know a verbal or written advance decision exists, healthcare professionals must determine whether:

- it is valid (see paragraph 9.40), and

- it is applicable to the proposed treatment (see paragraphs 9.41–9.44).

9.51   When establishing whether an advance decision applies to current circumstances, healthcare professionals should take special care if the decision does not seem to have been reviewed or updated for some time. If the person's current circumstances are significantly different from those when the decision was made, the advance decision may not be applicable. People close to the person concerned, or anyone named in the advance decision, may be able to help explain the person's prior wishes.

9.52 If healthcare professionals are satisfied that an advance decision to refuse treatment exists, is valid and is applicable, they must follow it and not provide the treatment refused in the advance decision.

9.53 If healthcare professionals are not satisfied that an advance decision exists that is both valid and applicable, they can treat the person without fear of liability. But treatment must be in the person's best interests (see chapter 5). They should make clear notes explaining why they have not followed an advance decision which they consider to be invalid or not applicable.

9.54 Sometimes professionals can give or continue treatment while they resolve doubts over an advance decision. It may be useful to get information from someone who can provide information about the person's capacity when they made the advance decision. The Court of Protection can settle disagreements about the existence, validity or applicability of an advance decision. Section 26 of the Act allows healthcare professionals to give necessary treatment, including life-sustaining treatment, to stop a person's condition getting seriously worse while the court decides.

Do advance decisions apply in emergencies?

9.55 A healthcare professional must provide treatment in the patient's best interests, unless they are satisfied that there is a advance decision that is:

- valid, and
- applicable in the circumstances.

9.56 Healthcare professionals should not delay emergency treatment to look for an advance decision if there is no clear indication that one exists. But if it is clear that a person has made an advance decision that is likely to be relevant, healthcare professionals should assess its validity and applicability as soon as possible. Sometimes the urgency of treatment decisions will make this difficult.

When can healthcare professionals be found liable?

9.57 Healthcare professionals must follow an advance decision if they are satisfied that it exists, is valid and is applicable to their circumstances. Failure to follow an advance decision in this situation could lead to a claim for damages for battery or a criminal charge of assault.

9.58 But they are protected from liability if they are not:

- aware of an advance decision, or

- satisfied that an advance decision exists, is valid and is applicable to the particular treatment and the current circumstances (section 26(2)).

If healthcare professionals have genuine doubts, and are therefore not 'satisfied', about the existence, validity or applicability of the advance decision, treatment can be provided without incurring liability.

9.59 Healthcare professionals will be protected from liability for failing to provide treatment if they 'reasonably believe' that a valid and applicable advance decision to refuse that treatment exists. But they must be able to demonstrate that their belief was reasonable (section 26(3)) and point to reasonable grounds showing why they believe this. Healthcare professionals can only base their decision on the evidence that is available at the time they need consider an advance decision.

9.60 Some situations might be enough in themselves to raise concern about the existence, validity or applicability of an advance decision to refuse treatment. These could include situations when:

- a disagreement between relatives and healthcare professionals about whether verbal comments were really an advance decision

- evidence about the person's state of mind raises questions about their capacity at the time they made the decision (see paragraphs 9.7–9.9)

- evidence of important changes in the person's behaviour before they lost capacity that might suggest a change of mind.

In cases where serious doubt remains and cannot be resolved in any other way, it will be possible to seek a declaration from the court.

What if a healthcare professional has a conscientious objection to stopping or providing life-sustaining treatment?

9.61 Some healthcare professionals may disagree in principle with patients' rights to refuse life-sustaining treatment. The Act does not change the current legal situation. They do not have to do something that goes against their beliefs. But they must not simply abandon patients or cause their care to suffer.

9.62   Healthcare professionals should make their views clear to the patient and the healthcare team as soon as someone raises the subject of withholding, stopping or providing life-sustaining treatment. Patients who still have capacity should then have the option of transferring their care to another healthcare professional, if it is possible to do this without affecting their care.

9.63   In cases where the patient now lacks capacity but has made a valid and applicable advance decision to refuse treatment which a doctor or health professional cannot, for reasons of conscience, comply with, arrangements should be made for the management of the patient's care to be transferred to another healthcare professional.[36] Where a transfer cannot be agreed, the Court of Protection can direct those responsible for the person's healthcare (for example, a Trust, doctor or other health professional) to make arrangements to take over responsibility for the person's healthcare (section 17(1)(e)).

What happens if there is a disagreement about an advance decision?

9.64   It is ultimately the responsibility of the healthcare professional who is in charge of the person's care when the treatment is required to decide whether there is an advance decision which is valid and applicable in the circumstances. In the event of disagreement about an advance decision between healthcare professionals, or between healthcare professionals and family members or others close to the person, the senior clinician must consider all the available evidence. This is likely to be a hospital consultant or the GP where the person is being treated in the community.

9.65   The senior clinician may need to consult with relevant colleagues and others who are close to or familiar with the patient. All staff involved in the person's care should be given the opportunity to express their views. If the person is in hospital, their GP may also have relevant information.

9.66   The point of such discussions should not be to try to overrule the person's advance decision but rather to seek evidence concerning its validity and to confirm its scope and its applicability to the current circumstances. Details of these discussions should be recorded in the person's healthcare records. Where the senior clinician has a reasonable belief that an advance decision to refuse medical treatment is both valid and applicable, the person's advance decision should be complied with.

---

[36] *Re B (Adult: Refusal of Medical Treatment)* [2002] EWHC 429 (Fam) at paragraph 100(viii)

When can somebody apply to the Court of Protection?

9.67   The Court of Protection can make a decision where there is genuine doubt or disagreement about an advance decision's existence, validity or applicability. But the court does not have the power to overturn a valid and applicable advance decision.

Chapter 9

What does the Act say about advance decisions to refuse treatment?

9.68   The court has a range of powers (sections 16–17) to resolve disputes concerning the personal care and medical treatment of a person who lacks capacity (see chapter 8). It can decide whether:

- a person has capacity to accept or refuse treatment at the time it is proposed

- an advance decision to refuse treatment is valid

- an advance decision is applicable to the proposed treatment in the current circumstances.

9.69   While the court decides, healthcare professionals can provide life-sustaining treatment or treatment to stop a serious deterioration in their condition. The court has emergency procedures which operate 24 hours a day to deal with urgent cases quickly. See chapter 8 for guidance on applying to the court.

10 What is the new Independent Mental Capacity Advocate service and how does it work?

This chapter describes the new Independent Mental Capacity Advocate (IMCA) service created under the Act. The purpose of the IMCA service is to help particularly vulnerable people who lack the capacity to make important decisions about serious medical treatment and changes of accommodation, and who have no family or friends that it would be appropriate to consult about those decisions. IMCAs will work with and support people who lack capacity, and represent their views to those who are working out their best interests.

The chapter provides guidance both for IMCAs and for everyone who may need to instruct an IMCA. It explains how IMCAs should be appointed. It also explains the IMCA's duties and the situations when an IMCA should be instructed. Both IMCAs and decision-makers are required to have regard to the Code of Practice.

> In this chapter, as throughout the Code, a person's capacity (or lack of capacity) refers specifically to their capacity to make a particular decision at the time it needs to be made.

Quick summary

Understanding the role of the IMCA service

- The aim of the IMCA service is to provide independent safeguards for people who lack capacity to make certain important decisions and, at the time such decisions need to be made, have no-one else (other than paid staff) to support or represent them or be consulted.

- IMCAs must be independent.

Instructing and consulting an IMCA

- An IMCA *must* be instructed, and then consulted, for people lacking capacity who have no-one else to support them (other than paid staff), whenever:

  - an NHS body is proposing to provide serious medical treatment, or

  - an NHS body or local authority is proposing to arrange accommodation (or a change of accommodation) in hospital or a care home, and

- the person will stay in hospital longer than 28 days, or

- they will stay in the care home for more than eight weeks.

- An IMCA *may* be instructed to support someone who lacks capacity to make decisions concerning:

  - care reviews, where no-one else is available to be consulted

  - adult protection cases, whether or not family, friends or others are involved

Chapter 10

What is the new Independent Mental Capacity Advocate service and how does it work?

Ensuring an IMCA's views are taken into consideration

- The IMCA's role is to support and represent the person who lacks capacity. Because of this, IMCAs have the right to see relevant healthcare and social care records.

- Any information or reports provided by an IMCA must be taken into account as part of the process of working out whether a proposed decision is in the person's best interests.

What is the IMCA service?

10.1 Sections 35–41 of the Act set up a new IMCA service that provides safeguards for people who:

- lack capacity to make a specified decision at the time it needs to be made

- are facing a decision on a long-term move or about serious medical treatment and

- have nobody else who is willing and able to represent them or be consulted in the process of working out their best interests.

10.2 Regulations made under the Act also state that IMCAs may be involved in other decisions, concerning:

- a care review, or

- an adult protection case.

In adult protection cases, an IMCA may be appointed even where family members or others are available to be consulted.

10.3 Most people who lack capacity to make a specific decision will have people to support them (for example, family members or friends who take an interest in their welfare). Anybody working out a person's best interests must consult these people, where possible, and take their views into account (see chapter 5). But if a person who lacks capacity has nobody to represent them or no-one who it is appropriate to consult, an IMCA must be instructed in prescribed circumstances. The prescribed circumstances are:

- providing, withholding or stopping serious medical treatment
- moving a person into long-term care in hospital or a care home (see 10.11 for definition), or
- moving the person to a different hospital or care home.

The only exception to this can be in situations where an urgent decision is needed. Further details on the situations where there is a duty to instruct an IMCA are given in paragraphs 10.40–10.58.

In other circumstances, an IMCA *may* be appointed for the person (see paragraphs 10.59–10.68). These include:

- care reviews or
- adult protection cases.

10.4 The IMCA will:

- be independent of the person making the decision
- provide support for the person who lacks capacity
- represent the person without capacity in discussions to work out whether the proposed decision is in the person's best interests
- provide information to help work out what is in the person's best interests (see chapter 5), and
- raise questions or challenge decisions which appear not to be in the best interests of the person.

The information the IMCA provides must be taken into account by decision-makers whenever they are working out what is in a person's best interests. See paragraphs 10.20–10.39 for more information on an IMCA's role. For more information on who is a decision-maker, see chapter 5.

10.5 The IMCA service will build on good practice in the independent advocacy sector. But IMCAs have a different role from many other advocates. They:

- provide statutory advocacy

- are instructed to support and represent people who lack capacity to make decisions on specific issues

- have a right to meet in private the person they are supporting

- are allowed access to relevant healthcare records and social care records

- provide support and representation specifically while the decision is being made, and

- act quickly so their report can form part of decision-making.

Chapter 10

What is the new Independent Mental Capacity Advocate service and how does it work?

Who is responsible for delivering the service?

10.6   The IMCA service is available in England and Wales. Both countries have regulations for setting up and managing the service.

- England's regulations[37] are available at www.opsi.gov.uk/si/ si200618.htm and www.opsi.gov.uk/si/dsis2006.htm.

- The regulations for Wales[38] are available at www.new.wales.gov.uk/ consultations/closed/healandsoccarecloscons/.

Guidance has been issued to local health boards and local authorities involved in commissioning IMCA services for their area.

---

[37] *The Mental Capacity Act 2005 (Independent Mental Capacity Advocate) (General) Regulations 2006 SI: 2006 /No 1832*. The 'General Regulations'. These regulations set out the details on how the IMCA will be appointed, the functions of the IMCA, including their role in challenging the decision-maker and include definitions of 'serious medical treatment' and 'NHS body'.

The Mental Capacity Act 2005 (Independent Mental Capacity Advocate) (Expansion of Role) Regulations 2006 SI: 2883. The 'Expansion Regulations'. These regulations specify the circumstances in which local authorities and NHS bodies may provide the IMCA service on a discretionary basis. These include involving the IMCA in a care review and in adult protection cases.

[38] *The Mental Capacity Act 2005 (Independent Mental Capacity Advocate) (Wales) Regulations 2007 SI: /No (W.)*. These regulations will remain in draft form until they are made by the National Assembly for Wales. The target coming into force date is 1 October 2007. Unlike the two sets of English regulations there will be one set only for Wales. Although the Welsh regulations will remain in draft form until the coming into force date, these have been drafted to give effect to similar and corresponding provisions to the regulations in England.

10.7 In England the Secretary of State for Health delivers the service through local authorities, who work in partnership with NHS organisations. Local authorities have financial responsibility for the service. In Wales the National Assembly for Wales delivers the service through local health boards, who have financial responsibility for the service and work in partnership with local authority social services departments and other NHS organisations. The service is commissioned from independent organisations, usually advocacy organisations.

10.8 Local authorities or NHS organisations are responsible for instructing an IMCA to represent a person who lacks capacity. In these circumstances they are called the 'responsible body'.

10.9 For decisions about serious medical treatment, the responsible body will be the NHS organisation providing the person's healthcare or treatment. But if the person is in an independent or voluntary sector hospital, the responsible body will be the NHS organisation arranging and funding the person's care, which should have arrangements in place with the independent or voluntary sector hospital to ensure an IMCA is appointed promptly.

10.10 For decisions about admission to accommodation in hospital for 28 days or more, the responsible body will be the NHS body that manages the hospital. For admission to an independent or voluntary sector hospital for 28 days or more, the responsible body will be the NHS organisation arranging and funding the person's care. The independent or voluntary hospital must have arrangements in place with the NHS organisation to ensure that an IMCA can be appointed without delay.

10.11 For decisions about moves into long-term accommodation[39] (for eight weeks or longer), or about a change of accommodation, the responsible body will be either:

- the NHS body that proposes the move or change of accommodation (e.g. a nursing home), or

- the local authority that has carried out an assessment of the person under the NHS and Community Care Act 1990 and decided the move may be necessary.

---

[39] This may be accommodation in a care home, nursing home, ordinary and sheltered housing, housing association or other registered social housing or in private sector housing provided by a local authority or in hostel accommodation.

10.12 Sometimes NHS organisations and local authorities will make decisions together about moving a person into long-term care. In these cases, the organisation that must instruct the IMCA is the one that is ultimately responsible for the decision to move the person. The IMCA to be instructed is the one who works wherever the person is at the time that the person needs support and representation.

Chapter 10

What is the new Independent Mental Capacity Advocate service and how does it work?

What are the responsible body's duties?

10.13 The responsible body:

- *must* instruct an IMCA to support and represent a person in the situations set out in paragraphs 10.40–10.58

- *may* decide to instruct an IMCA in situations described in paragraphs 10.59–10.68

- *must*, in all circumstances when an IMCA is instructed, take properly into account the information that the IMCA provides when working out whether the particular decision (such as giving, withholding or stopping treatment, changing a person's accommodation, or carrying out a recommendation following a care review or an allegation requiring adult protection) is in the best interests of the person who lacks capacity.

10.14 The responsible body should also have procedures, training and awareness programmes to make sure that:

- all relevant staff know when they need to instruct an IMCA and are able to do so promptly

- all relevant staff know how to get in touch with the IMCA service and know the procedure for instructing an IMCA

- they record an IMCA's involvement in a case and any information the IMCA provides to help decision-making

- they also record how a decision-maker has taken into account the IMCA's report and information as part of the process of working out the person's best interests (this should include reasons for disagreeing with that advice, if relevant)

- they give access to relevant records when requested by an IMCA under section 35(6)(b) of the Act

- the IMCA gets information about changes that may affect the support and representation the IMCA provides

- decision-makers let all relevant people know when an IMCA is working on a person's case, and

- decision-makers inform the IMCA of the final decision taken and the reason for it.

10.15 Sometimes an IMCA and staff working for the responsible body might disagree. If this happens, they should try to settle the disagreement through discussion and negotiation as soon as possible. If they cannot do this, they should then follow the responsible body's formal procedures for settling disputes or complaints (see paragraphs 10.34 to 10.39 below).

10.16 In some situations the IMCA may challenge a responsible body's decision, or they may help somebody who is challenging a decision. The General Regulations in England and the Regulations in Wales set out when this may happen (see also chapter 15). If there is no other way of resolving the disagreement, the decision may be challenged in the Court of Protection.

Who can be an IMCA?

10.17 In England, a person can only be an IMCA if the local authority approves their appointment. In Wales, the local health board will provide approval. Qualified employees of an approved organisation can act as IMCAs. Local authorities and health boards will usually commission independent advocacy organisations to provide the IMCA service. These organisations will work to appropriate organisational standards set through the contracting/commissioning process.

10.18 Individual IMCAs must:

- have specific experience
- have IMCA training
- have integrity and a good character, and
- be able to act independently.

All IMCAs must complete the IMCA training in order that they can work as an independent mental capacity advocate. A national advocacy qualification is also being developed, which will include the IMCA training.

Before a local authority or health board appoints an IMCA, they must carry out checks with the Criminal Records Bureau (CRB) to get a criminal record certificate or enhanced criminal record certificate for that individual.[40]

---

40 IMCAs were named as a group that is subject to mandatory checking under the new vetting and barring system in the Safeguarding Vulnerable Groups Act 2006. Roll-out of the bulk of the scheme will take place in 2008.

10.19 IMCAs must be independent. People cannot act as IMCAs if they:

Chapter 10

What is the new Independent Mental Capacity Advocate service and how does it work?

- care for or treat (in a paid or professional capacity) the person they will be representing (this does not apply if they are an existing advocate acting for that person), or
- have links to the person instructing them, to the decision-maker or to other individuals involved in the person's care or treatment that may affect their independence.

What is an IMCA's role?

10.20 An IMCA must decide how best to represent and support the person who lacks capacity that they are helping. They:

- must confirm that the person instructing them has the authority to do so
- should interview or meet in private the person who lacks capacity, if possible
- must act in accordance with the principles of the Act (as set out in section 1 of the Act and chapter 2 of the Code) and take account of relevant guidance in the Code
- may examine any relevant records that section 35(6) of the Act gives them access to
- should get the views of professionals and paid workers providing care or treatment for the person who lacks capacity
- should get the views of anybody else who can give information about the wishes and feelings, beliefs or values of the person who lacks capacity
- should get hold of any other information they think will be necessary
- must find out what support a person who lacks capacity has had to help them make the specific decision
- must try to find out what the person's wishes and feelings, beliefs and values would be likely to be if the person had capacity
- should find out what alternative options there are
- should consider whether getting another medical opinion would help the person who lacks capacity, and
- must write a report on their findings for the local authority or NHS body.

10.21 Where possible, decision-makers should make decisions based on a full understanding of a person's past and present wishes. The IMCA should provide the decision-maker with as much of this information as possible – and anything else they think is relevant. The report they give the decision-maker may include questions about the proposed action or may include suggested alternatives, if they think that these would be better suited to the person's wishes and feelings.

10.22 Another important part of the IMCA's role is communicating their findings. Decision-makers should find the most effective way to enable them to do this. In some of the IMCA pilot areas,[41] hospital discharge teams added a 'Need to instruct an IMCA?' question on their patient or service user forms. This allowed staff to identify the need for an IMCA as early as possible, and to discuss the timetable for the decision to be made. Some decisions need a very quick IMCA response, others will allow more time. In the pilot areas, IMCA involvement led to better informed discharge planning, with a clearer focus on the best interests of a person who lacked capacity. It did not cause additional delays in the hospital discharge.

Representing and supporting the person who lacks capacity

10.23 IMCAs should take account of the guidance in chapter 5.

- IMCAs should find out whether the decision-maker has given all practical and appropriate support to help the person who lacks capacity to be involved as much as possible in decision-making. If the person has communication difficulties, the IMCA should also find out if the decision-maker has obtained any specialist help (for example, from a speech and language therapist).

- Sometimes an IMCA may find information to suggest a person might regain capacity in the future, either so they can make the decision themselves or be more involved in decision-making. In such a situation, the IMCA can ask the decision-maker to delay the decision, if it is not urgent.

- The IMCA will need to get as much information as possible about the person's wishes, feelings, beliefs and values – both past and present. They should also consider the person's religion and any cultural factors that may influence the decision.

---

[41] For further information see www.dh.gov.uk/imca

10.24 Sometimes a responsible body will not have time to instruct an IMCA (for example in an emergency or if a decision is urgent). If this is the case, this should be recorded, with the reason an IMCA has not been instructed. Where the decision concerns a move of accommodation, the local authority must appoint an IMCA as soon as possible afterwards. Sometimes the IMCA will not have time to carry out full investigations. In these situations, the IMCA must make a judgement about what they can achieve in the time available to support and represent the person who lacks capacity.

Chapter 10

What is the new Independent Mental Capacity Advocate service and how does it work?

10.25 Sometimes an IMCA might not be able to get a good picture of what the person might want. They should still try to make sure the decision-maker considers all relevant information by:

- raising relevant issues and questions, and

- providing additional, relevant information to help the final decision.

Finding and evaluating information

10.26 Section 35(6) provides IMCAs with certain powers to enable them to carry out their duties. These include:

- the right to have an interview in private with the person who lacks capacity, and

- the right to examine, and take copies of, any records that the person holding the record thinks are relevant to the investigation (for example, clinical records, care plans, social care assessment documents or care home records).

10.27 The IMCA may also need to meet professionals or paid carers providing care or treatment for the person who lacks capacity. These people can help assess the information in case records or other sources. They can also comment on possible alternative courses of action. Ultimately, it is the decision-maker's responsibility to decide whether a proposed course of action is in the person's best interests. However, the Act requires the decision-maker to take account of the reports made and information given by the IMCA. In most cases a decision on the person's best interests will be made through discussion involving all the relevant people who are providing care or treatment, as well as the IMCA.

Finding out the person's wishes and feelings, beliefs and values

10.28 The IMCA needs to try and find out what the person's wishes and feelings might be, and what their underlying beliefs and values might also be. The IMCA should try to communicate both verbally and non-verbally with the person who may lack capacity, as appropriate. For example, this might mean using pictures or photographs. But there will be cases where the person cannot communicate at all (for example, if they are unconscious). The IMCA may also talk to other professionals or paid carers directly involved in providing present or past care or treatment. The IMCA might also need to examine health and social care records and any written statements of preferences the person may have made while they still had capacity to do so.

Chapter 5 contains further guidance on finding out the views of people who lack capacity. Chapter 3 contains further guidance on helping someone to make their own decision.

Considering alternative courses of action

10.29 The IMCA will need to check whether the decision-maker has considered all possible options. They should also ask whether the proposed option is less restrictive of the person's rights or future choices or would allow them more freedom (chapter 2, principle 5).

10.30 The IMCA may wish to discuss possible options with other professionals or paid carers directly involved in providing care or treatment for the person. But they must respect the confidentiality of the person they are representing.

Chapter 10

What is the new
Independent
Mental Capacity
Advocate service
and how does it
work?

Scenario: Using an IMCA

Mrs Nolan has dementia. She is being discharged from hospital. She has
no close family or friends. She also lacks the capacity to decide whether
she should return home or move to a care home. The local authority
instructs an IMCA.

Mrs Nolan tells the IMCA that she wants to go back to her own home,
which she can remember and describe. But the hospital care team
thinks she needs additional support, which can only be provided in a
care home.

The IMCA reviewed all the assessments of Mrs Nolan's needs, spoke to
people involved in her care and wrote a report stating that Mrs Nolan had
strong and clear wishes. The IMCA also suggested that a care package
could be provided to support Mrs Nolan if she were allowed to return
home. The care manager now has to decide what is in Mrs Nolan's best
interests. He must consider the views of the hospital care team and the
IMCA's report.

Getting a second medical opinion

10.31 For decisions about serious medical treatment, the IMCA may consider
seeking a second medical opinion from a doctor with appropriate
expertise. This puts a person who lacks the capacity to make a specific
decision in the same position as a person who has capacity, who has
the right to request a second opinion.

What happens if the IMCA disagrees with the decision-maker?

10.32 The IMCA's role is to support and represent their client. They may do
this through asking questions, raising issues, offering information and
writing a report. They will often take part in a meeting involving different
healthcare and social care staff to work out what is in the person's best
interests. There may sometimes be cases when an IMCA thinks that a
decision-maker has not paid enough attention to their report and other
relevant information and is particularly concerned about the decision
made. They may then need to challenge the decision.

10.33 An IMCA has the same rights to challenge a decision as any other
person caring for the person or interested in his welfare. The right
of challenge applies both to decisions about lack of capacity and a
person's best interests.

10.34 Chapter 15 sets out how disagreements can be settled. The approach will vary, depending on the type and urgency of the disagreement. It could be a formal or informal approach.

Disagreements about health care or treatment

- Consult the Patient Advice and Liaison Service (England)
- Consult the Community Health Council (Wales)
- Use the NHS Complaints Procedure
- Refer the matter to the local continuing care review panel
- Engage the services of the Independent Complaints Advocacy Service (England) or another advocate.

Disagreements about social care

- Use the care home's complaints procedure (if the person is in a care home)
- Use the local authority complaints procedure.

10.35 Before using these formal methods, the IMCA and the decision-maker should discuss the areas they disagree about – particularly those that might have a serious impact on the person the IMCA is representing. The IMCA and decision-maker should make time to listen to each other's views and to understand the reason for the differences. Sometimes these discussions can help settle a disagreement.

10.36 Sometimes an IMCA service will have a steering group, with representatives from the local NHS organisations and the local authority. These representatives can sometimes negotiate between two differing views. Or they can clarify policy on a certain issue. They should also be involved if an IMCA believes they have discovered poor practice on an important issue.

10.37 IMCAs may use complaints procedures as necessary to try to settle a disagreement – and they can pursue a complaint as far as the relevant ombudsman if needed. In particularly serious or urgent cases, an IMCA may seek permission to refer a case to the Court of Protection for a decision. The Court will make a decision in the best interests of the person who lacks capacity.

10.38 The first step in making a formal challenge is to approach the Official Solicitor (OS) with the facts of the case. The OS can decide to apply to the court as a litigation friend (acting on behalf of the person the IMCA is representing). If the OS decides not to apply himself, the IMCA can ask for permission to apply to the Court of Protection. The OS can still be asked to act as a litigation friend for the person who lacks capacity.

Chapter 10

What is the new Independent Mental Capacity Advocate service and how does it work?

10.39 In extremely serious cases, the IMCA might want to consider an application for judicial review in the High Court. This might happen if the IMCA thinks there are very serious consequences to a decision that has been made by a public authority. There are time limits for making an application, and the IMCA would have to instruct solicitors – and may be liable for the costs of the case going to court. So IMCAs should get legal advice before choosing this approach. The IMCA can also ask the OS to consider making the claim.

What decisions require an IMCA?

10.40 There are three types of decisions which require an IMCA to be instructed for people who lack capacity. These are:

- decisions about providing, withholding or stopping serious medical treatment

- decisions about whether to place people into accommodation (for example a care home or a long stay hospital), and

- decisions about whether to move people to different long stay accommodation.

For these decisions all local authorities and all health bodies must refer the same kinds of decisions to an IMCA for anyone who lacks capacity and qualifies for the IMCA service.

10.41 There are two further types of decisions where the responsible body has the power to instruct an IMCA for a person who lacks capacity. These are decisions relating to:

- care reviews and

- adult protection cases.

In such cases, the relevant local authority or NHS body must decide in each individual case whether it would be of particular benefit to the person who lacks capacity to have an IMCA to support them. The factors which should be considered are explained in paragraphs 10.59–10.68.[42]

Decisions about serious medical treatment

10.42 Where a serious medical treatment decision is being considered for a person who lacks the capacity to consent, and who qualifies for additional safeguards, section 37 of the Act imposes a duty on the NHS body to instruct an IMCA. NHS bodies must instruct an IMCA whenever they are proposing to take a decision about 'serious medical treatment', or proposing that another organisation (such as a private hospital) carry out the treatment on their behalf, if:

- the person concerned does not have the capacity to make a decision about the treatment, and

- there is no-one appropriate to consult about whether the decision is in the person's best interests, other than paid care staff.

10.43 Regulations for England and Wales set out the definition of 'serious medical treatment' for decisions that require an IMCA. It includes treatments for both mental and physical conditions.

Serious medical treatment is defined as treatment which involves giving new treatment, stopping treatment that has already started or withholding treatment that could be offered in circumstances where:

- if a single treatment is proposed there is a fine balance between the likely benefits and the burdens to the patient and the risks involved

- a decision between a choice of treatments is finely balanced, or

- what is proposed is likely to have serious consequences for the patient.

10.44 'Serious consequences' are those which could have a serious impact on the patient, either from the effects of the treatment itself or its wider implications. This may include treatments which:

- cause serious and prolonged pain, distress or side effects

---

[42] See chapter 11 for information about the role of 'consultees' when research is proposed involving a person who lacks capacity to make a decision about whether to agree to take part in research. In certain situations IMCAs may be involved as consultees for research purposes.

- have potentially major consequences for the patient (for example, stopping life-sustaining treatment or having major surgery such as heart surgery), or

- have a serious impact on the patient's future life choices (for example, interventions for ovarian cancer).

10.45 It is impossible to set out all types of procedures that may amount to 'serious medical treatment', although some examples of medical treatments that might be considered serious include:

- chemotherapy and surgery for cancer

- electro-convulsive therapy

- therapeutic sterilisation

- major surgery (such as open-heart surgery or brain/neuro-surgery)

- major amputations (for example, loss of an arm or leg)

- treatments which will result in permanent loss of hearing or sight

- withholding or stopping artificial nutrition and hydration, and

- termination of pregnancy.

These are illustrative examples only, and whether these or other procedures are considered serious medical treatment in any given case, will depend on the circumstances and the consequences for the patient. There are also many more treatments which will be defined as serious medical treatments under the Act's regulations. Decision-makers who are not sure whether they need to instruct an IMCA should consult their colleagues.

10.46 The only situation in which the duty to instruct an IMCA need not be followed, is when an urgent decision is needed (for example, to save the person's life). This decision must be recorded with the reason for the non-referral. Responsible bodies will however still need to instruct an IMCA for any serious treatment that follows the emergency treatment.

10.47 While a decision-maker is waiting for the IMCA's report, they must still act in the person's best interests (for example, to give treatment that stops the person's condition getting worse).

Chapter 10

What is the new Independent Mental Capacity Advocate service and how does it work?

Scenario: Using an IMCA for serious medical treatment

Mr Jones had a fall and suffered serious head injuries. Hospital staff could not find any family or friends. He needed urgent surgery, but afterwards still lacked capacity to accept or refuse medical treatment.

The hospital did not involve an IMCA in the decision to operate, because it needed to make an emergency decision. But it did instruct an IMCA when it needed to carry out further serious medical treatment.

The IMCA met with Mr Jones looked at his case notes and reviewed the options with the consultant. The decision-maker then made the clinical decision about Mr Jones' best interests taking into account the IMCA's report.

10.48 Some decisions about medical treatment are so serious that the courts need to make them (see chapter 8). But responsible bodies should still instruct an IMCA in these cases. The OS may be involved as a litigation friend of the person who lacks capacity.

10.49 Responsible bodies do not have to instruct an IMCA for patients detained under the Mental Health Act 1983, if:

- the treatment is for mental disorder, and

- they can give it without the patient's consent under that Act.

10.50 If serious medical treatment proposed for the detained patient is not for their mental disorder, the patient then has a right to an IMCA – as long as they meet the Mental Capacity Act's requirements. So a detained patient without capacity to consent to cancer treatment, for example, should qualify for an IMCA if there are no family or friends whom it would be appropriate to consult.

Decisions about accommodation or changes of residence

10.51 The Act imposes similar duties on NHS bodies and local authorities who are responsible for long-term accommodation decisions for a person who lacks the capacity to agree to the placement and who qualifies for the additional safeguard of an IMCA. The right to an IMCA applies to decisions about long-term accommodation in a hospital or care home if it is:

- provided or arranged by the NHS, or

- residential care that is provided or arranged by the local authority or provided under section 117 of the Mental Health Act 1983, or

- a move between such accommodation.

Chapter 10

What is the new Independent Mental Capacity Advocate service and how does it work?

10.52 Responsible bodies have a duty to instruct an IMCA if:

- an NHS organisation proposes to place a person who lacks capacity in a hospital – or to move them to another hospital – for longer than 28 days, or

- an NHS organisation proposes to place a person who lacks capacity in a care home – or to move them to a different care home – for what is likely to be longer than eight weeks.

In either situation the other qualifying conditions apply. So, if the accommodation is for less than 28 days in a hospital or less than 8 weeks in a care home, then an IMCA need not be appointed.

10.53 The duty also applies if a local authority carries out an assessment under section 47 of the NHS and Community Care Act 1990, and it decides to:

- provide care services for a person who lacks capacity in the form of residential accommodation in a care home or its equivalent (see paragraph 10.11) which is likely to be longer than eight weeks, or

- move a person who lacks capacity to another care home or its equivalent for a period likely to exceed eight weeks.

10.54 In some cases, a care home may decide to de-register so that they can provide accommodation and care in a different way. If a local authority makes the new arrangements, then an IMCA should still be instructed if a patient lacks capacity and meets the other qualifying conditions.

10.55 Sometimes a person's placement will be longer than expected. The responsible body should involve an IMCA as soon as they realise the stay will be longer than 28 days or eight weeks, as appropriate.

10.56 People who fund themselves in long-term accommodation have the same rights to an IMCA as others, if the local authority:

- carries out an assessment under section 47 of the NHS and Community Care Act 1990, and

- decides it has a duty to the person (under either section 21 or 29 of the National Assistance Act 1947 or section 117 of the Mental Health Act 1983).

10.57 Responsible bodies can only put aside the duty to involve an IMCA if the placement or move is urgent (for example, an emergency admission to hospital or possible homelessness). The decision-maker must involve an IMCA as soon as possible after making an emergency decision, if:

- the person is likely to stay in hospital for longer than 28 days, or

- they will stay in other accommodation for longer than eight weeks.

10.58 Responsible bodies do not have to involve IMCAs if the person in question is going to be required to stay in the accommodation under the Mental Health Act 1983. But if a person is discharged from detention, they have a right to an IMCA in future accommodation decisions (if they meet the usual conditions set out in the Act).

When can a local authority or NHS body decide to instruct an IMCA?

10.59 The Expansion Regulations have given local authorities and NHS bodies the power to apply the IMCA role to two further types of decisions:

- a care review, and

- adult protection cases that involve vulnerable people.

10.60 In these situations, the responsible body must consider in each individual case whether to instruct an IMCA. Where an IMCA is instructed:

- the decision-maker must be satisfied that having an IMCA will be of particular benefit to the person who lacks capacity

- the decision-maker must also follow the best interests checklist, including getting the views of anyone engaged in caring for a person when assessing their best interests, and

- the decision-maker must consider the IMCA's report and related information when making a decision.

Chapter 10

What is the new Independent Mental Capacity Advocate service and how does it work?

10.61 Responsible bodies are expected to take a strategic approach in deciding when they will use IMCAs in these two additional situations. They should establish a policy locally for determining these decisions, setting out the criteria for appointing an IMCA including the issues to be taken into account when deciding if an IMCA will be of particular benefit to the person concerned. However, decision-makers will need to consider each case separately to see if the criteria are met. Local authorities or NHS bodies may want to publish their approach for ease of access, setting out the ways they intend to use these additional powers and review it periodically.

Involving an IMCA in care reviews

10.62 A responsible body can instruct an IMCA to support and represent a person who lacks capacity when:

- they have arranged accommodation for that person
- they aim to review the arrangements (as part of a care plan or otherwise), and
- there are no family or friends who it would be appropriate to consult.

10.63 Section 7 of the Local Authority Social Services Act 1970 sets out current requirements for care reviews. It states that there should be a review 'within three months of help being provided or major changes made to services'. There should then be a review every year – or more often, if needed.

10.64 Reviews should relate to decisions about accommodation:

- for someone who lacks capacity to make a decision about accommodation
- that will be provided for a continuous period of more than 12 weeks
- that are not the result of an obligation under the Mental Health Act 1983, and
- that do not relate to circumstances where sections 37 to 39 of the Act would apply.

10.65 Where the person is to be detained or required to live in accommodation under the Mental Health Act 1983, an IMCA will not be needed since the safeguards available under that Act will apply.

Involving IMCAs in adult protection cases

10.66 Responsible bodies have powers to instruct an IMCA to support and represent a person who lacks capacity where it is alleged that:

- the person is or has been abused or neglected by another person, or

- the person is abusing or has abused another person.

The responsible bodies can only instruct an IMCA if they propose to take, or have already taken, protective measures. This is in accordance with adult protection procedures set up under statutory guidance.[43]

10.67 In adult protection cases (and no other cases), access to IMCAs is not restricted to people who have no-one else to support or represent them. People who lack capacity who have family and friends can still have an IMCA to support them in the adult protection procedures.

10.68 In some situations, a case may start out as an adult protection case where a local authority may consider whether or not to involve an IMCA under the criteria they have set – but may then become a case where the allegations or evidence give rise to the question of whether the person should be moved in their best interests. In these situations the case has become one where an IMCA must be involved if there is no-one else appropriate to support and represent the person in this decision.

Who qualifies for an IMCA?

10.69 Apart from the adult protection cases discussed above, IMCAs are only available to people who:

- lack capacity to make a specific decision about serious medical treatment or long-term accommodation, *and*

- have no family or friends who are available and appropriate to support or represent them apart from professionals or paid workers providing care or treatment, *and*

- have not previously named someone who could help with a decision, *and*

---

[43] Published guidance: *No secrets: Guidance on developing and implementing multi-agency policies and procedures to protect vulnerable adults from abuse* for England (on the Department of Health website) and *In safe hands* in Wales.

No secrets applies to adults aged 18 or over. The Children Act 1989 applies to 16 and 17 year olds who may be facing abuse. Part V of the Act covers the Protection of Children, which includes at section 47 the duty to investigate by a local authority in order to decide whether they should take any action to safeguard or promote a child's welfare where he or she requires protection or may suffer harm. See also chapter 12 of this Code.

- have not made a Lasting Power of Attorney or Enduring Power of Attorney (see paragraph 10.70 below).

Chapter 10

What is the new Independent Mental Capacity Advocate service and how does it work?

10.70 The Act says that IMCAs cannot be instructed if:

- a person who now lacks capacity previously named a person that should be consulted about decisions that affect them, and that person is available and willing to help

- the person who lacks capacity has appointed an attorney, either under a Lasting Power of Attorney or an Enduring Power of Attorney, and the attorney continues to manage the person's affairs

- the Court of Protection has appointed a deputy, who continues to act on the person's behalf.

10.71 However, where a person has no family or friends to represent them, but does have an attorney or deputy who has been appointed solely to deal with their property and affairs, they should not be denied access to an IMCA. The Government is seeking to amend the Act at the earliest opportunity to ensure that, in such circumstances, an IMCA should always be appointed to represent the person's views when they lack the capacity to make decisions relating to serious medical treatment or long-term accommodation moves.

10.72 A responsible body can still instruct an IMCA if the Court of Protection is deciding on a deputy, but none is in place when a decision needs to be made.

Scenario: Qualifying for an IMCA

Ms Lewis, a woman with a history of mental health problems has lived in a care home for several years. Her home will soon close, and she has no-one who could help her. She has become very anxious and now lacks capacity to make a decision about future accommodation. The local authority instructs an IMCA to support her. The IMCA visits Ms Lewis, talks to staff who have been involved in her care and reviews her case notes.

In his report, the IMCA includes the information that Ms Lewis is very close to another client in the care home. The IMCA notes that they could move together – if it is also in the interests of the other client. The local authority now has to decide on the best interests of the client, considering the information that the IMCA has provided.

Will IMCAs be available to people in prisons?

10.73 IMCAs should be available to people who are in prison and lack capacity to make decisions about serious medical treatment or long-term accommodation.

Who is it 'appropriate to consult'?

10.74 The IMCA is a safeguard for those people who lack capacity, who have no-one close to them who 'it would be appropriate to consult'. (This is apart from adult protection cases where this criterion does not apply.) The safeguard is intended to apply to those people who have little or no network of support, such as close family or friends, who take an interest in their welfare or no-one willing or able to be formally consulted in decision-making processes.

10.75 The Act does not define those 'whom it would be appropriate to consult' and the evaluation of the IMCA pilots reported that decision-makers in the local authority and in the NHS, whose decision it is to determine this, sometimes found it difficult to establish when an IMCA was required.[44] Section 4(7) provides that consultation about a person's best interests shall include among others, anyone:

- named by the person as someone to be consulted on a relevant decision

- engaged in caring for them, or

- interested in their welfare (see chapter 4).

10.76 The decision-maker must determine if it is possible and practical to speak to these people, and those described in paragraph 10.70 when working out whether the proposed decision is in the person's best interests. If it is not possible, practical and appropriate to consult anyone, an IMCA should be instructed.

10.77 There may be situations where a person who lacks capacity has family or friends, but it is not practical or appropriate to consult them. For example, an elderly person with dementia may have an adult child who now lives in Australia, or an older person may have relatives who very rarely visit. Or, a family member may simply refuse to be consulted. In such cases, decision-makers must instruct an IMCA – for serious medical treatment and care moves and record the reason for the decision.

---

[44] see www.dh.gov.uk/PolicyAndGuidance/HealthAndSocialCareTopics/SocialCare/IMCA/fs/en

10.78   The person who lacks capacity may have friends or neighbours who know their wishes and feelings but are not willing or able to help with the specific decision to be made. They may think it is too much of a responsibility. If they are elderly and frail themselves, it may be too difficult for them to attend case conferences and participate formally. In this situation, the responsible body should instruct an IMCA, and the IMCA may visit them and enable them to be involved more informally.

Chapter 10

What is the new Independent Mental Capacity Advocate service and how does it work?

10.79   If a family disagrees with a decision-maker's proposed action, this is not grounds for concluding that there is nobody whose views are relevant to the decision.

10.80   A person who lacks capacity and already has an advocate may still be entitled to an IMCA. The IMCA would consult with the advocate. Where that advocate meets the appointment criteria for the IMCA service, they may be appointed to fulfil the IMCA role for this person in addition to their other duties.

11 How does the Act affect research projects involving a person who lacks capacity?

It is important that research involving people who lack capacity can be carried out, and that is carried out properly. Without it, we would not improve our knowledge of what causes a person to lack or lose capacity, and the diagnosis, treatment, care and needs of people who lack capacity.

This chapter gives guidance on involving people who lack capacity to consent to take part in research. It sets out:

- what the Act means by 'research'
- the requirements that people must meet if their research project involves somebody who lacks capacity
- the specific responsibilities of researchers, and
- how the Act applies to research that started before the Act came into force.

This chapter only deals with research in relation to adults. Further guidance will be provided on how the Act applies in relation to research involving those under the age of 18.

> In this chapter, as throughout the Code, a person's capacity (or lack of capacity) refers specifically to their capacity to make a particular decision at the time it needs to be made.

Quick summary

The Act's rules for research that includes people who lack capacity to consent to their involvement cover:

- when research can be carried out
- the ethical approval process
- respecting the wishes and feelings of people who lack capacity
- other safeguards to protect people who lack capacity
- how to engage with a person who lacks capacity
- how to engage with carers and other relevant people.

This chapter also explains:

- the specific rules that apply to research involving human tissue and

- what to do if research projects have already been given the go-ahead.

Chapter 11

How does
the Act affect
research projects
involving a
person who lack
capacity?

The Act applies to all research that is intrusive. 'Intrusive' means research that would be unlawful if it involved a person who had capacity but had not consented to take part. The Act does not apply to research involving clinical trials (testing new drugs).

Why does the Act cover research?

11.1   Because the Act is intended to assist and support people who may lack capacity, the Act protects people who take part in research projects but lack capacity to make decisions about their involvement. It makes sure that researchers respect their wishes and feelings. The Act does not apply to research that involves clinical trials of medicines – because these are covered by other rules.[45]

How can research involving people who lack capacity help?

A high percentage of patients with Down's syndrome lack capacity to agree or refuse to take part in research. Research involving patients with Down's syndrome has shown that they are more likely than other people to get pre-senile dementia. Research has also shown that when this happens the pathological changes that occur in a person with Down's syndrome (changes affecting their body and brain) are similar to those that occur in someone with Alzheimer's disease. This means that we now know that treatment similar to that used for memory disorders in patients with Alzheimer's is appropriate to treat dementia in those with Down's syndrome.

What is 'research'?

11.2   The Act does not have a specific definition for 'research'. The Department of Health and National Assembly for Wales publications *Research governance framework for health and social care* both state:

'research can be defined as the attempt to derive generalisable new knowledge by addressing clearly defined questions with systematic and rigorous methods.'[46]

---

[45] The Medicines for Human Use (Clinical Trials) Regulations 2004.

[46] www.dh.gov.uk/PublicationsAndStatistics/Publications/PublicationsPolicyAndGuidance/
PublicationsPolicyAndGuidanceArticle/fs/en?CONTENT_ID=4008777&chk=dMRd/5 and
www.word.wales.gov.uk/content/governance/governance-e.htm

Research may:

- provide information that can be applied generally to an illness, disorder or condition
- demonstrate how effective and safe a new treatment is
- add to evidence that one form of treatment works better than another
- add to evidence that one form of treatment is safer than another, or
- examine wider issues (for example, the factors that affect someone's capacity to make a decision).

11.3 Researchers must state clearly if an activity is part of someone's care and not part of the research. Sometimes experimental medicine or treatment may be performed for the person's benefit and be the best option for their care. But in these cases, it may be difficult to decide whether treatment is research or care. Where there is doubt, the researcher should seek legal advice.

What assumptions can a researcher make about capacity?

11.4 Researchers should assume that a person has capacity, unless there is proof that they lack capacity to make a specific decision (see chapter 3). The person must also receive support to try to help them make their own decision (see chapter 2). The person whose capacity is in question has the right to make decisions that others might not agree with, and they have the right not to take part in research.

What research does the Act cover?

11.5 It is expected that most of the researchers who ask for their research to be approved under the Act will be medical or social care researchers. However, the Act can cover more than just medical and social care research. Intrusive research which does not meet the requirements of the Act cannot be carried out lawfully in relation to people who lack capacity.

11.6 The Act applies to research that:

Chapter 11

How does the Act affect research projects involving a person who lacks capacity?

- is 'intrusive' (if a person taking part had capacity, the researcher would need to get their consent to involve them)

- involves people who have an impairment of, or a disturbance in the functioning of, their mind or brain which makes them unable to decide whether or not to agree to take part in the research (i.e. they lack capacity to consent), and

- is not a clinical trial covered under the Medicines for Human Use (Clinical Trials) Regulations 2004.

11.7 There are circumstances where no consent is needed to lawfully involve a person in research. These apply to all persons, whether they have capacity or not:

- Sometimes research only involves data that has been anonymised (it cannot be traced back to individuals). Confidentiality and data protection laws do not apply in this case.

- Under the Human Tissue Act 2004, research that deals only with human tissue that has been anonymised does not require consent (see paragraphs 11.37–11.40). This applies to both those who have capacity and those who do not. But the research must have ethical approval, and the tissue must come from a living person.[47]

- If researchers collected human tissue samples before 31 August 2006, they do not need a person's consent to work on them. But they will normally have to get ethical approval.

- Regulations[48] made under section 251 of the NHS Act 2006 (formerly known as section 60 of the Health and Social Care Act 2001[49]) allow people to use confidential patient information without breaking the law on confidentiality by applying to the Patient Information Advisory Group for approval on behalf of the Secretary of State.[50]

Who is responsible for making sure research meets the Act's requirements?

11.8 Responsibility for meeting the Act's requirements lies with:

---

[47] Human Tissue Act 2004 section 1(9).

[48] Health Service (Control of Patient Information) Regulations 2002 Section I. 2002/1438.

[49] Section 60 of the Health and Social Care Act 2001 was included in the NHS Act 2006 which consolidated all the previous health legislation still in force.

[50] The Patient Information Advisory Group considers applications on behalf of the Secretary of State to allow the common law duty of confidentiality to be aside. It was established under section 61 of the Health and Social Care Act 2006 (now known as section 252 of the NHS Act 2006). Further information can be found at www.advisorybodies.doh.gov.uk/PIAG.

- the 'appropriate body', as defined in regulations made by the Secretary of State (for regulations applying in England) or the National Assembly for Wales (for regulations applying in Wales) (see paragraph 11.10), and

- the researchers carrying out the research (see paragraphs 11.20–11.40).

How can research get approval?

11.9　Research covered by the Act cannot include people who lack capacity to consent to the research unless:

- it has the approval of 'the appropriate body', and

- it follows other requirements in the Act to:

  - consider the views of carers and other relevant people

  - treat the person's interests as more important than those of science and society, and

  - respect any objections a person who lacks capacity makes during research.

11.10　An 'appropriate body' is an organisation that can approve research projects. In England, the 'appropriate body' must be a research ethics committee recognised by the Secretary of State.[51] In Wales, the 'appropriate body' must be a research ethics committee recognised by the Welsh Assembly Government.

11.11　The appropriate body can only approve a research project if the research is linked to:

- an impairing condition that affects the person who lacks capacity, or

- the treatment of that condition (see paragraph 11.17)

and:

- there are reasonable grounds for believing that the research would be less effective if only people with capacity are involved, and

- the research project has made arrangements to consult carers and to follow the other requirements of the Act.

---

[51]　Mental Capacity Act 2005 (Appropriate Body) (England) Regulations 2006

11.12 Research must also meet one of two requirements:

Chapter 11

How does
the Act affect
research projects
involving a
person who lacks
capacity?

1. The research must have some chance of benefiting the person who lacks capacity, as set out in paragraph 11.14 below. The benefit must be in proportion to any burden caused by taking part, or

2. The aim of the research must be to provide knowledge about the cause of, or treatment or care of people with, the same impairing condition – or a similar condition.

If researchers are relying on the second requirement, the Act sets out further requirements that must be met:

- the risk to the person who lacks capacity must be negligible

- there must be no significant interference with the freedom of action or privacy of the person who lacks capacity, and

- nothing must be done to or in relation to the person who lacks capacity which is unduly invasive or restrictive (see paragraphs 11.16–11.19 below).

11.13 An impairing condition:

- is caused by (or may be caused by) an impairment of, or disturbance in the functioning of, the person's mind or brain

- causes (or may cause) an impairment or disturbance of the mind or brain, or

- contributes to (or may contribute to) an impairment or disturbance of the mind or brain.

Balancing the benefit and burden of research

11.14 Potential benefits of research for a person who lacks capacity could include:

- developing more effective ways of treating a person or managing their condition

- improving the quality of healthcare, social care or other services that they have access to

- discovering the cause of their condition, if they would benefit from that knowledge, or

- reducing the risk of the person being harmed, excluded or disadvantaged.

11.15 Benefits may be direct or indirect (for example, the person might benefit at a later date if policies or care packages affecting them are changed because of the research). It might be that participation in the research itself will be of benefit to the person in particular circumstances. For example, if the research involves interviews and the person has the opportunity to express their views, this could be considered of real benefit to a particular individual.

Providing knowledge about causes, treatment or care of people with the same impairing condition or a similar condition

11.16 It is possible for research to be carried out which doesn't actually benefit the person taking part, as long as it aims to provide knowledge about the causes, treatment or care of people with the same impairing condition, or a similar condition. *'Care'* and *'treatment'* are not limited to medical care and treatment. For example, research could examine how day-to-day life in prison affects prisoners with mental health conditions.

11.17 It is the person's actual condition that must be the same or similar in research, not the underlying cause. A *'similar condition'* may therefore have a different cause to that suffered by the participant. For example, research into ways of supporting people with learning disabilities to live more independently might involve a person with a learning disability caused by a head trauma. But its findings might help people with similar learning disabilities that have different causes.

Scenario: Research that helps find a cause or treatment

Mr Neal has Down's syndrome. For many years he has lived in supported housing and worked in a local supermarket. But several months ago, he became aggressive, forgetful and he started to make mistakes at work. His consultant believes that this may indicate the start of Alzheimer's disease.

Mr Neal's condition is now so bad that he does not have capacity to consent to treatment or make other decisions about his care. A research team is researching the cause of dementia in people with Down's syndrome. They would like to involve Mr Neal. The research satisfies the Act's requirement that it is intended to provide knowledge of the causes or treatment of that condition, even though it may not directly benefit Mr Neal. So the approving body might give permission – if the research meets other requirements.

Chapter 11

How does
the Act affect
research projects
involving a
person who lacks
capacity?

11.18 Any risk to people involved in this category of research must be 'negligible' (minimal). This means that a person should suffer no harm or distress by taking part. Researchers must consider risks to psychological wellbeing as well as physical wellbeing. This is particularly relevant for research related to observations or interviews.

11.19 Research in this category also must not affect a person's freedom of action or privacy in a significant way, and it should not be unduly invasive or restrictive. What will be considered as unduly invasive will be different for different people and different types of research. For example, in psychological research some people may think a specific question is intrusive, but others would not. Actions will not usually be classed as unduly invasive if they do not go beyond the experience of daily life, a routine medical examination or a psychological examination.

Scenario: Assessing the risk to research participants

A research project is studying:

* how well people with a learning disability make financial decisions, and

* communication techniques that may improve their decision-making capacity.

Some of the participants lack capacity to agree to take part. The Research Ethics Committee is satisfied that some of these participants may benefit from the study because their capacity to make financial decisions may be improved. For those who will not gain any personal benefit, the Committee is satisfied that:

* the research meets the other conditions of the Act

* the research methods (psychological testing and different communication techniques) involve no risk to participants, and

* the research could not have been carried out as effectively with people who have capacity.

11.20 Before starting the research, the research team must make arrangements to:

- obtain approval for the research from the 'appropriate body'

- get the views of any carers and other relevant people before involving a person who lacks capacity in research (see paragraphs 11.22–11.28). There is an exception to this consultation requirement in situations where urgent treatment needs to be given or is about to be given

- respect the objections, wishes and feelings of the person, and

- place more importance on the person's interests than on those of science and society.

11.21 The research proposal must give enough information about what the team will do if a person who lacks capacity needs urgent treatment during research and it is not possible to speak to the person's carer or someone else who acts or makes decisions on behalf of the person (see paragraphs 11.32–11.36).

Consulting carers

11.22 Once it has been established that a person lacks capacity to agree to participate, then before they are included in research the researcher must consult with specified people in accordance with section 32 of the Act to determine whether the person should be included in the research.

Who can researchers consult?

11.23 The researcher should as a matter of good practice take reasonable steps to identify someone to consult. That person (the consultee) must be involved in the person's care, interested in their welfare and must be willing to help. They must not be a professional or paid care worker. They will probably be a family member, but could be another person.

11.24 The researcher must take into account previous wishes and feelings that the person might have expressed about who they would, or would not, like involved in future decisions.

11.25 A person is not prevented from being consulted if they are an attorney authorised under a registered Lasting Power of Attorney or are a deputy appointed by the Court of Protection. But that person must not be acting in a professional or paid capacity (for example, person's solicitor).

Chapter 11

How does
the Act affect
research projects
involving a
person who lacks
capacity?

11.26 Where there is no-one who meets the conditions mentioned at paragraphs 11.23 and 11.25, the researcher must nominate a person to be the consulted. In this situation, they must follow guidance from the Secretary of State for Health in England or the National Assembly for Wales (the guidance will be available from mid-2007). The person who is nominated must have no connection with the research project.

11.27 The researcher must provide the consultee with information about the research project and ask them:

- for advice about whether the person who lacks capacity should take part in the project, and

- what they think the person's feelings and wishes would be, if they had capacity to decide whether to take part.

11.28 Sometimes the consultee will say that the person would probably not take part in the project or that they would ask to be withdrawn. In this situation, the researcher must not include the person in the project, or they should withdraw them from it. But if the project has started, and the person is getting treatment as part of the research, the researcher may decide that the person should not be withdrawn if the researcher reasonably believes that this would cause a significant risk to the person's health. The researcher may decide that the person should continue with the research while the risk exists. But they should stop any parts of the study that are not related to the risk to the person's health.

What other safeguards does the Act require?

11.29 Even when a consultee agrees that a person can take part in research, the researcher must still consider the person's wishes and feelings.

11.30 Researchers must not do anything the person who lacks capacity objects to. They must not do anything to go against any advance decision to refuse treatment or other statement the person has previously made expressing preferences about their care or treatment. They must assume that the person's interests in this matter are more important than those of science and society.

11.31 A researcher must withdraw someone from a project if:

- they indicate in any way that they want to be withdrawn from the project (for example, if they become upset or distressed), or

- any of the Act's requirements are no longer met.

What happens if urgent decisions are required during the research project?

11.32 Anyone responsible for caring for a person must give them urgent treatment if they need it. In some circumstances, it may not be possible to separate the research from the urgent treatment.

11.33 A research proposal should explain to the appropriate body how researchers will deal with urgent decisions which may occur during the project, when there may not be time to carry out the consultations required under the Act. For example, after a patient has arrived in intensive care, the doctor may want to chart the course of an injury by taking samples or measurements immediately and then taking further samples after some type of treatment to compare with the first set.

11.34 Special rules apply where a person who lacks capacity is getting, or about to get, urgent treatment and researchers want to include them in a research project. If in these circumstances a researcher thinks that it is necessary to take urgent action for the purposes of the research, and they think it is not practical to consult someone about it, the researcher can take that action if:

- they get agreement from a registered medical practitioner not involved with the research, or

- they follow a procedure that the appropriate body agreed to at approval stage.

11.35 The medical practitioner may have a connection to the person who lacks capacity (for example, they might be their doctor). But they must not be involved in the research project in any way. This is to avoid conflicts of interest.

11.36 This exception to the duty to consult only applies:

- for as long as the person needs urgent treatment, and

- when the researcher needs to take action urgently for research to be valid.

It is likely to be limited to research into procedures or treatments used in emergencies. It does not apply where the researcher simply wants to act quickly.

What happens for research involving human tissue?

Chapter 11

How does
the Act affect
research projects
involving a
person who lacks
capacity?

11.37 A person with capacity has to give their permission for someone to remove tissue from their body (for example, taking a biopsy (a sample) for diagnosis or removal of tissue in surgery). The Act allows the removal of tissue from the body of a person who lacks capacity, if it is in their best interests (see chapter 5).

11.38 People with capacity must also give permission for the storage or use of tissue for certain purposes, set out in the Human Tissue Act 2004, (for example, transplants and research). But there are situations in which permission is not required by law:

- research where the samples are anonymised and the research has ethical approval[52]

- clinical audit

- education or training relating to human health

- performance assessment

- public health monitoring, and

- quality assurance.

11.39 If an adult lacks capacity to consent, the Human Tissue Act 2004 says that tissue can be stored or used without seeking permission if the storage or use is:

- to get information relevant to the health of another individual (for example, before conducting a transplant), as long as the researcher or healthcare professional storing or using the human tissue believes they are doing it in the best interests of the person who lacks capacity to consent

- for a clinical trial approved and carried out under the Medicines for Human Use (Clinical Trials) Regulations 2004, or

- for intrusive research:

  – after the Mental Capacity Act comes into force

  – that meets the Act's requirements, and

  – that has ethical approval.

[52] Section 1(9) of the Human Tissue Act 2004

11.40 Tissue samples that were obtained before 31 August 2006 are existing holdings under the Human Tissue Act. Researchers can work with these tissues without seeking permission. But they will still need to get ethical approval. Guidance is available in the Human Tissue Authority Code of Practice on consent.[53]

What should happen to research that started before the Act came into force?

What if a person has capacity when research starts but loses capacity?

11.41 Some people with capacity will agree to take part in research but may then lose capacity before the end of the project. In this situation, researchers will be able to continue research as long as they comply with the conditions set out in the Mental Capacity Act 2005 (Loss of Capacity During Research Project) (England) Regulations 2007 or equivalent Welsh regulations.

The regulations only apply to tissue and data collected before the loss of capacity from a person who gave consent before 31 March 2008 to join a project that starts before 1 October 2007.

11.42 The regulations do not cover research involving direct intervention (for example, taking of further blood pressure readings) or the taking of further tissue after loss of capacity. Such research must comply with sections 30 to 33 of the Act to be lawful.

11.43 Where the regulations do apply, research can only continue if the project already has procedures to deal with people who lose capacity during the project. An appropriate body must have approved the procedures. The researcher must follow the procedures that have been approved.

11.44 The researcher must also:

- seek out the views of someone involved in the person's care or interested in their welfare and if a carer can't be found they must nominate a consultee (see paragraphs 11.22–11.28)

- respect advance decisions and expressed preferences, wishes or objections that the person has made in the past, and

- treat the person's interests as more important than those of science and society.

---

[53] www.hta.gov.uk

The appropriate body must be satisfied that the research project has reasonable arrangements to meet these requirements.

Chapter 11

How does the Act affect research projects involving a person who lacks capacity?

11.45 If at any time the researcher believes that procedures are no longer in place or the appropriate body no longer approves the research, they must stop research on the person immediately.

11.46 Where regulations do apply, research does not have to:

- be linked to an impairing condition of the person

- have the potential to benefit that person, or

- aim to provide knowledge relevant to others with the same or a similar condition.

What happens to existing projects that a person never had capacity to agree to?

11.47 There are no regulations for projects that:

- started before the Act comes into force, and

- a person never had the capacity to agree to.

Projects that already have ethical approval will need to obtain approval from an appropriate body under sections 30 and 31 of the Mental Capacity Act and to comply with the requirements of sections 32 and 33 of that Act by 1 October 2008. Research that does not have ethical approval must get approval from an appropriate body by 1 October 2007 to continue lawfully. This is the case in England and it is expected that similar arrangements will apply in Wales.

12 How does the Act apply to children and young people?

This chapter looks at the few parts of the Act that may affect children under 16 years of age. It also explains the position of young people aged 16 and 17 years and the overlapping laws that affect them.

This chapter does not deal with research. Further guidance will be provided on how the Act applies in relation to research involving those under the age of 18.

Within this Code of Practice, 'children' refers to people aged below 16. 'Young people' refers to people aged 16–17. This differs from the Children Act 1989 and the law more generally, where the term 'child' is used to refer to people aged under 18.

> In this chapter, as throughout the Code, a person's capacity (or lack of capacity) refers specifically to their capacity to make a particular decision at the time it needs to be made.

Quick summary

Children under 16

- The Act does not generally apply to people under the age of 16.
- There are two exceptions:
  - The Court of Protection can make decisions about a child's property or finances (or appoint a deputy to make these decisions) if the child lacks capacity to make such decisions within section 2(1) of the Act and is likely to still lack capacity to make financial decisions when they reach the age of 18 (section 18(3)).
  - Offences of ill treatment or wilful neglect of a person who lacks capacity within section 2(1) can also apply to victims younger than 16 (section 44).

Young people aged 16–17 years

- Most of the Act applies to young people aged 16–17 years, who may lack capacity within section 2(1) to make specific decisions.
- There are three exceptions:
  - Only people aged 18 and over can make a Lasting Power of Attorney (LPA).

- Only people aged 18 and over can make an advance decision to refuse medical treatment.

- The Court of Protection may only make a statutory will for a person aged 18 and over.

Care or treatment for young people aged 16–17

- People carrying out acts in connection with the care or treatment of a young person aged 16–17 who lacks capacity to consent within section 2(1) will generally have protection from liability (section 5), as long as the person carrying out the act:

  - has taken reasonable steps to establish that the young person lacks capacity

  - reasonably believes that the young person lacks capacity and that the act is in the young person's best interests, and

  - follows the Act's principles.

- When assessing the young person's best interests (see chapter 5), the person providing care or treatment must consult those involved in the young person's care and anyone interested in their welfare – if it is practical and appropriate to do so. This may include the young person's parents. Care should be taken not to unlawfully breach the young person's right to confidentiality (see chapter 16).

- Nothing in section 5 excludes a person's civil liability for loss or damage, or his criminal liability, resulting from his negligence in carrying out the act.

Legal proceedings involving young people aged 16-17

- Sometimes there will be disagreements about the care, treatment or welfare of a young person aged 16 or 17 who lacks capacity to make relevant decisions. Depending on the circumstances, the case may be heard in the family courts or the Court of Protection.

- The Court of Protection may transfer a case to the family courts, and vice versa.

Does the Act apply to children?

12.1   Section 2(5) of the Act states that, with the exception of section 2(6), as explained below, no powers under the Act may be exercised in relation to a child under 16.

12.2   Care and treatment of children under the age of 16 is generally governed by common law principles. Further information is provide at www.dh.gov.uk/consent.

Can the Act help with decisions about a child's property or finances?

12.3   Section 2(6) makes an exception for some decisions about a child's property and financial affairs. The Court of Protection can make decisions about property and affairs of those under 16 in cases where the person is likely to still lack capacity to make financial decisions after reaching the age of 18. The court's ruling will still apply when the person reaches the age of 18, which means there will not be a need for further court proceedings once the person reaches the age of 18.

12.4   The Court of Protection can:

- make an order (for example, concerning the investment of an award of compensation for the child), and/or

- appoint a deputy to manage the child's property and affairs and to make ongoing financial decisions on the child's behalf.

In making a decision, the court must follow the Act's principles and decide in the child's best interests as set out in chapter 5 of the Code.

Scenario: Applying the Act to children

Tom was nine when a drunk driver knocked him off his bicycle. He suffered severe head injuries and permanent brain damage. He received a large amount of money in compensation. He is unlikely to recover enough to be able to make financial decisions when he is 18. So the Court of Protection appoints Tom's father as deputy to manage his financial affairs in order to pay for the care Tom will need in the future.

What if somebody mistreats or neglects a child who lacks capacity?

12.5   Section 44 covers the offences of ill treatment or wilful neglect of a person who lacks capacity to make relevant decisions (see chapter 14). This section also applies to children under 16 and young people aged 16 or 17. But it only applies if the child's lack of capacity to make a decision for themselves is caused by an impairment or disturbance that affects how their mind or brain works (see chapter 4). If the lack of capacity is solely the result of the child's youth or immaturity, then the ill treatment or wilful neglect would be dealt with under the separate offences of child cruelty or neglect.

Does the Act apply to young people aged 16–17?

12.6 Most of the Act applies to people aged 16 years and over. There is an overlap with the Children Act 1989. For the Act to apply to a young person, they must lack capacity to make a particular decision (in line with the Act's definition of lack of capacity described in chapter 4). In such situations either this Act or the Children Act 1989 may apply, depending upon the particular circumstances.

However, there may also be situations where neither of these Acts provides an appropriate solution. In such cases, it may be necessary to look to the powers available under the Mental Health Act 1983 or the High Court's inherent powers to deal with cases involving young people.

12.7 There are currently no specific rules for deciding when to use either the Children Act 1989 or the Mental Capacity Act 2005 or when to apply to the High Court. But, the examples below show circumstances where this Act may be the most appropriate (see also paragraphs 12.21–12.23 below).

- In unusual circumstances it might be in a young person's best interests for the Court of Protection to make an order and/or appoint a property and affairs deputy. For example, this might occur when a young person receives financial compensation and the court appoints a parent or a solicitor as a property and affairs deputy.

- It may be appropriate for the Court of Protection to make a welfare decision concerning a young person who lacks capacity to decide for themselves (for example, about where the young person should live) if the court decides that the parents are not acting in the young person's best interests.

- It might be appropriate to refer a case to the Court of Protection where there is disagreement between a person interested in the care and welfare of a young person and the young person's medical team about the young person's best interests or capacity.

Do any parts of the Act not apply to young people aged 16 or 17?

LPAs

12.8 Only people aged 18 or over can make a Lasting Power of Attorney (LPA) (section 9(2)(c)).

Advance decisions to refuse treatment

12.9 Information on decisions to refuse treatment made in advance by young people under the age of 18 will be available at www.dh.gov.uk/consent.

Making a will

12.10 The law generally does not allow anyone below the age of 18 to make a will. So section 18(2) confirms that the Court of Protection can only make a statutory will on behalf of those aged 18 and over.

What does the Act say about care or treatment of young people aged 16 or 17?

Background information concerning competent young people

12.11 The Family Law Reform Act 1969 presumes that young people have the legal capacity to agree to surgical, medical or dental treatment.[54] This also applies to any associated procedures (for example, investigations, anaesthesia or nursing care).

12.12 It does not apply to some rarer types of procedure (for example, organ donation or other procedures which are not therapeutic for the young person) or research. In those cases, anyone under 18 is presumed to lack legal capacity, subject to the test of 'Gillick competence' (testing whether they are mature and intelligent enough to understand a proposed treatment or procedure).[55]

12.13 Even where a young person is presumed to have legal capacity to consent to treatment, they may not necessarily be able to make the relevant decision. As with adults, decision-makers should assess the young person's capacity to consent to the proposed care or treatment (see chapter 4). If a young person lacks capacity to consent within section 2(1) of the Act because of an impairment of, or a disturbance in the functioning of, the mind or brain then the Mental Capacity Act will apply in the same way as it does to those who are 18 and over. If however they are unable to make the decision for some other reason, for example because they are overwhelmed by the implications of the decision, the Act will not apply to them and the legality of any treatment should be assessed under common law principles.

54 Family Law Reform Act 1969, section 8(1)

55 In the case of Gillick v West Norfolk and Wisbech Area Health Authority [1986] 1 AC 112 the court found that a child below 16 years of age will be competent to consent to medical treatment if they have sufficient intelligence and understanding to understand what is proposed. This test applies in relation to all people under 18 where there is no presumption of competence in relation to the procedure – for example where the procedure is not one referred to in section 8 of the Family Law Reform Act 1969, e.g. organ donation.

12.14 If a young person has capacity to agree to treatment, their decision to consent must be respected. Difficult issues can arise if a young person has legal and mental capacity and refuses consent – especially if a person with parental responsibility wishes to give consent on the young person's behalf. The Family Division of the High Court can hear cases where there is disagreement. The Court of Protection has no power to settle a dispute about a young person who is said to have the mental capacity to make the specific decision.

Chapter 12

How does the Act apply to children and young people?

12.15 It may be unclear whether a young person lacks capacity within section 2(1) of the Act. In those circumstances, it would be prudent for the person providing care or treatment for the young person to seek a declaration from the court.

If the young person lacks capacity to make care or treatment decisions

12.16 Under the common law, a person with parental responsibility for a young person is generally able to consent to the young person receiving care or medical treatment where they lack capacity under section 2(1) of the Act. They should act in the young person's best interests.

12.17 However if a young person lacks the mental capacity to make a specific care or treatment decision within section 2(1) of the Act, healthcare staff providing treatment, or a person providing care to the young person, can carry out treatment or care with protection from liability (section 5) whether or not a person with parental responsibility consents.[56] They must follow the Act's principles and make sure that the actions they carry out are in the young person's best interests. They must make every effort to work out and consider the young person's wishes, feelings, beliefs and values – both past and present – and consider all other factors in the best interests checklist (see chapter 5).

12.18 When assessing a young person's best interests, healthcare staff must take into account the views of anyone involved in caring for the young person and anyone interested in their welfare, where it is practical and appropriate to do so. This may include the young person's parents and others with parental responsibility for the young person. Care should be taken not to unlawfully breach the young person's right to confidentiality (see chapter 16).

---

[56] Nothing in section 5 excludes a person's civil liability for loss or damage, or his criminal liability, resulting from his negligence in doing the Act.

12.19 If a young person has said they do not want their parents to be consulted, it may not be appropriate to involve them (for example, where there have been allegations of abuse).

12.20 If there is a disagreement about whether the proposed care or treatment is in the best interests of a young person, or there is disagreement about whether the young person lacks capacity and there is no other way of resolving the matter, it would be prudent for those in disagreement to seek a declaration or other order from the appropriate court (see paragraphs 12.23–12.25 below).

Scenario: Working out a young person's best interests

Mary is 16 and has Down's syndrome. Her mother wants Mary to have dental treatment that will improve her appearance but is not otherwise necessary.

To be protected under section 5 of the Act, the dentist must consider whether Mary has capacity to agree to the treatment and what would be in her best interests. He decides that she is unable to understand what is involved or the possible consequences of the proposed treatment and so lacks capacity to make the decision.

But Mary seems to want the treatment, so he takes her views into account in deciding whether the treatment is in her best interests. He also consults with both her parents and with her teacher and GP to see if there are other relevant factors to take into account.

He decides that the treatment is likely to improve Mary's confidence and self-esteem and is in her best interests.

12.21 There may be particular difficulties where young people with mental health problems require in-patient psychiatric treatment, and are treated informally rather than detained under the Mental Health Act 1983. The Mental Capacity Act and its principles apply to decisions related to the care and treatment of young people who lack mental capacity to consent, including treatment for mental disorder. As with any other form of treatment, somebody assessing a young person's best interests should consult anyone involved in caring for the young person or anyone interested in their welfare, as far as is practical and appropriate. This may include the young person's parents or those with parental responsibility for the young person.

But the Act does not allow any actions that result in a young person being deprived of their liberty (see chapter 6). In such circumstances, detention under the Mental Health Act 1983 and the safeguards provided under that Act might be appropriate (see also chapter 13).

12.22 People may disagree about a young person's capacity to make the specific decision or about their best interests, or it may not be clear whether they lack capacity within section 2(1) or for some other reason. In this situation, legal proceedings may be necessary if there is no other way of settling the disagreement (see chapters 8 and 15). If those involved in caring for the young person or who are interested in the young person's welfare do not agree with the proposed treatment, it may be necessary for an interested party to make an application to the appropriate court.

What powers do the courts have in cases involving young people?

12.23 A case involving a young person who lacks mental capacity to make a specific decision could be heard in the family courts (probably in the Family Division of the High Court) or in the Court of Protection.

12.24 If a case might require an ongoing order (because the young person is likely to still lack capacity when they are 18), it may be more appropriate for the Court of Protection to hear the case. For one-off cases not involving property or finances, the Family Division may be more appropriate.

12.25 So that the appropriate court hears a case, the Court of Protection can transfer cases to the family courts, and vice versa (section 21).

Scenario: Hearing cases in the appropriate court

Shola is 17. She has serious learning disabilities and lacks the capacity to decide where she should live. Her parents are involved in a bitter divorce. They cannot agree on several issues concerning Shola's care – including where she should live. Her mother wants to continue to look after Shola at home. But her father wants Shola to move into a care home.

In this case, it may be more appropriate for the Court of Protection to deal with the case. This is because an order made in the Court of Protection could continue into Shola's adulthood. However an order made by the family court under the Children Act 1989 would end on Shola's eighteenth birthday.

This chapter explains the relationship between the Mental Capacity Act 2005 (MCA) and the Mental Health Act 1983 (MHA). It:

- sets out when it may be appropriate to detain someone under the MHA rather than to rely on the MCA

- describes how the MCA affects people lacking capacity who are also subject to the MHA

- explains when doctors cannot give certain treatments for a mental disorder (in particular, psychosurgery) to someone who lacks capacity to consent to it, and

- sets out changes that the Government is planning to make to both Acts.

It does not provide a full description of the MHA. The MHA has its own Memorandum to explain the Act and its own Code of Practice to guide people about how to use it.[57]

> In this chapter, as throughout the Code, a person's capacity (or lack of capacity) refers specifically to their capacity to make a particular decision at the time it needs to be made.

Quick summary

- Professionals may need to think about using the MHA to detain and treat somebody who lacks capacity to consent to treatment (rather than use the MCA), if:

  - it is not possible to give the person the care or treatment they need without doing something that might deprive them of their liberty

  - the person needs treatment that cannot be given under the MCA (for example, because the person has made a valid and applicable advance decision to refuse an essential part of treatment)

  - the person may need to be restrained in a way that is not allowed under the MCA

---

57 Department of Health & Welsh Office, *Mental Health Act 1983 Code of Practice* (TSO, 1999), www.dh.gov.uk/assetRoot/04/07/49/61/04074961.pdf

- it is not possible to assess or treat the person safely or effectively without treatment being compulsory (perhaps because the person is expected to regain capacity to consent, but might then refuse to give consent)

- the person lacks capacity to decide on some elements of the treatment but has capacity to refuse a vital part of it – and they have done so, or

- there is some other reason why the person might not get treatment, and they or somebody else might suffer harm as a result.

- Before making an application under the MHA, decision-makers should consider whether they could achieve their aims safely and effectively by using the MCA instead.

- Compulsory treatment under the MHA is not an option if:

- the patient's mental disorder does not justify detention in hospital, or

- the patient needs treatment only for a physical illness or disability.

- The MCA applies to people subject to the MHA in the same way as it applies to anyone else, with four exceptions:

- if someone is detained under the MHA, decision-makers cannot normally rely on the MCA to give treatment for mental disorder or make decisions about that treatment on that person's behalf

- if somebody can be treated for their mental disorder without their consent because they are detained under the MHA, healthcare staff can treat them even if it goes against an advance decision to refuse that treatment

- if a person is subject to guardianship, the guardian has the exclusive right to take certain decisions, including where the person is to live, and

- Independent Mental Capacity Advocates do not have to be involved in decisions about serious medical treatment or accommodation, if those decisions are made under the MHA.

- Healthcare staff cannot give psychosurgery (i.e. neurosurgery for mental disorder) to a person who lacks capacity to agree to it. This applies whether or not the person is otherwise subject to the MHA.

Who does the MHA apply to?

13.1 The MHA provides ways of assessing, treating and caring for people who have a serious mental disorder that puts them or other people at risk. It sets out when:

- people with mental disorders can be detained in hospital for assessment or treatment

- people who are detained can be given treatment for their mental disorder without their consent (it also sets out the safeguards people must get in this situation), and

- people with mental disorders can be made subject to guardianship or after-care under supervision to protect them or other people.

Chapter 13

What is the relationship between the Mental Capacity Act and the Mental Health Act 1983?

13.2 Most of the MHA does not distinguish between people who have the capacity to make decisions and those who do not. Many people covered by the MHA have the capacity to make decisions for themselves. Most people who lack capacity to make decisions about their treatment will never be affected by the MHA, even if they need treatment for a mental disorder.

13.3 But there are cases where decision-makers will need to decide whether to use the MHA or MCA, or both, to meet the needs of people with mental health problems who lack capacity to make decisions about their own treatment.

What are the MCA's limits?

13.4 Section 5 of the MCA provides legal protection for people who care for or treat someone who lacks capacity (see chapter 6). But they must follow the Act's principles and may only take action that is in a person's best interests (see chapter 5). This applies to care or treatment for physical and mental conditions. So it can apply to treatment for people with mental disorders, however serious those disorders are.

13.5 But section 5 does have its limits. For example, somebody using restraint only has protection if the restraint is:

- necessary to protect the person who lacks capacity from harm, and

- in proportion to the likelihood and seriousness of that harm.

13.6 There is no protection under section 5 for actions that deprive a person of their liberty (see chapter 6 for guidance). Similarly, the MCA does not allow giving treatment that goes against a valid and applicable advance decision to refuse treatment (see chapter 9).

13.7 None of these restrictions apply to treatment for mental disorder given under the MHA – but other restrictions do.

When can a person be detained under the MHA?

13.8 A person may be taken into hospital and detained for assessment under section 2 of the MHA for up to 28 days if:

- they have a mental disorder that is serious enough for them to be detained in a hospital for assessment (or for assessment followed by treatment) for at least a limited period, and

- they need to be detained to protect their health or safety, or to protect others.

13.9 A patient may be admitted to hospital and detained for treatment under section 3 of the MHA if:

- they have a mental illness, severe mental impairment, psychopathic disorder or mental impairment (the MHA sets out definitions for these last three terms)

- their mental disorder is serious enough to need treatment in hospital

- treatment is needed for the person's health or safety, or for the protection of other people – and it cannot be provided without detention under this section, and

- (if the person has a mental impairment or psychopathic disorder) treatment is likely to improve their condition or stop it getting worse.

13.10 Decision-makers should consider using the MHA if, in their professional judgment, they are not sure it will be possible, or sufficient, to rely on the MCA. They do not have to ask the Court of Protection to rule that the MCA does not apply before using the MHA.

13.11 If a clinician believes that they can safely assess or treat a person under the MCA, they do not need to consider using the MHA. In this situation, it would be difficult to meet the requirements of the MHA anyway.

13.12 It might be necessary to consider using the MHA rather than the MCA if:

- it is not possible to give the person the care or treatment they need without carrying out an action that might deprive them of their liberty

- the person needs treatment that cannot be given under the MCA (for example, because the person has made a valid and applicable advance decision to refuse all or part of that treatment)

- the person may need to be restrained in a way that is not allowed under the MCA

- it is not possible to assess or treat the person safely or effectively without treatment being compulsory (perhaps because the person is expected to regain capacity to consent, but might then refuse to give consent)

- the person lacks capacity to decide on some elements of the treatment but has capacity to refuse a vital part of it – and they have done so, or

- there is some other reason why the person might not get the treatment they need, and they or somebody else might suffer harm as a result.

Chapter 13

What is the relationship between the Mental Capacity Act and the Mental Health Act 1983?

13.13 But it is important to remember that a person cannot be treated under the MHA unless they meet the relevant criteria for being detained. Unless they are sent to hospital under Part 3 of the MHA in connection with a criminal offence, people can only be detained where:

- the conditions summarised in paragraph 13.8 or 13.9 are met

- the relevant people agree that an application is necessary (normally two doctors and an approved social worker), and

- (in the case of section 3) the patient's nearest relative has not objected to the application.

'Nearest relative' is defined in section 26 of the MHA. It is usually, but not always, a family member.

Scenario: Using the MHA

Mr Oliver has a learning disability. For the last four years, he has had depression from time to time, and has twice had treatment for it at a psychiatric hospital. He is now seriously depressed and his care workers are worried about him.

Mr Oliver's consultant has given him medication and is considering electro-convulsive therapy. The consultant thinks this care plan will only work if Mr Oliver is detained in hospital. This will allow close observation and Mr Oliver will be stopped if he tries to leave. The consultant thinks an application should be made under section 3 of the MHA.

The consultant also speaks to Mr Oliver's nearest relative, his mother. She asks why Mr Oliver needs to be detained when he has not needed to be in the past. But after she hears the consultant's reasons, she does not object to the application. An approved social worker makes the application and obtains a second medical recommendation. Mr Oliver is then detained and taken to hospital for his treatment for depression to begin.

13.14 Compulsory treatment under the MHA is not an option if:

- the patient's mental disorder does not justify detention in hospital, or
- the patient needs treatment only for a physical illness or disability.

13.15 There will be some cases where a person who lacks capacity cannot be treated either under the MHA or the MCA – even if the treatment is for mental disorder.

Chapter 13

What is the relationship between the Mental Capacity Act and the Mental Health Act 1983?

Scenario: Deciding whether to use the MHA or MCA

Mrs Carter is in her 80s and has dementia. Somebody finds her wandering in the street, very confused and angry. A neighbour takes her home and calls her doctor. At home, it looks like she has been deliberately smashing things. There are cuts on her hands and arms, but she won't let the doctor touch them, and she hasn't been taking her medication.

Her doctor wants to admit her to hospital for assessment. Mrs Carter gets angry and says that they'll never keep her in hospital. So the doctor thinks that it might be necessary to use the MHA. He arranges for an approved social worker to visit. The social worker discovers that Mrs Carter was expecting her son this morning, but he has not turned up. They find out that he has been delayed, but could not call because Mrs Carter's telephone has become unplugged.

When she is told that her son is on his way, Mrs Carter brightens up. She lets the doctor treat her cuts – which the doctor thinks it is in her best interests to do as soon as possible. When Mrs Carter's son arrives, the social worker explains the doctor is very worried, especially that Mrs Carter is not taking her medication. The son explains that he will help his mother take it in future. It is agreed that the MCA will allow him to do that. The social worker arranges to return a week later and calls the doctor to say that she thinks Mrs Carter can get the care she needs without being detained under the MHA. The doctor agrees.

How does the MCA apply to a patient subject to guardianship under the MHA?

13.16 Guardianship gives someone (usually a local authority social services department) the exclusive right to decide where a person should live – but in doing this they cannot deprive the person of their liberty. The guardian can also require the person to attend for treatment, work, training or education at specific times and places, and they can demand that a doctor, approved social worker or another relevant person have access to the person wherever they live. Guardianship can apply whether or not the person has the capacity to make decisions about care and treatment. It does not give anyone the right to treat the person without their permission or to consent to treatment on their behalf.

13.17 An application can be made for a person who has a mental disorder to be received into guardianship under section 7 of the MHA when:

- the situation meets the conditions summarised in paragraph 13.18
- the relevant people agree an application for guardianship should be made (normally two doctors and an approved social worker), and
- the person's nearest relative does not object.

13.18 An application can be made in relation to any person who is 16 years or over if:

- they have a mental illness, severe mental impairment, psychopathic disorder or mental impairment that is serious enough to justify guardianship (see paragraph 13.20 below), and
- guardianship is necessary in the interests of the welfare of the patient or to protect other people.

13.19 Applicants (usually approved social workers) and doctors supporting the application will need to determine whether they could achieve their aims without guardianship. For patients who lack capacity, the obvious alternative will be action under the MCA.

13.20 But the fact that the person lacks capacity to make relevant decision is not the only factor that applicants need to consider. They need to consider all the circumstances of the case. They may conclude that guardianship is the best option for a person with a mental disorder who lacks capacity to make those decisions if, for example:

- they think it is important that one person or authority should be in charge of making decisions about where the person should live (for example, where there have been long-running or difficult disagreements about where the person should live)
- they think the person will probably respond well to the authority and attention of a guardian, and so be more prepared to accept treatment for the mental disorder (whether they are able to consent to it or it is being provided for them under the MCA), or
- they need authority to return the person to the place they are to live (for example, a care home) if they were to go absent.

Decision-makers must never consider guardianship as a way to avoid applying the MCA.

13.21 A guardian has the exclusive right to decide where a person lives, so nobody else can use the MCA to arrange for the person to live elsewhere. Somebody who knowingly helps a person leave the place a guardian requires them to stay may be committing a criminal offence under the MHA. A guardian also has the exclusive power to require the person to attend set times and places for treatment, occupation, education or training. This does not stop other people using the MCA to make similar arrangements or to treat the person in their best interests. But people cannot use the MCA in any way that conflicts with decisions which a guardian has a legal right to make under the MHA. See paragraph 13.16 above for general information about a guardian's powers.

Chapter 13

What is the relationship between the Mental Capacity Act and the Mental Health Act 1983?

How does the MCA apply to a patient subject to after-care under supervision under the MHA?

13.22 When people are discharged from detention for medical treatment under the MHA, their responsible medical officer may decide to place them on after-care under supervision. The responsible medical officer is usually the person's consultant psychiatrist. Another doctor and an approved social worker must support their application.

13.23 After-care under supervision means:

- the person can be required to live at a specified place (where they can be taken to and returned, if necessary)

- the person can be required to attend for treatment, occupation, education or training at a specific time and place (where they can be taken, if necessary), and

- their supervisor, any doctor or approved social worker or any other relevant person must be given access to them wherever they live.

13.24 Responsible medical officers can apply for after-care under supervision under section 25A of the MHA if:

- the person is 16 or older and is liable to be detained in a hospital for treatment under section 3 (and certain other sections) of the MHA

- the person has a mental illness, severe mental impairment, psychopathic disorder or mental impairment

- without after-care under supervision the person's health or safety would be at risk of serious harm, they would be at risk of serious exploitation, or other people's safety would be at risk of serious harm, and

- after-care under supervision is likely to help make sure the person gets the after-care services they need.

'Liable to be detained' means that a hospital is allowed to detain them. Patients who are liable to be detained are not always actually in hospital, because they may have been given permission to leave hospital for a time.

13.25 After-care under supervision can be used whether or not the person lacks capacity to make relevant decisions. But if a person lacks capacity, decision-makers will need to decide whether action under the MCA could achieve their aims before making an application. The kinds of cases in which after-care under supervision might be considered for patients who lack capacity to take decisions about their own care and treatment are similar to those for guardianship.

How does the Mental Capacity Act affect people covered by the Mental Health Act?

13.26 There is no reason to assume a person lacks capacity to make their own decisions just because they are subject (under the MHA) to:

- detention
- guardianship, or
- after-care under supervision.

13.27 People who lack capacity to make specific decisions are still protected by the MCA even if they are subject to the MHA (this includes people who are subject to the MHA as a result of court proceedings). But there are four important exceptions:

- if someone is liable to be detained under the MHA, decision-makers cannot normally rely on the MCA to give mental health treatment or make decisions about that treatment on someone's behalf
- if somebody can be given mental health treatment without their consent because they are liable to be detained under the MHA, they can also be given mental health treatment that goes against an advance decision to refuse treatment
- if a person is subject to guardianship, the guardian has the exclusive right to take certain decisions, including where the person is to live, and

- Independent Mental Capacity Advocates do not have to be involved in decisions about serious medical treatment or accommodation, if those decisions are made under the MHA.

Chapter 13

What is the relationship between the Mental Capacity Act and the Mental Health Act 1983?

What are the implications for people who need treatment for a mental disorder?

13.28 Subject to certain conditions, Part 4 of the MHA allows doctors to give patients who are liable to be detained treatment for mental disorders without their consent – whether or not they have the capacity to give that consent. Paragraph 13.31 below lists a few important exceptions.

13.29 Where Part 4 of the MHA applies, the MCA cannot be used to give medical treatment for a mental disorder to patients who lack capacity to consent. Nor can anyone else, like an attorney or a deputy, use the MCA to give consent for that treatment. This is because Part 4 of the MHA already allows clinicians, if they comply with the relevant rules, to give patients medical treatment for mental disorder even though they lack the capacity to consent. In this context, medical treatment includes nursing and care, habilitation and rehabilitation under medical supervision.

13.30 But clinicians treating people for mental disorder under the MHA cannot simply ignore a person's capacity to consent to treatment. As a matter of good practice (and in some cases in order to comply with the MHA) they will always need to assess and record:

- whether patients have capacity to consent to treatment, and

- if so, whether they have consented to or refused that treatment.

For more information, see the MHA Code of Practice.

13.31 Part 4 of the MHA does not apply to patients:

- admitted in an emergency under section 4(4)(a) of the MHA, following a single medical recommendation and awaiting a second recommendation

- temporarily detained (held in hospital) under section 5 of the MHA while awaiting an application for detention under section 2 or section 3

- remanded by a court to hospital for a report on their medical condition under section 35 of the MHA

- detained under section 37(4), 135 or 136 of the MHA in a place of safety, or

- who have been conditionally discharged by the Mental Health Review Tribunal (and not recalled to hospital).

13.32 Since the MHA does not allow treatment for these patients without their consent, the MCA applies in the normal way, even if the treatment is for mental disorder.

13.33 Even when the MHA allows patients to be treated for mental disorders, the MCA applies in the normal way to treatment for physical disorders. But sometimes healthcare staff may decide to focus first on treating a detained patient's mental disorder in the hope that they will get back the capacity to make a decision about treatment for the physical disorder.

13.34 Where people are subject to guardianship or after-care under supervision under the MHA, the MCA applies as normal to all treatment. Guardianship and after-care under supervision do not give people the right to treat patients without consent.

Scenario: Using the MCA to treat a patient who is detained under the MHA

Mr Peters is detained in hospital under section 3 of the MHA and is receiving treatment under Part 4 of the MHA. Mr Peters has paranoid schizophrenia, delusions, hallucinations and thought disorder. He refuses all medical treatment. Mr Peters has recently developed blood in his urine and staff persuaded him to have an ultrasound scan. The scan revealed suspected renal carcinoma.

His consultant believes that he needs a CT scan and treatment for the carcinoma. But Mr Peters refuses a general anaesthetic and other medical procedures. The consultant assesses Mr Peters as lacking capacity to consent to treatment under the MCA's test of capacity. The MHA is not relevant here, because the CT scan is not part of Mr Peters' treatment for mental disorder.

Under section 5 of the MCA, doctors can provide treatment without consent. But they must follow the principles of the Act and believe that treatment is in Mr Peters' best interests.

How does the Mental Health Act affect advance decisions to refuse treatment?

Chapter 13

What is the relationship between the Mental Capacity Act and the Mental Health Act 1983?

13.35 The MHA does not affect a person's advance decision to refuse treatment, unless Part 4 of the MHA means the person can be treated for mental disorder without their consent. In this situation healthcare staff can treat patients for their mental disorder, even if they have made an advance decision to refuse such treatment.

13.36 But even then healthcare staff must treat a valid and applicable advance decision as they would a decision made by a person with capacity at the time they are asked to consent to treatment. For example, they should consider whether they could use a different type of treatment which the patient has not refused in advance. If healthcare staff do not follow an advance decision, they should record in the patient's notes why they have chosen not to follow it.

13.37 Even if a patient is being treated without their consent under Part 4 of the MHA, an advance decision to refuse other forms of treatment is still valid. Being subject to guardianship or after-care under supervision does not affect an advance decision in any way. See chapter 9 for further guidance on advance decisions to refuse treatment.

Scenario: Deciding on whether to follow an advance decision to refuse treatment

Miss Khan gets depression from time to time and has old physical injuries that cause her pain. She does not like the side effects of medication, and manages her health through diet and exercise. She knows that healthcare staff might doubt her decision-making capacity when she is depressed. So she makes an advance decision to refuse all medication for her physical pain and depression.

A year later, she gets major depression and is detained under the MHA. Her GP (family doctor) tells her responsible medical officer (RMO) at the hospital about her advance decision. But Miss Khan's condition gets so bad that she will not discuss treatment. So the RMO decides to prescribe medication for her depression, despite her advance decision. This is possible because Miss Khan is detained under the MHA.

The RMO also believes that Miss Khan now lacks capacity to consent to medication for her physical pain. He assesses the validity of the advance decision to refuse medication for the physical pain. Her GP says that Miss Khan seemed perfectly well when she made the decision and seemed to understand what it meant. In the GP's view, Miss Khan had the capacity to make the advance decision. The RMO decides that the advance decision is valid and applicable, and does not prescribe medication for Miss Khan's pain – even though he thinks it would be in her best interests. When Miss Khan's condition improves, the consultant will be able to discuss whether she would like to change her mind about treatment for her physical pain.

Does the MHA affect the duties of attorneys and deputies?

13.38 In general, the MHA does not affect the powers of attorneys and deputies. But there are two exceptions:

- they will not be able to give consent on a patient's behalf for treatment under Part 4 of the MHA, where the patient is liable to be detained under the MHA (see 13.28–13.34 above), and

- they will not be able to take decisions:

    - about where a person subject to guardianship should live, or

    - that conflict with decisions that a guardian has a legal right to make.

13.39 Being subject to the MHA does not stop patients creating new Lasting Powers of Attorney (if they have the capacity to do so). Nor does it stop the Court of Protection from appointing a deputy for them.

Chapter 13

What is the relationship between the Mental Capacity Act and the Mental Health Act 1983?

13.40 In certain cases, people subject to the MHA may be required to meet specific conditions relating to:

- leave of absence from hospital

- after-care under supervision, or

- conditional discharge.

Conditions vary from case to case, but could include a requirement to:

- live in a particular place

- maintain contact with health services, or

- avoid a particular area.

13.41 If an attorney or deputy takes a decision that goes against one of these conditions, the patient will be taken to have gone against the condition. The MHA sets out the actions that could be taken in such circumstances. In the case of leave of absence or conditional discharge, this might involve the patient being recalled to hospital.

13.42 Attorneys and deputies are able to exercise patients' rights under the MHA on their behalf, if they have the relevant authority. In particular, some personal welfare attorneys and deputies may be able to apply to the Mental Health Review Tribunal (MHRT) for the patient's discharge from detention, guardianship or after-care under supervision.

13.43 The MHA also gives various rights to a patient's nearest relative. These include the right to:

- insist that a local authority social services department instructs an approved social worker to consider whether the patient should be made subject to the MHA

- apply for the patient to be admitted to hospital or guardianship

- object to an application for admission for treatment

- order the patient's discharge from hospital (subject to certain conditions) and

- order the patient's discharge from guardianship.

13.44 Attorneys and deputies may not exercise these rights, unless they are themselves the nearest relative. If the nearest relative and an attorney or deputy disagree, it may be helpful for them to discuss the issue, perhaps with the assistance of the patient's clinicians or social worker. But ultimately they have different roles and both must act as they think best. An attorney or deputy must act in the patient's best interests.

13.45 It is good practice for clinicians and others involved in the assessment or treatment of patients under the MHA to try to find out if the person has an attorney or deputy. But this may not always be possible. So attorneys and deputies should contact either:

- the healthcare professional responsible for the patient's treatment (generally known as the patient's RMO)

- the managers of the hospital where the patient is detained

- the person's guardian (normally the local authority social services department), or

- the person's supervisor (if the patient is subject to after-care under supervision).

Hospitals that treat detained patients normally have a Mental Health Act Administrator's office, which may be a useful first point of contact.

Does the MHA affect when Independent Mental Capacity Advocates must be instructed?

13.46 As explained in chapter 10, there is no duty to instruct an Independent Mental Capacity Advocate (IMCA) for decisions about serious medical treatment which is to be given under Part 4 of the MHA. Nor is there a duty to do so in respect of a move into accommodation, or a change of accommodation, if the person in question is to be required to live in it because of an obligation under the MHA. That obligation might be a condition of leave of absence or conditional discharge from hospital or a requirement imposed by a guardian or a supervisor.

13.47 However, the rules for instructing an IMCA for patients subject to the MHA who might undergo serious medical treatment not related to their mental disorder are the same as for any other patient.

13.48 The duty to instruct an IMCA would also apply as normal if accommodation is being planned as part of the after-care under section 117 of the MHA following the person's discharge from detention (and the person is not going to be required to live in it as a condition of after-care under supervision). This is because the person does not have to accept that accommodation.

Chapter 13

What is the relationship between the Mental Capacity Act and the Mental Health Act 1983?

What is the effect of section 57 of the Mental Health Act on the MCA?

13.49 Section 57 of the MHA states that psychosurgery (neurosurgery for mental disorder) requires:

- the consent of the patient, and

- the approval of an independent doctor and two other people appointed by the Mental Health Act Commission.

Psychosurgery is any surgical operation that destroys brain tissue or the function of brain tissue.

13.50 The same rules apply to other treatments specified in regulations under section 57. Currently, the only treatment included in regulations is the surgical implantation of hormones to reduce a man's sex drive.

13.51 The combined effect of section 57 of the MHA and section 28 of the MCA is, effectively, that a person who lacks the capacity to consent to one of these treatments for mental disorder may never be given it. Healthcare staff cannot use the MCA as an alternative way of giving these kinds of treatment. Nor can an attorney or deputy give permission for them on a person's behalf.

What changes does the Government plan to make to the MHA and the MCA?

13.52 The Government has introduced a Mental Health Bill into Parliament in order to modernise the MHA. Among the changes it proposes to make are:

- some amendments to the criteria for detention, including a new requirement that appropriate medical treatment be available for patients before they can be detained for treatment

- the introduction of supervised treatment in the community for suitable patients following a period of detention and treatment in hospital. This will help make sure that patients get the treatment they need and help stop them relapsing and returning to hospital

- the replacement of the approved social worker with the approved mental health professional. This will open up the possibility of approved mental healthcare professionals being drawn from other disciplines as well as social work. Other changes will open up the possibility of clinicians who are not doctors being approved to take on the role of the responsible medical officer. This role will be renamed the responsible clinician.

- provisions to make it possible for patients to apply to the county court for an unsuitable nearest relative to be replaced, and

- the abolition of after-care under supervision.

13.53 The Bill will also amend the MCA to introduce new procedures and provisions to make relevant decisions but who need to be deprived of their liberty, in their best interests, otherwise than under the Mental Health Act 1983 (the so-called 'Bournewood provisions').[58]

13.54 This chapter, as well as chapter 6, will be fully revised in due course to reflect those changes. Information about the Government's current proposals in respect of the Bournewood safeguards is available on the Department of Health website. This information includes draft illustrative Code of Practice guidance about the proposed safeguards.[59]

13.55 In the meantime, people taking decisions under both the MCA and the MHA must base those decisions on the Acts as they stand now.

---

[58] This refers to the European Court of Human Rights judgement (5 October 2004) in the case of *HL v The United Kingdom* (Application no, 45508/99).

[59] See www.dh.gov.uk/PublicationsAndStatistics/Publications/ PublicationsPolicyAndGuidance/PublicationsPolicyAndGuidanceArticle/fs/en?CONTENT_ ID=4141656&chk=jlw07L

14 What means of protection exist for people who lack capacity to make decisions for themselves?

This chapter describes the different agencies that exist to help make sure that adults who lack capacity to make decisions for themselves are protected from abuse. It also explains the services those agencies provide and how they supervise people who provide care for or make decisions on behalf of people who lack capacity. Finally, it explains what somebody should do if they suspect that somebody is abusing a vulnerable adult who lacks capacity.

> In this chapter, as throughout the Code, a person's capacity (or lack of capacity) refers specifically to their capacity to make a particular decision at the time it needs to be made.

Quick summary

- Always report suspicions of abuse of a person who lacks capacity to the relevant agency.

Concerns about an appointee

- When someone is concerned about the collection or use of social security benefits by an appointee on behalf a person who lacks capacity, they should contact the local Jobcentre Plus. If the appointee is for someone who is over the age of 60, contact The Pension Service.

Concerns about an attorney or deputy

- If someone is concerned about the actions of an attorney or deputy, they should contact the Office of the Public Guardian.

Concerns about a possible criminal offence

- If there is a good reason to suspect that someone has committed a crime against a vulnerable person, such as theft or physical or sexual assault, contact the police.
- In addition, social services should also be contacted, so that they can support the vulnerable person during the investigation.

Concerns about possible ill-treatment or wilful neglect

- The Act introduces new criminal offences of ill treatment or wilful neglect of a person who lacks capacity to make relevant decisions (section 44).
- If someone is not being looked after properly, contact social services.
- In serious cases, contact the police.

Concerns about care standards

- In cases of concern about the standard of care in a care home or an adult placement scheme, or about the care provided by a home care worker, contact social services.
- It may also be appropriate to contact the Commission for Social Care Inspection (in England) or the Care and Social Services Inspectorate for Wales.

Concerns about healthcare or treatment

- If someone is concerned about the care or treatment given to the person in any NHS setting (such as an NHS hospital or clinic) contact the managers of the service.
- It may also be appropriate to make a formal complaint through the NHS complaints procedure (see chapter 15).

What is abuse?

14.1   The word 'abuse' covers a wide range of actions. In some cases, abuse is clearly deliberate and intentionally unkind. But sometimes abuse happens because somebody does not know how to act correctly – or they haven't got appropriate help and support. It is important to prevent abuse, wherever possible. If somebody is abused, it is important to investigate the abuse and take steps to stop it happening.

14.2   Abuse is anything that goes against a person's human and civil rights. This includes sexual, physical, verbal, financial and emotional abuse. Abuse can be:

- a single act
- a series of repeated acts
- a failure to provide necessary care, or
- neglect.

Abuse can take place anywhere (for example, in a person's own home, a care home or a hospital).

14.3   The main types of abuse are:

Chapter 14

What means of
protection exist
for people who
lack capacity to
make decisions
for themselves?

Type of abuse	Examples
Financial	• theft • fraud • undue pressure • misuse of property, possessions or benefits • dishonest gain of property, possessions or benefits.
Physical	• slapping, pushing, kicking or other forms of violence • misuse of medication (for example, increasing dosage to make someone drowsy) • inappropriate punishments (for example, not giving someone a meal because they have been 'bad').
Sexual	• rape • sexual assault • sexual acts without consent (this includes if a person is not able to give consent or the abuser used pressure).
Psychological	• emotional abuse • threats of harm, restraint or abandonment • refusing contact with other people • intimidation • threats to restrict someone's liberty.
Neglect and acts of omission	• ignoring the person's medical or physical care needs • failing to get healthcare or social care • withholding medication, food or heating.

14.4   The Department of Health and the National Assembly for Wales have produced separate guidance on protecting vulnerable adults from abuse. *No secrets*[60] (England) and *In safe hands*[61] (Wales) both define vulnerable adults as people aged 18 and over who:

- need community care services due to a mental disability, other disability, age or illness, and

- may be unable to take care of themselves or protect themselves against serious harm or exploitation.

This description applies to many people who lack capacity to make decisions for themselves.

14.5   Anyone who thinks that someone might be abusing a vulnerable adult who lacks capacity should:

- contact the local social services (see paragraphs 14.27–14.28 below)

- contact the Office of the Public Guardian (see paragraph 14.8 below), or

- seek advice from a relevant telephone helpline[62] or through the Community Legal Service.[63]

Full contact details are provided in Annex A.

14.6   In most cases, local adult protection procedures will say who should take action (see paragraphs 14.28–14.29 below). But some abuse will be a criminal offence, such as physical assault, sexual assault or rape, theft, fraud and some other forms of financial exploitation. In these cases, the person who suspects abuse should contact the police urgently. The criminal investigation may take priority over all other forms of investigation. So all agencies will have to work together to plan the best way to investigate possible abuse.

---

[60] Department of Health and Home Office, *No secrets: Guidance on developing and implementing multi-agency policies and procedures to protect vulnerable adults from abuse*, (2000) www.dh.gov.uk/assetRoot/04/07/45/40/04074540.pdf

[61] National Assembly for Wales, *In safe hands: Implementing adult protection procedures in Wales* (2000), http://new.wales.gov.uk.about.departments/dhss/publications/social_services_publications/reports/insafehands?lang=en

[62] For example, the Action on Elder Abuse (0808 808 8141), Age Concern (0800 009966) or CarersLine (0808 808 7777)

[63] Community Legal Service Direct www.clsdirect.org.uk

14.7 The Fraud Act 2006 (due to come into force in 2007) creates a new offence of 'fraud by abuse of position'. This new offence may apply to a range of people, including:

Chapter 14

What means of protection exist for people who lack capacity to make decisions for themselves?

- attorneys under a Lasting Power of Attorney (LPA) or an Enduring Power of Attorney (EPA), or

- deputies appointed by the Court of Protection to make financial decisions on behalf of a person who lacks capacity.

Attorneys and deputies may be guilty of fraud if they dishonestly abuse their position, intend to benefit themselves or others, and cause loss or expose a person to the risk of loss. People who suspect fraud should report the case to the police.

How does the Act protect people from abuse?

The Office of the Public Guardian

14.8 Section 57 of the Act creates a new Public Guardian, supported by staff of the Office of the Public Guardian (OPG). The Public Guardian helps protect people who lack capacity by:

- setting up and managing a register of LPAs

- setting up and managing a register of EPAs

- setting up and managing a register of court orders that appoint deputies

- supervising deputies, working with other relevant organisations (for example, social services, if the person who lacks capacity is receiving social care)

- sending Court of Protection Visitors to visit people who may lack capacity to make particular decisions and those who have formal powers to act on their behalf (see paragraphs 14.10–14.11 below)

- receiving reports from attorneys acting under LPAs and from deputies

- providing reports to the Court of Protection, as requested, and

- dealing with representations (including complaints) about the way in which attorneys or deputies carry out their duties.

14.9 Section 59 of the Act creates a Public Guardian Board to oversee and review how the Public Guardian carries out these duties.

Court of Protection Visitors

14.10 The role of a Court of Protection Visitor is to provide independent advice to the court and the Public Guardian. They advise on how anyone given power under the Act should be, and is, carrying out their duties and responsibilities. There are two types of visitor: General Visitors and Special Visitors. Special visitors are registered medical practitioners with relevant expertise. The court or Public Guardian can send whichever type of visitor is most appropriate to visit and interview a person who may lack capacity. Visitors can also interview attorneys or deputies and inspect any relevant healthcare or social care records. Attorneys and deputies must co-operate with the visitors and provide them with all relevant information. If attorneys or deputies do not co-operate, the court can cancel their appointment, where it thinks that they have not acted in the person's best interests.

Scenario: Using a General Visitor

Mrs Quinn made an LPA appointing her nephew, Ian, as her financial attorney. She recently lost capacity to make her own financial decisions, and Ian has registered the LPA. He has taken control of Mrs Quinn's financial affairs.

But Mrs Quinn's niece suspects that Ian is using Mrs Quinn's money to pay off his own debts. She contacts the OPG, which sends a General Visitor to visit Mrs Quinn and Ian. The visitor's report will assess the facts. It might suggest the case go to court to consider whether Ian has behaved in a way which:

- goes against his authority under the LPA, or
- is not in Mrs Quinn's best interests.

The Public Guardian will decide whether the court should be involved in the matter. The court will then decide if it requires further evidence. If it thinks that Ian is abusing his position, the court may cancel the LPA.

14.11 Court of Protection Visitors have an important part to play in investigating possible abuse. But their role is much wider than this. They can also check on the general wellbeing of the person who lacks capacity, and they can give support to attorneys and deputies who need help to carry out their duties.

How does the Public Guardian oversee LPAs?

Chapter 14

What means of protection exist for people who lack capacity to make decisions for themselves?

14.12 An LPA is a private arrangement between the donor and the attorney (see chapter 7). Donors should only choose attorneys that they can trust. The OPG provides information to help potential donors understand:

- the impact of making an LPA
- what they can give an attorney authority to do
- what to consider when choosing an attorney.

14.13 The Public Guardian must make sure that an LPA meets the Act's requirements. Before registering an LPA, the OPG will check documentation. For property and affairs LPAs, it will check whether an attorney appointed under the LPA is bankrupt since this would revoke the authority.

14.14 The Public Guardian will not usually get involved once somebody has registered an LPA – unless someone is worried about how an attorney is carrying out their duties. If concerns are raised about an attorney, the OPG works closely with organisations such as local authorities and NHS Trusts to carry out investigations.

How does the Public Guardian supervise deputies?

14.15 Individuals do not choose who will act as a deputy for them. The court will make the decision. There are measures to make sure that the court appoints an appropriate deputy. The OPG will then supervise deputies and support them in carrying out their duties, while also making sure they do not abuse their position.

14.16 When a case comes before the Court of Protection, the Act states that the court should make a decision to settle the matter rather than appoint a deputy, if possible. Deputies are most likely to be needed for financial matters where someone needs continued authority to make decisions about the person's money or other assets. It will be easier for the courts to make decisions in cases where a one-off decision is needed about a person's welfare, so there are likely to be fewer personal welfare deputies. But there will be occasions where ongoing decisions about a person's welfare will be required, and so the court will appoint a personal welfare deputy (see chapter 8).

Scenario: Appointing deputies

Peter was in a motorbike accident that left him permanently and seriously brain-damaged. He has minimal awareness of his surroundings and an assessment has shown that he lacks capacity to make most decisions for himself.

Somebody needs to make several decisions about what treatment Peter needs and where he should be treated. His parents feel that healthcare staff do not always consider their views in decisions about what treatment is in Peter's best interests. So they make an application to the court to be appointed as joint personal welfare deputies.

There will be many care or treatment decisions for Peter in the future. The court decides it would not be practical to make a separate decision on each of them. It also thinks Peter needs some continuity in decision-making. So it appoints Peter's parents as joint personal welfare deputies.

14.17 The OPG may run checks on potential deputies if requested to by the court. It will carry out a risk assessment to determine what kind of supervision a deputy will need once they are appointed.

14.18 Deputies are accountable to the court. The OPG supervises the deputy's actions on the court's behalf, and the court may want the deputy to provide financial accounts or other reports to the OPG. The Public Guardian deals with complaints about the way deputies carry out their duties. It works with other relevant agencies to investigate them. Chapter 8 gives detailed information about the responsibilities of deputies.

What happens if someone says they are worried about an attorney or deputy?

14.19 Many people who lack capacity are likely to get care or support from a range of agencies. Even when an attorney or deputy is acting on behalf of a person who lacks capacity, the other carers still have a responsibility to the person to provide care and act in the person's best interests. Anybody who is caring for a person who lacks capacity, whether in a paid or unpaid role, who is worried about how attorneys or deputies carry out their duties should contact the Public Guardian.

Chapter 14

What means of
protection exist
for people who
lack capacity to
make decisions
for themselves?

14.20 The OPG will not always be the most appropriate organisation to investigate all complaints. It may investigate a case jointly with:

- healthcare or social care professionals

- social services

- NHS bodies

- the Commission for Social Care Inspection in England or the Care and Social Services Inspectorate for Wales (CSSIW)[64]

- the Healthcare Commission in England or the Healthcare Inspectorate for Wales, and

- in some cases, the police.

14.21 The OPG will usually refer concerns about personal welfare LPAs or personal welfare deputies to the relevant agency. In certain circumstances it will alert the police about a case. When it makes a referral, the OPG will make sure that the relevant agency keeps it informed of the action it takes. It will also make sure that the court has all the information it needs to take possible action against the attorney or deputy.

14.22 Examples of situations in which a referral might be necessary include where:

- someone has complained that a welfare attorney is physically abusing a donor – the OPG would refer this case to the relevant local authority adult protection procedures and possibly the police

- the OPG has found that a solicitor appointed as a financial deputy for an elderly woman has defrauded her estate – the OPG would refer this case to the police and the Law Society Consumer Complaints Service.

How does the Act deal with ill treatment and wilful neglect?

14.23 The Act introduces two new criminal offences: ill treatment and wilful neglect of a person who lacks capacity to make relevant decisions (section 44). The offences may apply to:

---

[64] In April 2007, the Care Standards Inspectorate for Wales (CSIW) and the Social Services Inspectorate for Wales (SSIW) came together to form the Care and Social Services Inspectorate for Wales.

- anyone caring for a person who lacks capacity – this includes family carers, healthcare and social care staff in hospital or care homes and those providing care in a person's home
- an attorney appointed under an LPA or an EPA, or
- a deputy appointed for the person by the court.

14.24 These people may be guilty of an offence if they ill-treat or wilfully neglect the person they care for or represent. Penalties will range from a fine to a sentence of imprisonment of up to five years – or both.

14.25 Ill treatment and neglect are separate offences.[65] For a person to be found guilty of ill treatment, they must either:

- have deliberately ill-treated the person, or
- be reckless in the way they were ill-treating the person or not.

It does not matter whether the behaviour was likely to cause, or actually caused, harm or damage to the victim's health.

14.26 The meaning of 'wilful neglect' varies depending on the circumstances. But it usually means that a person has deliberately failed to carry out an act they knew they had a duty to do.

Scenario: Reporting abuse

Norma is 95 and has Alzheimer's disease. Her son, Brendan, is her personal welfare attorney under an LPA. A district nurse has noticed that Norma has bruises and other injuries. She suspects Brendan may be assaulting his mother when he is drunk. She alerts the police and the local Adult Protection Committee.

Following a criminal investigation, Brendan is charged with ill-treating his mother. The Public Guardian applies to the court to cancel the LPA. Social services start to make alternative arrangements for Norma's care.

---

[65] *R v Newington (1990) 91 Cr App R 247, CA*

What other measures protect people from abuse?

Chapter 14

What means of
protection exist
for people who
lack capacity to
make decisions
for themselves?

14.27 Local agencies have procedures that allow them to work together (called multi-agency working) to protect vulnerable adults – in care settings and elsewhere. Most areas have Adult Protection Committees. These committees:

- create policy (including reporting procedures)
- oversee investigations and other activity between agencies
- carry out joint training, and
- monitor and review progress.

Other local authorities have developed multi-agency Adult Protection Procedures, which are managed by a dedicated Adult Protection Co-ordinator.

14.28 Adult Protection Committees and Procedures (APCP) involve representatives from the NHS, social services, housing, the police and other relevant agencies. In England, they are essential points of contact for anyone who suspects abuse or ill treatment of a vulnerable adult. They can also give advice to the OPG if it is uncertain whether an intervention is necessary in a case of suspected abuse. In Wales, APCPs are not necessarily points of contact themselves, but they publish details of points of contact.

Who should check that staff are safe to work with vulnerable adults?

14.29 Under the Safeguarding Vulnerable Groups Act 2006, criminal record checks are now compulsory for staff who:

- have contact with service users in registered care homes
- provide personal care services in someone's home, and
- are involved in providing adult placement schemes.

14.30 Potential employers must carry out a pre-employment criminal record check with the Criminal Records Bureau (CRB) for all potential new healthcare and social care staff. This includes nursing agency staff and home care agency staff.

See Annex A for sources of more detailed information.

14.31 The Protection of Vulnerable Adults (POVA) list has the names of people who have been barred from working with vulnerable adults (in England and Wales). Employers providing care in a residential setting or a person's own home must check whether potential employees are on the list.[66] If they are on the list, they must:

- refuse to employ them, or

- employ them in a position that does not give them regular contact with vulnerable adults.

It is an offence for anyone on the list to apply for a care position. In such cases, the employer should report the person making the application.

Who is responsible for monitoring the standard of care providers?

14.32 All care providers covered by the Care Standards Act 2000 must register with the Commission for Social Care Inspection in England (CSCI) or the Care and Social Services Inspectorate for Wales (CSSIW).[67] These agencies make sure that care providers meet certain standards. They require care providers to have procedures to protect people from harm or abuse. These agencies can take action if they discover dangerous or unsafe practices that could place people at risk.

14.33 Care providers must also have effective complaints procedures. If providers cannot settle complaints, CSCI or CSSIW can look into them.

14.34 CSCI or CSSIW assesses the effectiveness of local adult protection procedures. They will also monitor the arrangements local councils make in response to the Care Standards Act.

---

[66] www.dh.gov.uk/PublicationsAndStatistics/Publications/PublicationsPolicyAndGuidance/ PublicationsPolicyAndGuidanceArticle/fs/en?CONTENT_ID=4085855&chk=p0kQeS

[67] See note 64 above regarding the merger of the Care Standards Inspectorate for Wales and the Social Services Inspectorate for Wales.

What is an appointee, and who monitors them?

14.35 The Department for Work and Pensions (DWP) can appoint someone (an appointee) to claim and spend benefits on a person's behalf[68] if that person:

- gets social security benefits or pensions
- lacks the capacity to act for themselves
- has not made a property and affairs LPA or an EPA, and
- the court has not appointed a property and affairs deputy.

14.36 The DWP checks that an appointee is trustworthy. It also investigates any allegations that an appointee is not acting appropriately or in the person's interests. It can remove an appointee who abuses their position. Concerns about appointees should be raised with the relevant DWP agency (the local Jobcentre Plus, or if the person is aged 60 or over, The Pension Service).

Are there any other means of protection that people should be aware of?

14.37 There are a number of additional means that exist to protect people who lack capacity to make decisions for themselves. Healthcare and social care staff, attorneys and deputies should be aware of:

- National Minimum Standards (for example, for healthcare, care homes, and home care agencies) which apply to both England and Wales (see paragraph 14.38)
- National Service Frameworks, which set out national standards for specific health and care services for particular groups (for example, for mental health services[69] or services for older people[70])
- complaints procedures for all NHS bodies and local councils (see chapter 15)

Chapter 14

What means of protection exist for people who lack capacity to make decisions for themselves?

---

[68] www.dwp.gov.uk/publications/dwp/2005/gl21_apr.pdf

[69] www.dh.gov.uk/assetRoot/04/07/72/09/04077209.pdf and www.wales.nhs.uk/sites3/page.cfm?orgid=438&pid=11071

[70] www.dh.gov.uk/assetRoot/04/07/12/83/04071283.pdf and www.wales.nhs.uk/sites3/home.cfm?orgid=439&redirect=yes&CFID=298511&CFTOKEN=6985382

- Stop Now Orders (also known as Enforcement Orders) that allow consumer protection bodies to apply for court orders to stop poor trading practices (for example, unfair door-step selling or rogue traders).[71]

- The Public Interest Disclosure Act 1998, which encourages people to report malpractice in the workplace and protects people who report malpractice from being sacked or victimised.

14.38 Information about all national minimum standards are available on the CSCI[72] and Healthcare Commission websites[73] and the Welsh Assembly Government website. Chapter 15 gives guidance on complaints procedures. Individual local authorities will have their own complaints system in place.

---

[71] www.oft.gov.uk/Business/Legal/Stop+Now+Regulations.htm

[72] www.csci.org.uk/information_for_service_providers/national_minimum_standards/default.htm

[73] www.healthcarecommission.org.uk/_db/_documents/The_annual_health_check_in_2006_2007_assessing_and_rating_the_NHS_200609225143.pdf

15 What are the best ways to settle disagreements and disputes about issues covered in the Act?

Sometimes people will disagree about:

- a person's capacity to make a decision
- their best interests
- a decision someone is making on their behalf, or
- an action someone is taking on their behalf.

It is in everybody's interests to settle disagreements and disputes quickly and effectively, with minimal stress and cost. This chapter sets out the different options available for settling disagreements. It also suggests ways to avoid letting a disagreement become a serious dispute. Finally, it sets out when it might be necessary to apply to the Court of Protection and when somebody can get legal funding.

> In this chapter, as throughout the Code, a person's capacity (or lack of capacity) refers specifically to their capacity to make a particular decision at the time it needs to be made.

Quick summary

- When disagreements occur about issues that are covered in the Act, it is usually best to try and settle them before they become serious.
- Advocates can help someone who finds it difficult to communicate their point of view. (This may be someone who has been assessed as lacking capacity.)
- Some disagreements can be effectively resolved by mediation.
- Where there is a concern about healthcare or social care provided to a person who lacks capacity, there are formal and informal ways of complaining about the care or treatment.
- The Health Service Ombudsman or the Local Government Ombudsman (in England) or the Public Services Ombudsman (in Wales) can be asked to investigate some problems that have not been resolved through formal complaints procedures.

- Disputes about the finances of a person who lacks capacity should usually be referred to the Office of the Public Guardian (OPG).

- When other methods of resolving disagreements are not appropriate, the matter can be referred to the Court of Protection.

- There are some decisions that are so serious that the Court of Protection should always make them.

What options are there for settling disagreements?

15.1 Disagreements about healthcare, social or other welfare services may be between:

- people who have assessed a person as lacking capacity to make a decision and the person they have assessed (see chapter 4 for how to challenge an assessment of lack of capacity)

- family members or other people concerned with the care and welfare of a person who lacks capacity

- family members and healthcare or social care staff involved in providing care or treatment

- healthcare and social care staff who have different views about what is in the best interests of a person who lacks capacity.

15.2 In general, disagreements can be resolved by either formal or informal procedures, and there is more information on both in this chapter. However, there are some disagreements and some subjects that are so serious they can only be resolved by the Court of Protection.

15.3 It is usually best to try and settle disagreements before they become serious disputes. Many people settle them by communicating effectively and taking the time to listen and to address worries. Disagreements between family members are often best settled informally, or sometimes through mediation. When professionals are in disagreement with a person's family, it is a good idea to start by:

- setting out the different options in a way that is easy to understand

- inviting a colleague to talk to the family and offer a second opinion

- offering to get independent expert advice

- using an advocate to support and represent the person who lacks capacity

- arranging a case conference or meeting to discuss matters in detail
- listening to, acknowledging and addressing worries, and
- where the situation is not urgent, allowing the family time to think it over.

Further guidance on how to deal with problems without going to court may also be found in the Community Legal Services Information Leaflet 'Alternatives to Court'.[74]

Chapter 15

What are the best ways to settle disagreements and disputes about issues covered in the Act?

When is an advocate useful?

15.4 An advocate helps communicate the feelings and views of someone who has communication difficulties. The definition of advocacy set out in the Advocacy Charter adopted by most advocacy schemes is as follows: 'Advocacy is taking action to help people say what they want, secure their rights, represent their interests and obtain services they need. Advocates and advocacy schemes work in partnership with the people they support and take their side. Advocacy promotes social inclusion, equality and social justice.'[75]

An advocate may be able to help settle a disagreement simply by presenting a person's feelings to their family, carers or professionals. Most advocacy services are provided by the voluntary sector and are arranged at a local level. They have no link to any agency involved with the person.

15.5 Using advocates can help people who find it difficult to communicate (including those who have been assessed as lacking capacity) to:

- say what they want
- claim their rights
- represent their interests, and
- get the services they need.

15.6 Advocates may also be involved in supporting the person during mediation (see paragraphs 15.7–15.13 below) or helping with complaints procedures. Sometimes people who lack capacity or have been assessed as lacking capacity have a legal right to an advocate, for example:

---

[74] CLS (Community Legal Services) Direct Information Leaflet Number 23, www.clsdirect.org.uk/legalhelp/leaflet23.jsp?lang=en

[75] Advocacy across London, *Advocacy Charter* (2002)

- when making a formal complaint against the NHS (see paragraph 15.18), and

- where the Act requires the involvement of an Independent Mental Capacity Advocate (IMCA) (see chapter 10).

When is mediation useful?

15.7 A mediator helps people to come to an agreement that is acceptable to all parties. Mediation can help solve a problem at an early stage. It offers a wider range of solutions than the court can – and it may be less stressful for all parties, more cost-effective and quicker. People who come to an agreement through mediation are more likely to keep to it, because they have taken part in decision-making.

15.8 Mediators are independent. They have no personal interest in the outcome of a case. They do not make decisions or impose solutions. The mediator will decide whether the case is suitable for mediation. They will consider the likely chances of success and the need to protect the interests of the person who lacks capacity.

15.9 Any case that can be settled through negotiation is likely to benefit from mediation. It is most suitable when people are not communicating well or not understanding each other's point of view. It can improve relationships and stop future disputes, so it is a good option when it is in the person's interests for people to have a good relationship in the future.

Scenario: Using mediation

Mrs Roberts has dementia and lacks capacity to decide where she should live. She currently lives with her son. But her daughter has found a care home where she thinks her mother will get better care. Her brother disagrees.

Mrs Roberts is upset by this family dispute, and so her son and daughter decide to try mediation. The mediator believes that Mrs Roberts is able to communicate her feelings and agrees to take on the case. During the sessions, the mediator helps them to focus on their mother's best interests rather than imposing their own views. In the end, everybody agrees that Mrs Roberts should continue to live with her son. But they agree to review the situation again in six months to see if the care home might then be better for her.

15.10 In mediation, everybody needs to take part as equally as possible so that a mediator can help everyone involved to focus on the person's best interests. It might also be appropriate to involve an advocate to help communicate the wishes of the person who lacks capacity.

Chapter 15

What are the best ways to settle disagreements and disputes about issues covered in the Act?

15.11 The National Mediation Helpline[76] helps callers to identify an effective means of resolving their difficulty without going to court. It will arrange an appointment with a trained and accredited mediator. The Family Mediation Helpline[77] can provide information on family mediation and referrals to local family mediation services. Family mediators are trained to deal with the emotional, practical and financial needs of those going through relationship breakdown.

15.12 Healthcare and social care staff may also take part in mediation processes. But it may be more appropriate to follow the relevant healthcare or social care complaints procedures (see paragraphs 15.14–15.32).

15.13 In certain situations (mainly family mediation), legal aid may be available to fund mediation for people who meet the qualifying criteria (see paragraphs 15.38–15.44).

How can someone complain about healthcare?

15.14 There are formal and informal ways of complaining about a patient's healthcare or treatment. Healthcare staff and others need to know which methods are suitable in which situations.

15.15 In England, the Patient Advice and Liaison Service (PALS) provides an informal way of dealing with problems before they reach the complaints stage. PALS operate in every NHS and Primary Care Trust in England. They provide advice and information to patients (or their relatives or carers) to try to solve problems quickly. They can direct people to specialist support services (for example, advocates, mental health support teams, social services or interpreting services). PALS do not investigate complaints. Their role is to explain complaints procedures and direct people to the formal NHS complaints process, if necessary. NHS complaints procedures deal with complaints about something that happened in the past that requires an apology or explanation. A court cannot help in this situation, but court proceedings may be necessary in some clinical negligence cases (see paragraph 15.22).

---

[76] National Mediation Helpline, Tel: 0845 60 30 809, www.nationalmediationhelpline.com

[77] Family Mediation Helpline, Tel: 0845 60 26 627, www.familymediationhelpline.co.uk

15.16 In Wales, complaints advocates based at Community Health Councils provide advice and support to anyone with concerns about treatment they have had.

Disagreements about proposed treatments

15.17 If a case is not urgent, the supportive atmosphere of the PALS may help settle it. In Wales, the local Community Health Council may be able to help. But urgent cases about proposed serious treatment may need to go to the Court of Protection (see paragraphs 15.35–15.36).

Scenario: Disagreeing about treatment or an assessment

Mrs Thompson has Alzheimer's and does not want a flu jab. Her daughter thinks she should have the injection. The doctor does not want to go against the wishes of his patient, because he believes she has capacity to refuse treatment.

Mrs Thompson's daughter goes to PALS. A member of staff gives her information and advice about what is meant by capacity to consent to or refuse treatment, and tells her how to find out about the flu jab. The PALS staff speak to the doctor, and then they explain his clinical assessment to Mrs Thompson's daughter.

The daughter is still unhappy. PALS staff advise her that the Independent Complaints Advocacy Service can help if she wishes to make a formal complaint.

The formal NHS complaints procedure

15.18 The formal NHS complaints procedure deals with complaints about NHS services provided by NHS organisations or primary care practitioners. As a first step, people should try to settle a disagreement through an informal discussion between:

- the healthcare staff involved
- the person who may lack capacity to make the decision in question (with support if necessary)
- their carers, and
- any appropriate relatives.

If the person who is complaining is not satisfied, the Independent Complaints Advocacy Service (ICAS) may help. In Wales, the complaints advocates based at Community Health Councils will support and advise anyone who wants to make a complaint.

Chapter 15

What are the best ways to settle disagreements and disputes about issues covered in the Act?

15.19 In England, if the person is still unhappy after a local investigation, they can ask for an independent review by the Healthcare Commission. If the patient involved in the complaint was or is detained under the Mental Health Act 1983, the Mental Health Act Commission can be asked to look into the complaint. If people are still unhappy after this stage, they can go to the Health Service Ombudsman. More information on how to make a complaint in England is available from the Department of Health.

15.20 In Wales, if patients are still unhappy after a local investigation, they can ask for an independent review of their complaint by independent lay reviewers. After this, they can take their case to the Public Services Ombudsman for Wales. People can take their complaint direct to the Ombudsman if:

- the complaint is about care or treatment that took place after 1 April 2006, and

- they have tried to settle the problem locally first.

The Mental Health Act Commission may also investigate complaints about the care or treatment of detained patients in Wales, if attempts have been made to settle the complaint locally without success.

15.21 Regulations about first trying to settle complaints locally do not apply to NHS Foundation Trusts. But these Trusts are covered by the independent review stage operated by the Healthcare Commission and by the Health Service Ombudsman. People who have a complaint about an NHS Foundation Trust should contact the Trust for advice on how to make a complaint.

Cases of clinical negligence

15.22 The NHS Litigation Authority oversees all clinical negligence cases brought against the NHS in England. It actively encourages people to try other forms of settling complaints before going to court. The National Assembly for Wales also encourages people to try other forms of settling complaints before going to court.

How can somebody complain about social care?

15.23 The social services complaints procedure has been reformed. The reformed procedure came into effect on 1 September 2006 in England and on 1 April 2006 in Wales.

15.24 A service provider's own complaints procedure should deal with complaints about:

- the way in which care services are delivered
- the type of services provided, or
- a failure to provide services.

15.25 Care agencies contracted by local authorities or registered with the Commission for Social Care Inspection (CSCI) in England or Care and Social Services Inspectorate for Wales (CSSIW) are legally obliged to have their own written complaints procedures. This includes residential homes, agencies providing care in people's homes, nursing agencies and adult placement schemes. The procedures should set out how to make a complaint and what to do with a complaint that cannot be settled locally.

Local authority complaints procedures

15.26 For services contracted by a local authority, it may be more appropriate to use the local authority's complaints procedure. A simple example would be a situation where a local authority places a person in a care home and the person's family are not happy with the placement. If their complaint is not about the services the home provides (for example, it might be about the local authority's assessment of the person's needs), it might be more appropriate to use the local authority's complaints procedure.

15.27 As a first step, people should try to settle a disagreement through an informal discussion, involving:

- the professionals involved
- the person who may lack capacity to make the decision in question (with support if necessary)
- their carers, and
- any appropriate relatives.

15.28 If the person making the complaint is not satisfied, the local authority will carry out a formal investigation using its complaints procedure. In England, after this stage, a social service Complaints Review Panel can hear the case. In Wales complaints can be referred to the National Assembly for Wales for hearing by an independent panel.

Other complaints about social care

15.29 People can take their complaint to the CSCI in England or the CSSIW in Wales, if:

- the complaint is about regulations or national minimum standards not being met, and

- the complainants are not happy with the provider's own complaints procedure or the response to their complaint.

15.30 If a complaint is about a local authority's administration, it may be referred to the Commission for Local Administration in England (the Local Government Ombudsman) or the Public Services Ombudsman for Wales.

What if a complaint covers healthcare and social care?

15.31 Taking a complaint through NHS or local authority complaints procedures can be a complicated process – especially if the complaint covers a number of service providers or both healthcare and social care. In such situations, local authorities and the NHS must work together and agree which organisation will lead in handling the complaint. If a person is not happy with the outcome, they can take their case to the Health Service Ombudsman or to the Local Government Ombudsman (in England). There is guidance which sets out how organisations should work together to handle complaints that cover healthcare and social care (in England *Learning from Complaints* and in Wales *Listening and learning*). The Public Services Ombudsman for Wales handles complaints that cover both healthcare and social care.

Who can handle complaints about other welfare issues?

15.32 The Independent Housing Ombudsman deals with complaints about registered social landlords in England. This applies mostly to housing associations. But it also applies to many landlords who manage homes that were formerly run by local authorities and some private landlords. In Wales, the Public Services Ombudsman for Wales deals

Chapter 15

What are the best ways to settle disagreements and disputes about issues covered in the Act?

with complaints about registered social landlords. Complaints about local authorities may be referred to the Local Government Ombudsman in England or the Public Services Ombudsman for Wales. They look at complaints about decisions on council housing, social services, Housing Benefit and planning applications. More information about complaints to an Ombudsman is available on the relevant websites (see Annex A).

What is the best way to handle disagreement about a person's finances?

15.33 Some examples of disagreements about a person's finances are:

- disputes over the amount of money a person who lacks capacity should pay their carer

- disputes over whether a person who lacks capacity should sell their house

- somebody questioning the actions of a carer, who may be using the money of a person who lacks capacity inappropriately or without proper authority

- somebody questioning the actions of an attorney appointed under a Lasting Power of Attorney or an Enduring Power of Attorney or a deputy appointed by the court.

15.34 In all of the above circumstances, the most appropriate action would usually be to contact the Office of the Public Guardian (OPG) for guidance and advice. See chapter 14 for further details on the role of the OPG.

How can the Court of Protection help?

15.35 The Court of Protection deals with all areas of decision-making for adults who lack capacity to make particular decisions for themselves (see chapter 8 for more information about its roles and responsibilities). But the court is not always the right place to settle problems involving people who lack capacity. Other forms of settling disagreements may be more appropriate and less distressing.

15.36 There are some decisions that are so serious that the court should always make them. There are also other types of cases that the court should deal with when another method would generally not be suitable. See chapter 8 for more information about both kinds of cases.

Chapter 15

What are the best ways to settle disagreements and disputes about issues covered in the Act?

Right of Appeal

15.37 Section 53 of the Act describes the rights of appeal against any decision taken by the Court of Protection. There are further details in the Court of Protection Rules. It may be advisable for anyone who wishes to appeal a decision made by the court to seek legal advice.

Will public legal funding be available?

15.38 Depending on their financial situation, once the Act comes into force people may be entitled to:

- publicly funded legal advice from accredited solicitors or advice agencies

- legal representation before the new Court of Protection (in the most serious cases).

Information about solicitors and organisations who give advice on different areas of law is available from Community Legal Services Direct (CLS Direct).[78] Further information about legal aid and public funding can be obtained from the Legal Services Commission.[79] See Annex A for full contact details.

15.39 People who lack capacity to instruct a solicitor or conduct their own case will need a litigation friend. This person could be a relative, friend, attorney or the Official Solicitor (when no-one else is available). The litigation friend is able to instruct the solicitor and conduct the case on behalf of a person who lacks capacity to give instructions. If the person qualifies for public legal funding, the litigation friend can claim funding on their behalf.

---

[78] CLS Direct, Tel: 0845 345 4 345, www.clsdirect.org.uk

[79] www.legalservices.gov.uk

When can someone get legal help?

15.40 Legal help is a type of legal aid (public funding) that pays for advice and assistance on legal issues, including those affecting a person who lacks capacity. But it does not provide representation for a full court hearing, although there is a related form of funding called 'help at court' under which a legal representative can speak in court on a client's behalf on an informal basis. To qualify for legal help, applicants must show that:

- they get specific social security benefits, or they earn less than a specific amount and do not have savings or other financial assets in excess of a specific amount

- they would benefit sufficiently from legal advice to justify the amount it costs, and

- they cannot get another form of funding.

15.41 Legal help can include:

- help from a solicitor or other representative in writing letters

- in exceptional circumstances, getting a barrister's opinion, and

- assistance in preparing for Court of Protection hearings.

15.42 People cannot get legal help for making a Lasting Power of Attorney or an advance decision to refuse treatment. But they can get general help and information from the OPG. The OPG cannot give legal or specialist advice. For example, they will not be able to advise someone on what powers they should delegate to their attorney under an LPA.

When can someone get legal representation?

15.43 Public funding for legal representation in the Court of Protection will be available from solicitors with a relevant contract – but only for the most serious cases. To qualify, applicants will normally face the same test as for legal help to qualify financially (paragraph 15.40). They will generally have to satisfy more detailed criteria than applicants for legal help, relating, for instance, to their prospects of being successful, to whether legal representation is necessary and to the cost benefit of being represented. They will also have to establish that the case could not be brought or funded in another way and that there are not alternatives to court proceedings that should be explored first.

15.44 Serious personal welfare cases that were previously heard by the High Court will continue to have public funding for legal representation when they are transferred to the Court of Protection. These cases will normally be related to personal liberty, serious welfare decisions or medical treatment for a person who lacks capacity. But legal representation may also be available in other types of cases, depending on the particular circumstances.

Chapter 15

What are the best ways to settle disagreements and disputes about issues covered in the Act?

16 What rules govern access to information about a person who lacks capacity?

This chapter gives guidance on:

- what personal information about someone who lacks capacity people involved in their care have the right to see, and
- how they can get hold of that information.

This chapter is only a general guide. It does not give detailed information about the law. Nor does it replace professional guidance or the guidance of the Information Commissioner's Office on the Data Protection Act 1998 (this guidance is available on its website, see Annex A). Where necessary, people should take legal advice.

This chapter is mainly for people such as family carers and other carers, deputies and attorneys, who care for or represent someone who lacks capacity to make specific decisions and in particular, lacks capacity to allow information about them to be disclosed. Professionals have their own codes of conduct, and they may have the support of experts in their organisations.

> In this chapter, as throughout the Code, a person's capacity (or lack of capacity) refers specifically to their capacity to make a particular decision at the time it needs to be made.

Quick summary

Questions to ask when requesting personal information about someone who may lack capacity

- Am I acting under a Lasting Power of Attorney or as a deputy with specific authority?
- Does the person have capacity to agree that information can be disclosed? Have they previously agreed to disclose the information?
- What information do I need?

- Why do I need it?
- Who has the information?
- Can I show that:
  - I need the information to make a decision that is in the best interests of the person I am acting for, and
  - the person does not have the capacity to act for themselves?
- Do I need to share the information with anyone else to make a decision that is in the best interests of the person who lacks capacity?
- Should I keep a record of my decision or action?
- How long should I keep the information for?
- Do I have the right to request the information under section 7 of the Data Protection Act 1998?

Questions to ask when considering whether to disclose information

- Is the request covered by section 7 of the Data Protection Act 1998? Is the request being made by a formally authorised representative?

If not:

- Is the disclosure legal?
- Is the disclosure justified, having balanced the person's best interests and the public interest against the person's right to privacy?

Questions to ask to decide whether the disclosure is legal or justified

- Do I (or does my organisation) have the information?
- Am I satisfied that the person concerned lacks capacity to agree to disclosure?
- Does the person requesting the information have any formal authority to act on behalf of the person who lacks capacity?
- Am I satisfied that the person making the request:
  - is acting in the best interests of the person concerned?
  - needs the information to act properly?
  - will respect confidentiality?
  - will keep the information for no longer than necessary?
- Should I get written confirmation of these things?

Chapter 16

What rules govern access to information about a person who lacks capacity?

What laws and regulations affect access to information?

16.1 People caring for, or managing the finances of, someone who lacks capacity may need information to:

- assess the person's capacity to make a specific decision

- determine the person's best interests, and

- make appropriate decisions on the person's behalf.

16.2 The information they need varies depending on the circumstances. For example:

- a daughter providing full-time care for an elderly parent will make decisions based on her own experience and knowledge of her parent

- a deputy may need information from other people. For instance, if they were deciding whether a person needs to move into a care home or whether they should sell the person's home, they might need information from family members, the family doctor, the person's bank and their solicitor to make sure they are making the decision in the person's best interests.

16.3 Much of the information needed to make decisions under the Act is sensitive or confidential. It is regulated by:

- the Data Protection Act 1998

- the common law duty of confidentiality

- professional codes of conduct on confidentiality, and

- the Human Rights Act 1998 and European Convention on Human Rights, in particular Article 8 (the right to respect for private and family life), which means that it is only lawful to reveal someone's personal information if:

  – there is a legitimate aim in doing so

  – a democratic society would think it necessary to do so, and

  – the kind and amount of information disclosed is in relation to the need.

What information do people generally have a right to see?

16.4   Section 7 of the Data Protection Act 1998 gives everyone the right to see personal information that an organisation holds about them. They may also authorise someone else to access their information on their behalf. The person holding the information has a legal duty to release it. So, where possible, it is important to try to get a person's consent before requesting to see information about them.

16.5   A person may have the capacity to agree to someone seeing their personal information, even if they do not have the capacity to make other decisions. In some situations, a person may have previously given consent (while they still had capacity) for someone to see their personal information in the future.

16.6   Doctors and lawyers cannot share information about their clients, or that clients have given them, without the client's consent. Sometimes it is fair to assume that a doctor or lawyer already has someone's consent (for example, patients do not usually expect healthcare staff or legal professionals to get consent every time they share information with a colleague – but staff may choose to get clients' consent in writing when they begin treating or acting for that person). But in other circumstances, doctors and lawyers must get specific consent to 'disclose' information (share it with someone else).

16.7   If someone's capacity changes from time to time, the person needing the information may want to wait until that person can give their consent. Or they may decide that it is not necessary to get access to information at all, if the person will be able to make a decision on their own in the future.

16.8   If someone lacks the capacity to give consent, someone else might still be able to see their personal information. This will depend on:

- whether the person requesting the information is acting as an agent (a representative recognised by the law, such as a deputy or attorney) for the person who lacks capacity

- whether disclosure is in the best interests of the person who lacks capacity, and

- what type of information has been requested.

Chapter 16

What rules govern access to information about a person who lacks capacity?

When can attorneys and deputies ask to see personal information?

16.9 An attorney acting under a valid LPA or EPA (and sometimes a deputy) can ask to see information concerning the person they are representing, as long as the information applies to decisions the attorney has the legal right to make.

16.10 In practice, an attorney or deputy may only require limited information and may not need to make a formal request. In such circumstances, they can approach the information holder informally. Once satisfied that the request comes from an attorney or deputy (having seen appropriate authority), the person holding information should be able to release it. The attorney or deputy can still make a formal request for information in the future.

16.11 The attorney or deputy must treat the information confidentially. They should be extremely careful to protect it. If they fail to do so, the court can cancel the LPA or deputyship.

16.12 Before the Act came into effect, only a few receivers were appointed with the general authority to manage a person's property and affairs. So they needed specific authority from the Court of Protection to ask for access to the person's personal information. Similarly, a deputy who only has authority to act in specific areas only has the right to ask for information relating to decisions in those specific areas. For information relating to other areas, the deputy will need to apply to the Court of Protection.

16.13 Requests for personal information must be in writing, and there might be a fee. Information holders should release it promptly (always within 40 calendar days). Fees may be particularly high for getting copies of healthcare records – particularly where information may be in unusual formats (for example, x-rays). The maximum fee is currently £50. Complaints about a failure to comply with the Data Protection Act 1998 should be directed to the Information Commissioner's Office (see Annex A for contact details).

What limitations are there?

16.14 Attorneys and deputies should only ask for information that will help them make a decision they need to make on behalf of the person who lacks capacity. For example, if the attorney needs to know when the person should take medication, they should not ask to see the entire healthcare record. The person who releases information must make sure that an attorney or deputy has official authority (they may ask for proof of identity and appointment). When asking to see personal information, attorneys and deputies should bear in mind that their decision must always be in the best interests of the person who lacks capacity to make that decision.

Chapter 16

What rules govern access to information about a person who lacks capacity?

16.15 The attorney or deputy may not know the kind of information that someone holds about the person they are representing. So sometimes it might be difficult for them to make a specific request. They might even need to see all the information to make a decision. But again, the 'best interests' principle applies.

Scenario: Giving attorneys access to personal information

Mr Yapp is in the later stages of Alzheimer's disease. His son is responsible for Mr Yapp's personal welfare under a Lasting Power of Attorney. Mr Yapp has been in residential care for a number of years. But his son does not think that the home is able to meet his father's current needs as his condition has recently deteriorated.

The son asks to see his father's records. He wants specific information about his father's care, so that he can make a decision about his father's best interests. But the manager of the care home refuses, saying that the Data Protection Act stops him releasing personal information.

Mr Yapp's son points out that he can see his father's records, because he is his personal welfare attorney and needs the information to make a decision. The Data Protection Act 1998 requires the care home manager to provide access to personal data held on Mr Yapp.

16.16 The deputy or attorney may find that some information is held back (for example, when this contains references to people other than the person who lacks capacity). This might be to protect another person's privacy, if that person is mentioned in the records. It is unlikely that information relating to another person would help an attorney make a decision on behalf of the person who lacks capacity. The information holder might also be obliged to keep information about the other person confidential. There might be another reason why the person does not want information about them to be released. Under these circumstances, the attorney does not have the right to see that information.

16.17 An information holder should not release information if doing so would cause serious physical or mental harm to anyone – including the person the information is about. This applies to information on health, social care and education records.

16.18 The Information Commissioner's Office can give further details on:

- how to request personal information
- restrictions on accessing information, and
- how to appeal against a decision not to release information.

When can someone see information about healthcare or social care?

16.19 Healthcare and social care staff may disclose information about somebody who lacks capacity only when it is in the best interests of the person concerned to do so, or when there is some other, lawful reason for them to do so.

16.20 The Act's requirement to consult relevant people when working out the best interests of a person who lacks capacity will encourage people to share the information that makes a consultation meaningful. But people who release information should be sure that they are acting lawfully and that they can justify releasing the information. They need to balance the person's right to privacy with what is in their best interests or the wider public interest (see paragraphs 16.24–16.25 below).

16.21 Sometimes it will be fairly obvious that staff should disclose information. For example, a doctor would need to tell a new care worker about what drugs a person needs or what allergies the person has. This is clearly in the person's best interests.

16.22 Other information may need to be disclosed as part of the process of working out someone's best interests. A social worker might decide to reveal information about someone's past when discussing their best interests with a close family member. But staff should always bear in mind that the Act requires them to consider the wishes and feelings of the person who lacks capacity.

16.23 In both these cases, staff should only disclose as much information as is relevant to the decision to be made.

Chapter 16

What rules govern access to information about a person who lacks capacity?

Scenario: Sharing appropriate information

Mr Jeremy has learning disabilities. His care home is about to close down. His care team carries out a careful assessment of his needs. They involve him as much as possible, and use the support of an Independent Mental Capacity Advocate. Following the assessment, he is placed with carers under an adult placement scheme.

The carers ask to see Mr Jeremy's case file, so that they can provide him with appropriate care in his best interests. The care manager seeks Mr Jeremy's consent to disclosure of his notes, but believes that Mr Jeremy lacks capacity to make this decision. She recognises that it is appropriate to provide the carers with sufficient information to enable them to act in Mr Jeremy's best interests. But it is not appropriate for them to see all the information on the case file. Much of it is not relevant to his current care needs. The care manager therefore only passes on relevant information from the file.

16.24 Sometimes a person's right to confidentiality will conflict with broader public concerns. Information can be released if it is in the public interest, even if it is not in the best interests of the person who lacks capacity. It can be difficult to decide in these cases, and information holders should consider each case on its merits. The NHS Code on Confidentiality gives examples of when disclosure is in the public interest. These include situations where disclosing information could prevent, or aid investigation of, serious crimes, or to prevent serious harm, such as spread of an infectious disease. It is then necessary to judge whether the public good that would be achieved by the disclosure outweighs *both* the obligation of confidentiality to the individual concerned *and* the broader public interest in the provision of a confidential service.

16.25 For disclosure to be in the public interest, it must be proportionate and limited to the relevant details. Healthcare or social care staff faced with this decision should seek advice from their legal advisers. It is not just things for 'the public's benefit' that are in the public interest – disclosure for the benefit of the person who lacks capacity can also be in the public interest (for example, to stop a person who lacks capacity suffering physical or mental harm).

What financial information can carers ask to see?

16.26 It is often more difficult to get financial information than it is to get information on a person's welfare. A bank manager, for example, is less likely to:

- know the individual concerned

- be able to make an assessment of the person's capacity to consent to disclosure, and

- be aware of the carer's relationship to the person.

So they are less likely than a doctor or social worker to be able to judge what is in a person's best interests and are bound by duties to keep clients' affairs confidential. It is likely that someone wanting financial information will need to apply to the Court of Protection for access to that information. This clearly does not apply to an attorney or a deputy appointed to manage the person's property and affairs, who will generally have the authority (because of their appointment) to obtain all relevant information about the person's property and affairs.

Is information still confidential after someone shares it?

16.27 Whenever a carer gets information, they should treat the information in confidence, and they should not share it with anyone else (unless there is a lawful basis for doing so). In some circumstances, the information holder might ask the carer to give a formal confirmation that they will keep information confidential.

16.28 Where the information is in written form, carers should store it carefully and not keep it for longer than necessary. In many cases, the need to keep the information will be temporary. So the carer should be able to reassure the information holder that they will not keep a permanent record of the information.

What is the best way to settle a disagreement about personal information?

16.29 A carer should always start by trying to get consent from the person whose information they are trying to access. If the person lacks capacity to consent, the carer should ask the information holder for the relevant information and explain why they need it. They may need to remind the information holder that they have to make a decision in the person's best interests and cannot do so without the relevant information.

16.30 This can be a sensitive area and disputes will inevitably arise. Healthcare and social care staff have a difficult judgement to make. They might feel strongly that disclosing the information would not be in the best interests of the person who lacks capacity and would amount to an invasion of their privacy. This may be upsetting for the carer who will probably have good motives for wanting the information. In all cases, an assessment of the interests and needs of the person who lacks capacity should determine whether staff should disclose information.

16.31 If a discussion fails to settle the matter, and the carer still is not happy, there are other ways to settle the disagreement (see chapter 15). The carer may need to use the appropriate complaints procedure. Since the complaint involves elements of data protection and confidentiality, as well as best interests, relevant experts should help deal with the complaint.

16.32 In cases where carers and staff cannot settle their disagreement, the carer can apply to the Court of Protection for the right to access to the specific information. The court would then need to decide if this was in the best interests of the person who lacks capacity to consent. In urgent cases, it might be necessary for the carer to apply directly to the court without going through the earlier stages.

Chapter 16

What rules govern access to information about a person who lacks capacity?

Key words and phrases used in the Code

The table below is not a full index or glossary. Instead, it is a list of key terms used in the Code or the Act, and the main references to them. References in bold indicate particularly valuable content for that term.

Acts in connection with care or treatment	Tasks carried out by carers, healthcare or social care staff which involve the personal care, healthcare or medical treatment of people who lack capacity to consent to them – referred to in the Act as 'section 5 acts'.	**Chapter 6** 2.13–2.14, 4.39 Best interests and _ 5.10, 5,39 Deprivation of liberty and _ 6.39. 6.49–6.52
Advance decision to refuse treatment	A decision to refuse specified treatment made in advance by a person who has capacity to do so. This decision will then apply at a future time when that person lacks capacity to consent to, or refuse, the specified treatment. This is set out in Section 24(1) of the Act. Specific rules apply to advance decisions to refuse life-sustaining treatment.	**Chapter 9 (all)** Best interests and _ 5.5, 5.35, 5.45 Protection from liability and _ 6.37–6.38 LPAs and _ 7.55 Deputies and _ 8.28 Research and _ 11.30 Young people and _ 12.9 Mental Health Act 13.35–13.37
Adult protection procedures	Procedures devised by local authorities, in conjunction with other relevant agencies, to investigate and deal with allegations of abuse or ill treatment of vulnerable adults, and to put in place safeguards to provide protection from abuse.	**Chapter 14** 14.6, 14.22, 14.27–28, 14.34 IMCAs and _ 10.66–10.67
After-care under supervision	Arrangements for supervision in the community following discharge from hospital of certain patients previously detained under the Mental Health Act 1983.	**Chapter 13** **13.22–13.25**, 13.34, 13.37, 13.40, 13.42, 13.45, 13.48, 13.52
Agent	A person authorised to act on behalf of another person under the law of agency. Attorneys appointed under an LPA or EPA are agents and court-appointed deputies are deemed to be agents and must undertake certain duties as agents.	LPAs and _ 7.58–7.68 Deputies and _ 8.55–8.68

Appointee	Someone appointed under Social Security Regulations to claim and collect social security benefits or pensions on behalf of a person who lacks capacity to manage their own benefits. An appointee is permitted to use the money claimed to meet the person's needs.	Role of _ 6:65–6.66 Deputies and _ 8.56 Concerns about _ 14:35–14.36
Appropriate body	A committee which is established to advise on, or on matters which include, the ethics of intrusive research in relation to people who lack capacity to consent to it, and is recognised for those purposes by the Secretary of State (in England) or the National Assembly for Wales (in Wales).	**Chapter 11** 11.8–11.11, 11.20, 11.33–11.34, 11.43–11.47.
Approved Social Worker (ASW)	A specially trained social worker with responsibility for assessing a person's needs for care and treatment under the Mental Health Act 1983. In particular, an ASW assesses whether the person should be admitted to hospital for assessment and/or treatment.	**Chapter 13** 13.16, 13.22–13.23, 13.43, 13.52
Artificial Nutrition and Hydration (ANH)	Artificial nutrition and hydration (ANH) has been recognised as a form of medical treatment. ANH involves using tubes to provide nutrition and fluids to someone who cannot take them by mouth. It bypasses the natural mechanisms that control hunger and thirst and requires clinical monitoring.	**9.26** 5.34 6.18 8.18
Attorney	Someone appointed under either a Lasting Power of Attorney (LPA) or an Enduring Power of Attorney (EPA), who has the legal right to make decisions within the scope of their authority on behalf of the person (the donor) who made the Power of Attorney.	**Chapter 7** Best interests principle and _ 5.2, 5.13, 5.49, 5.55 Protection from liability as _ 6.54–6.55 Court of Protection and _ 8.30 Advance decisions and _ 9.33 Mental Health Act and _ 13.38–13.45 Public Guardian and _ 14.7–14.14 Legal help and _ 15.39–15.42 Accessing personal information as _ 16.9–16.16

Key words

Key words and phrases used in the Code

Best interests	Any decisions made, or anything done for a person who lacks capacity to make specific decisions, must be in the person's best interests. There are standard minimum steps to follow when working out someone's best interests. These are set out in section 4 of the Act, and in the non-exhaustive checklist in 5.13.	**Chapter 2 (Principle 4) Chapter 5** Protection from liability and _ 6.4–6.18 Reasonable belief and _ 6.32–6.36 Deprivation of liberty and _ 6.51–6.53 Acting as an attorney and _ 7.19–7.20, 7.29, 7.53 Court of Protection and _ 8.14–8.26 Acting as a deputy and _ 8.50–8.52 Advance decisions and _ 9.4–9.5
Bournewood provisions	A name given to some proposed new procedures and safeguards for people who lack capacity to make relevant decisions but who need to be deprived of their liberty, in their best interests, otherwise than under the Mental Health Act 1983. The name refers to a case which was eventually decided by the European Court of Human Rights.	6.53–6.54 13.53–13.54
Capacity	The ability to make a decision about a particular matter at the time the decision needs to be made. The legal definition of a person who lacks capacity is set out in section 2 of the Act.	**Chapter 4**
Carer	Someone who provides *unpaid* care by looking after a friend or neighbour who needs support because of sickness, age or disability. In this document, the role of the carer is different from the role of a professional care worker.	**Acting as decision-maker 5.8–5.10 Protection from liability 6.20–6.24** Assessing capacity as _ 4.44–4.45 Acting with reasonable belief 6.29–6.34 Paying for goods and services 6.56–6.66 Accessing information 16.26–16.32

Care worker	Someone employed to provide personal care for people who need help because of sickness, age or disability. They could be employed by the person themselves, by someone acting on the person's behalf or by a care agency.	Assessing capacity as _4.38, 4.44–4.45 Protection from liability 6.20 Paying for goods and services 6.56–6.66 Acting as an attorney 7.10 Acting as a deputy 8.41
Children Act 1989	A law relating to children and those with parental responsibility for children.	**Chapter 12**
Complaints Review Panel	A panel of people set up to review and reconsider complaints about health or social care services which have not been resolved under the first stage of the relevant complaints procedure.	15.28
Consultee	A person who is consulted, for example about the involvement in a research project of a person who lacks capacity to consent to their participation in the research.	11.23, 11.28–29, 11.44
Court of Protection	The specialist Court for all issues relating to people who lack capacity to make specific decisions. The Court of Protection is established under section 45 of the Act.	**Chapter 8** _ must always make decisions about these issues 6.18 Decisions about life-sustaining treatment 5.33–5.36 LPAs and _ 7.45–7.49 Advance decisions and _ 9.35, 9.54, 9.67–9.69 Decisions regarding children and young people 12.3–12.4, 12.7, 12.10, 12.23–12.25 Access to legal help 15.40–15.44
Court of Protection Visitor	Someone who is appointed to report to the Court of Protection on how attorneys or deputies are carrying out their duties. Court of Protection Visitors are established under section 61 of the Act. They can also be directed by the Public Guardian to visit donors, attorney and deputies under section 58 (1) (d).	**14.10–14.11** Attorneys and _ 7.71 Deputies and _ 8.71

Key words

Key words and phrases used in the Code

283

Criminal Records Bureau (CRB)	An Executive Agency of the Home Office which provides access to criminal record information. Organisations in the public, private and voluntary sectors can ask for the CRB to check candidates for jobs to see if they have any criminal records which would make them unsuitable for certain work, especially that involves children or vulnerable adults. For some jobs, a CRB check is mandatory.	Checking healthcare and social care staff 14.29–14.30 Checking IMCAs 10.18
Data Protection Act 1998	A law controlling the handling of, and access to, personal information, such as medical records, files held by public bodies and financial information held by credit reference agencies.	**Chapter 16**
Decision-maker	Under the Act, many different people may be required to make decisions or act on behalf of someone who lacks capacity to make decisions for themselves. The person making the decision is referred to throughout the Code, as the 'decision-maker', and it is the decision-maker's responsibility to work out what would be in the best interests of the person who lacks capacity.	**Chapter 5** Working with IMCAs 10.4, 10.21–10.29 Applying the MHA 13.3, 13.10, 13.27
Declaration	A kind of order made by the Court of Protection. For example, a declaration could say whether a person has or lacks capacity to make a particular decision, or declaring that a particular act would or would not be lawful. The Court's power to make declarations is set out in section 15 of the Act.	**8.13–8.19** Advance decisions and _ 9.35
Deprivation of liberty	Deprivation of liberty is a term used in the European Convention on Human Rights about circumstances when a person's freedom is taken away. Its meaning in practice is being defined through case law.	**6.49–6.54** Protection from liability 6.13–6.14 Attorneys and _ 7.44 Mental Health Act and _ 13.12, 13.16

Deputy	Someone appointed by the Court of Protection with ongoing legal authority as prescribed by the Court to make decisions on behalf of a person who lacks capacity to make particular decisions as set out in Section 16(2) of the Act.	**Chapter 8** Best interests principle and _ 5.2, 5.13, 5.49, 5.55 Protection from liability as _ 6.54–6.55 Attorneys becoming _ 7.56 Advance decisions and _ 9.33 IMCAs and _ 10.70–72 Acting for children and young people 12.4, 12.7 Public Guardian and _ 14.15–14.18 Complaints about 14.19–14.25 Accessing personal information as _ 16.9–16.16
Donor	A person who makes a Lasting Power of Attorney or Enduring Power of Attorney.	**Chapter 7**
Enduring Power of Attorney (EPA)	A Power of Attorney created under the Enduring Powers of Attorney Act 1985 appointing an attorney to deal with the donor's property and financial affairs. Existing EPAs will continue to operate under Schedule 4 of the Act, which replaces the EPA Act 1985.	**Chapter 7** See also LPA
Family carer	A family member who looks after a relative who needs support because of sickness, age or disability. It does not mean a professional care-worker employed by a disabled person or a care assistant in a nursing home, for example.	See carer
Family Division of the High Court	The Division of the High Court that has the jurisdiction to deal with all matrimonial and civil partnership matters, family disputes, matters relating to children and some disputes about medical treatment.	12.14, 12.23
Fiduciary duty	Anyone acting under the law of agency will have this duty. In essence, it means that any decision taken or act done as an agent (such as an attorney or deputy) must not benefit themselves, but must benefit the person for whom they are acting.	_ for attorneys 7.58 _ for deputies 8.58

Guardianship	Arrangements, made under the Mental Health Act 1983, for a guardian to be appointed for a person with mental disorder to help ensure that the person gets the care they need in the community.	**13.16–13.21** 13.1, 13.25–13.27, 13.54
Health Service Ombudsman	An independent person whose organisation investigates complaints about National Health Service (NHS) care or treatment in England which have not been resolved through the NHS complaints procedure.	15.19, 15.21, 15.31
Human Rights Act 1998	A law largely incorporating into UK law the substantive rights set out in the European Convention on Human Rights.	6.49 16.3
Human Tissue Act 2004	A law to regulate issues relating to whole body donation and the taking, storage and use of human organs and tissue.	11.7 11.38–11.39
Ill treatment	Section 44 of the Act introduces a new offence of ill treatment of a person who lacks capacity by someone who is caring for them, or acting as a deputy or attorney for them. That person can be guilty of ill treatment if they have deliberately ill-treated a person who lacks capacity, or been reckless as to whether they were ill-treating the person or not. It does not matter whether the behaviour was likely to cause, or actually caused, harm or damage to the victim's health.	14.23–14.26
Independent Complaints Advocacy Service (ICAS)	In England, a service to support patients and their carers who wish to pursue a complaint about their NHS treatment or care.	15.18
Independent Mental Capacity Advocate (IMCA)	Someone who provides support and representation for a person who lacks capacity to make specific decisions, where the person has no-one else to support them. The IMCA service is established under section 35 of the Act and the functions of IMCAs are set out in section 36. It is not the same as an ordinary advocacy service.	**Chapter 10** Consulting to work out best interests 5.51 Involvement in changes of residence 6.9 Involvement in serious medical decisions 6.16 MHA and _ 13.46–13.48
Information Commissioner's Office	An independent authority set up to promote access to official information and to protect personal information. It has powers to ensure that the laws about information, such as the Data Protection Act 1998, are followed.	16.13 16.18

Lasting Power of Attorney (LPA)	A Power of Attorney created under the Act (see Section 9(1)) appointing an attorney (or attorneys) to make decisions about the donor's personal welfare (including healthcare) and/or deal with the donor's property and affairs.	**Chapter 7** Best interests principle and _ 5.2, 5.13, 5.49, 5.55 Protection from liability as _ 6.54–6.55 Court of Protection and _ 8.30 Advance decisions and _ 9.33 Mental Health Act and _ 13.38–13.45 Public Guardian and _ 14.7–14.14 Legal help and _ 15.39–15.42 Accessing personal information as _ 16.9–16.16
Life-sustaining treatment	Treatment that, in the view of the person providing healthcare, is necessary to keep a person alive See Section 4(10) of the Act.	**Providing or stopping _ in best interests 5.29–5.36 Advance decisions to refuse _ 9.10–9.11, 9.19–9.20, 9.24–9.28** Protection from liability when providing _ 6.16, 6.55 Attorneys and _ 7.22, 7.27, 7.29-7.30 Deputies and _ 8.17, 8.46 Conscientious objection to stopping _ 9.61–9.63 IMCAs and _ 10.44
Litigation friend	A person appointed by the court to conduct legal proceedings on behalf of, and in the name of, someone who lacks capacity to conduct the litigation or to instruct a lawyer themselves.	4.54 10.38 15.39
Local Government Ombudsman	In England, an independent organisation that investigates complaints about councils and local authorities on most council matters including housing, planning, education and social services.	15.30–15.32

Makaton	A language programme using signs and symbols, for the teaching of communication, language and literacy skills for people with communication and learning difficulties.	3.11
Mediation	A process for resolving disagreements in which an impartial third party (the mediator) helps people in dispute to find a mutually acceptable resolution.	15.7–15.13
Mental capacity	See capacity	
Mental Health Act 1983	A law mainly about the compulsory care and treatment of patients with mental health problems. In particular, it covers detention in hospital for mental health treatment.	**Chapter 13** Deprivation of liberty other than in line with _ 6.50–6.53, 7.44 Attorneys and _ 7.27 Advance decisions and _9.37 IMCAs and 10.44, 10.51, 10.56–10.58 Children and young people and _ 12.6, 12.21 Complaints regarding _ 15.19
Mental Health Review Tribunal	An independent judicial body with powers to direct the discharge of patients who are detained under the Mental Health Act 1983.	13.31 13.42
NHS Litigation Authority	A Special Health Authority (part of the NHS), responsible for handling negligence claims made against NHS bodies in England.	15.22
Office of the Public Guardian (OPG)	The Public Guardian is an officer established under Section 57 of the Act. The Public Guardian will be supported by the Office of the Public Guardian, which will supervise deputies, keep a register of deputies, Lasting Powers of Attorney and Enduring Powers of Attorney, check on what attorneys are doing, and investigate any complaints about attorneys or deputies. The OPG replaces the Public Guardianship Office (PGO) that has been in existence for many years.	**14.8–14.22** Registering LPAs with _ 7.14–7.17 Supervision of attorneys by _ 7.69–7.74 Registering EPAs with _ 7.78 Guidance for EPAs _ 7.79 Guidance for receivers_ 8.5 Panel of deputies of _ 8.35 Supervision of deputies by _ 8.69–8.77

Official Solicitor	Provides legal services for vulnerable persons, or in the interests of achieving justice. The Official Solicitor represents adults who lack capacity to conduct litigation in county court or High Court proceedings in England and Wales, and in the Court of Protection.	Helping with formal assessment of capacity 4.54 Acting in applications to the Court of Protection 8.10 Acting as litigation friend 10.38, 15.39
Patient Advice and Liaison Service (PALS)	In England, a service providing information, advice and support to help NHS patients, their families and carers. PALS act on behalf of service users when handling patient and family concerns and can liaise with staff, managers and, where appropriate, other relevant organisations, to find solutions.	15.15–15.17
Permanent vegetative state (PVS)	A condition caused by catastrophic brain damage whereby patients in PVS have a permanent and irreversible lack of awareness of their surroundings and no ability to interact at any level with those around them.	6.18 8.18
Personal welfare	Personal welfare decisions are any decisions about person's healthcare, where they live, what clothes they wear, what they eat and anything needed for their general care and well-being. Attorneys and deputies can be appointed to make decisions about personal welfare on behalf of a person who lacks capacity. Many acts of care are to do with personal welfare.	_ **LPAs 7.21–7.31** _ **deputies 8.38–8.39** Advance decisions about _ 9.4, 9.35 Role of High Court in decisions about _ 15.44
Property and affairs	Any possessions owned by a person (such as a house or flat, jewellery or other possessions), the money they have in income, savings or investments and any expenditure. Attorneys and deputies can be appointed to make decisions about property and affairs on behalf of a person who lacks capacity.	_ **LPAs 7.32–7.42** _ **deputies 8.34–8.37** Restrictions on _ LPA 7.56 Duties of _ attorney 7.58, 7.67–7.68 _ EPAs 7.76–7.77 OPG panel of _ deputies 8.35 Duties of _ deputy 8.56, 8.67–8.68 _ of children and young people 12.3–12.4, 12.7
Protection from liability	Legal protection, granted to anyone who has acted or made decisions in line with the Act's principles.	**Chapter 6**

Protection of Vulnerable Adults (POVA) list	A register of individuals who have abused, neglected or otherwise harmed vulnerable adults in their care or placed vulnerable adults at risk of harm. Providers of care must not offer such individuals employment in care positions.	14.31
Public Services Ombudsman for Wales	An independent body that investigates complaints about local government and NHS organisations in Wales, and the National Assembly for Wales, concerning matters such as housing, planning, education, social services and health services.	15.20 15.30–15.32
Receiver	Someone appointed by the former Court of Protection to manage the property and affairs of a person lacking capacity to manage their own affairs. Existing receivers continue as deputies with legal authority to deal with the person's property and affairs.	8.5 8.35
Restraint	See Section 6(4) of the Act. The use or threat of force to help do an act which the person resists, or the restriction of the person's liberty of movement, whether or not they resist. Restraint may only be used where it is necessary to protect the person from harm and is proportionate to the risk of harm.	**6.39–6.44, 6.47–53** Use of _ in moves between accommodation 6.11 Use of _ in healthcare and treatment decisions 6.15 Attorneys and _ 7.43-7.44 Deputies and _ 8.46 MHA and _ 13.5
Statutory principles	The five key principles are set out in Section 1 of the Act. They are designed to emphasise the fundamental concepts and core values of the Act and to provide a benchmark to guide decision-makers, professionals and carers acting under the Act's provisions. The principles generally apply to all actions and decisions taken under the Act.	**Chapter 2**
Two-stage test of capacity	Using sections 2 and 3 of the Act to assess whether or not a person has capacity to make a decision for themselves at that time.	**4.10–4.13** Protection from liability 6.27 Applying _ to advance decisions 9.39

Wilful neglect	An intentional or deliberate omission or failure to carry out an act of care by someone who has care of a person who lacks (or whom the person reasonably believes lacks) capacity to care for themselves. Section 44 introduces a new offence of wilful neglect of a person who lacks capacity.	14.23–14.26
Written statements of wishes and feelings	Written statements the person might have made before losing capacity about their wishes and feelings regarding issues such as the type of medical treatment they would want in the case of future illness, where they would prefer to live, or how they wish to be cared for. They should be used to help find out what someone's wishes and feelings might be, as part of working out their best interests. They are not the same as advance decisions to refuse treatment and are not binding.	5.34 5.37 5.42–5.44

Key words

Key words and phrases used in the Code

The following list provides contact details for some organisations that provide information, guidance or materials related to the Code of Practice and the Mental Capacity Act. The list is not exhaustive: many other organisations may also produce their own materials.

British Banking Association
Provides guidance for bank staff on *'Banking for mentally incapacitated and learning disabled customers'*.
Available from www.bba.org.uk/bba/jsp/polopoly.jsp?d=146&a=5757, price £10 (members) /£12 (non-members). Not inclusive of VAT.

web: www.bba.org.uk
telephone: 020 7216 8800

British Medical Association
Co-authors (with the Law Society) of *Assessment of Mental Capacity: Guidance for Doctors and Lawyers* (Second edition) (London: BMJ Books, 2004). www.bma.org.uk/ap.nsf/Content/Assessmentmental?OpenDocument& Highlight=2,mental, capacity

Available from BMJ Books (www.bmjbookshop.com), price £20.99

web: www.bma.org.uk
telephone: 020 7387 4499

British Psychological Society
Publishers of *Guidelines on assessing capacity* – professional guidance available online to members.

web: www.bps.org.uk
telephone: (0)116 254 9568

Commission for Social Care Inspection
The Commission for Social Care Inspection (CSCI) registers, inspects and reports on social care services in England.

web: www.csci.org.uk
telephone: 0845 015 0120 / 0191 233 3323
textphone: 0845 015 2255 / 0191 233 3588

Community Legal Services Direct

Provides free legal information to people living in England and Wales to help them deal with legal problems.

web: www.clsdirect.org.uk
telephone (helpline): 0845 345 4 345

Criminal Records Bureau (CRB)

The CRB runs criminal records checks on people who apply for jobs working with children and vulnerable adults.

web: www.crb.org.uk
telephone: 0870 90 90 811

Department for Constitutional Affairs

The government department with responsibility for the Mental Capacity Act and the Code of Practice. Also publishes guidance for specific audiences www.dca.gov.uk/legal-policy/mental-capacity/guidance.htm

Department of Health

Publishes guidance for healthcare and social care staff in England. Key publications referenced in the Code include:

- on using restraint with people with learning disabilities and autistic spectrum disorder, see *Guidance for restrictive physical interventions* www.dh.gov.uk/assetRoot/04/06/84/61/04068461.pdf
- on adult protection procedures, see *No secrets: Guidance on developing and implementing multi-agency policies and procedures to protect vulnerable adults from abuse* www.dh.gov.uk/assetRoot/04/07/45/44/04074544.pdf
- on consent to examination and treatment, including advance decisions to refuse treatment www.dh/gov.uk/consent
- on the proposed Bournewood safeguards, a draft illustrative Code of Practice www.dh.gov.uk/assetRoot/04/14/17/64/04141764.pdf
- on IMCAs and the IMCA pilots www.dh.gov.uk/imca

DH also is responsible for the *Mental Health Act 1983 Code of Practice* (TSO 1999) www.dh.gov.uk/assetRoot/04/07/49/61/04074961.pdf

Family Mediation Helpline

Provides general information on family mediation and contact details for mediation services in your local area.

web: www.familymediationhelpline.co.uk
telephone: 0845 60 26 627

Healthcare Commission

The health watchdog in England, undertaking reviews and investigations into the provision of NHS and private healthcare services.

web: www.healthcarecommission.org.uk
telephone helpline: 0845 601 3012
switchboard: 020 7448 9200

Healthcare Inspectorate for Wales

Undertakes reviews and investigations into the provision of NHS funded care, either by or for Welsh NHS organisations.

web: www.hiw.org.uk
email: hiw@wales.gsi.gov.uk
telephone: 029 2092 8850

Housing Ombudsman Service

The Housing Ombudsman Service considers complaints against member organisations, and deals with other housing disputes.

web: www.ihos.org.uk
email: info@housing-ombudsman.org.uk
telephone: 020 7421 3800

Information Commissioner's Office

The Information Commissioner's Office is the UK's independent authority set up to promote access to official information and to protect personal information.

web: www.ico.gov.uk
telephone helpline: 08456 30 60 60

Legal Services Commission

Looks after legal aid in England and Wales, and provides information, advice and legal representation.

web: www.legalservices.gov.uk
See also Community Legal Services Direct.

Local Government Ombudsman

The Local Government Ombudsmen investigate complaints about councils and certain other bodies.

web: www.lgo.org.uk
telephone: 0845 602 1983

National Mediation Helpline

Provides access to a simple, low cost method of resolving a wide range of disputes.

The National Mediation Helpline is operated on behalf of the Department for Constitutional Affairs (DCA) in conjunction with the Civil Mediation Council (CMC).

web: www.nationalmediationhelpline.com
telephone: 0845 60 30 809

Office of the Public Guardian

The new Public Guardian is established under the Act and will be supported by the Office of the Public Guardian, which will replace the current Public Guardianship Office (PGO). The OPG will be an executive agency of the Department for Constitutional Affairs. Amongst its other roles, it provides forms for LPAs and EPAs.

web: From October 2007, a new website will be created at
                www.publicguardian.gov.uk

Official Solicitor

Provides legal services for vulnerable people and is able to represent people who lack capacity and act as a litigation friend.

web: www.officialsolicitor.gov.uk
telephone: 020 7911 7127

Patient Advice and Liaison Service (PALS)

Provides information about the NHS and help resolve concerns or problems with the NHS, including support when making complaints.

web: www.pals.nhs.uk
                The site includes contact details for local PALS offices around
                the country.

Patient Information Advisory Group

Considers applications on behalf of the Secretary of State to allow the common law duty of confidentiality to be aside.

web: www.advisorybodies.doh.gov.uk/PIAG

Public Service Ombudsman for Wales

Investigates complaints about local authorities and NHS organisations in Wales, and about the National Assembly Government for Wales.

web: www.ombudsman-wales.org.uk
telephone: 01656 641 150

Welsh Assembly Government

Produces key pieces of guidance for healthcare and social care staff, including:

- *In safe hands – Implementing Adult Protection Procedures in Wales* (July 2000) http://new.wales.gov.uk/about/departments/ dhss/publications/social_services_publications/reports/ insafehands?lang=en
- *Framework for restrictive physical intervention policy and practice* (available at www.childrenfirst.wales.gov.uk/content/framework/ phys-int-e.pdf)